The Rise and

Fall of Gay Culture

The Rise
and Fall of
Gay Culture

Daniel Harris

HYPERION

NEW YORK

Portions of this book have appeared in Harper's, Salmagundi, the Antioch Review, the Baffler, Word, the Harvard Gay and Lesbian Review, and the Bay Area Reporter.

Library of Congress Cataloging-in-Publication Data

Harris, Daniel.
The rise and fall of gay culture / by Daniel Harris. — 1st ed.
p.   cm.
Includes bibliographical references.
ISBN 0-7868-6165-7
1. Gay men—United States. 2. Gay communities—United States.
3. Subculture—United States. 4. Popular culture—United States.
5. Assimilation (Sociology) I. Title.
HQ76.2.U5H347   1997
305.38'96642—dc21   96-47822
CIP

Book design by Brian Mulligan

First Edition

2   4   6   8   10   9   7   5   3   1

To Philip Shehadi

Contents

Acknowledgments

S EVERAL PEOPLE HAVE PROVIDED invaluable assistance in the research and preparation of this book. Most notably, I would like to thank Bill Walker at the Gay and Lesbian Historical Society of Northern California who was generous with both his time and expertise. His unmitigated cynicism and camp sense of humor made the hours I spent shivering in the dank basement of the Historical Society's less than glamorous offices much more tolerable than they might otherwise have been.

I would also like to thank my oldest and best friend Joaquin Martinez-Pizarro (aka Jackie Pizzazzo) for the careful attention he lavished on the manuscript. Joaquin is my most loyal and trustworthy reader, as well as the best friend a guy could ever possibly have. He is also one of the few critics I have met who not only damns with faint praise but praises with faint damnation.

This book could also not have been written without the loving skepticism and gentle severity of my former boyfriend Anthony Aziz and his current consort Sammy Cucher, both of whom I love more than they will ever know. My friend Christoph Lehner also read portions of the manuscript with great care.

The continued support of Bob and Peggy Boyers at *Salmagundi* has been of vital importance to me as a writer. Without the encouragement of the editors of small pioneering literary quarterlies, published with the help of the disinterested generosity of such schools as Skidmore College, writers like myself would never make it into print. I would also like to thank Robert Fogarty at the *Antioch Review* for his unqualified support.

My agent Malaga Baldi continues to work indefatigably on my behalf. I want to thank her for picking me out of her slush pile and sticking with me through the ordeal of getting into print.

I would also like to thank my tireless and forbearing editor Rick Kot at Hyperion for giving me the opportunity to devote my undivided attention to my writing for one glorious year without the distractions of a day job. He is another of that rare breed of critics who praises with faint damnation. He took enormous care with my manuscript and is a gifted editor whose judgment I trust implicitly. I would also like to thank his assistant Michael Liss for fielding all of my phone calls, answering all of my trivial and bothersome questions, and making sure that I avoided unforgivable oversights.

Danny Nicoletta's photographs of drag were very helpful in my research. Maurice Duran, the resident savant at the Superstar Video in San Francisco's Castro district, also helped me at several crucial junctures in this project with his encyclopedic knowledge of film.

This book is dedicated to the memory of my best friend Philip Shehadi. Philip was the bureau chief for Reuters in Algiers and was murdered during the Gulf War. He was a crusading journalist, an exemplary friend, and a passionate proponent of Palestinian rights. Philip won the love and affection of the countless numbers of people he encountered across the globe in the course of his short and tragic career, and it is still a source of pride to me that we remained so close for his entire life.

—Daniel Harris
Brooklyn, New York
November 1996

Introduction

I CAME OUT IN 1970 at the somewhat precocious age of 13. While my announcement coincided almost exactly with the Stonewall riots, they played no role in my decision to confront my parents with what should have been perfectly obvious to them ever since the third grade when, even as my peers were collecting baseball cards and winning merit badges in the Cub Scouts, I threw myself into a somewhat unconventional pastime: female impersonation. Although my mother tactfully refrained from interfering with what promised to be a brilliant career in the theater, the mad, one-woman show I regularly performed in the school auditorium before audiences of my delirious fellow students raised in her mind "certain doubts," as she later put it, "about my son's masculinity." When I finally did confirm these well-founded suspicions, which were further supported by my tendency to sashay around the house in brightly colored caftans and stalk regally through the corridors of Brighton Middle School in towering platform shoes, Stonewall was as yet merely a small footnote in gay activism and had not been assigned the mythological status it was to acquire only a few years later.

Far more important for the evolution of my own self-awareness was an event that has been all but forgotten in gay history, swallowed up in the sea of words in which the gay community has been deluged since the 1970s: the publication, some three years after Stonewall, of

George Weinberg's *Society and the Healthy Homosexual* (1972), a book that launched an entire genre of self-help literature that attempted to instill gay pride in its readers. Full of reassuring commonplaces, Weinberg's book was popular enough to make it onto the shelves of a B. Dalton's in Asheville, North Carolina, where it was promptly snatched up by a lonely gay adolescent who, brazening out the contemptuous looks of the store's cashier, guiltily brought it home and devoured it in a single sitting.

Given how instrumental the literature of the gay self-help movement was to my own political development, one would have expected that, years later, when I began reviewing gay books, I would have been eager to repay my debt to writers like Weinberg and enthusiastically praise the steady stream of gay pride manuals they were producing for the uninitiated. In fact, however, the exact opposite occurred. Far from feeling charitable, I found myself quickly losing patience with books that seemed to me to belabor the obvious, functioning as tour guides around a Sodom and Gomorrah that they had transformed into an immaculate theme park for the happy and the well adjusted. Books like Mary Borhek's *Coming Out to Parents* (1983), Ann Heron's *One Teenager in Ten* (1983), or Eric Rofe's *"I Thought People Like That Killed Themselves"* (1983) became inextricably linked in my mind, not only with my own adolescence, but with the adolescence of the entire subculture. The gay community seemed hopelessly mired in an emotionally stagnant state of euphoria, forever fixated on a single moment, the admittedly triumphant occasion of coming out, an event these writers were doomed to relive over and over again ad infinitum, digging themselves deeper and deeper into the same yawning intellectual rut.

For far too long, the book trade has provided gay readers with nothing more than the literary equivalent of a warm glow, a soothing linguistic salve for the walking wounded, as if we were all still 13 and were all still mustering the courage to come out, as if, after 25 years of gay liberation, we all still needed to be scolded and cajoled into self-acceptance. Boosterism has largely displaced real discussion about gay culture. It has weakened our fiction, much as the Stalinists undermined Soviet fiction (and for virtually the same reasons), and it has turned much of our nonfiction into hyperkinetic cheerleading by well-intentioned masters of interpersonal hype who treat their readers as if they were bedridden patients, moral invalids who need to be spoon-fed medicinal lessons about pride and oppression.

The assumption behind *The Rise and Fall of Gay Culture* is that homosexuals are not permanent intellectual convalescents. They are thriving, mentally, if not physically, and it is time that they remove their bandages, raise themselves off of the soft, snug, and commodious bed of uplifting ideology in which they have slept for decades, and face some important truths about a culture desperately in need of being shaken out of its complacency.

The Rise and Fall of Gay Culture investigates various aspects of the gay experience as they have evolved over time. My primary purpose is to document subtle shifts, from one decade to the next, in the meaning of rituals like drag, obsessions like divas, methods of communication like personal ads, commodities like pornography, political institutions like newspapers, and styles of bodily adornment like tattoos and piercings. Each chapter takes a single feature of gay culture—an artifact, a fetish, a piece of clothing, a method of political protest—and presents a before and after snapshot of it, i.e., literary pornography before Stonewall and literary pornography today; glossy magazines in the early 1970s and glossy magazines in the 1990s; gay motorcycle gangs before the sexual revolution and contemporary "leatherfolk"; underwear from the Ah Men catalog and underwear from the International Male catalog; glad-to-be-gay propaganda from the Mattachine era and the sepulchral tactics of ACT UP.

Essential elements of gay culture have not only changed, I argue, they have changed into their opposites: the love of actresses has become the ridicule of actresses; butch, tattooed bodies have become effeminate, "decorated" ones; exotic, playful drag queens have become mean, militarized gender fuckers; sadistic leathermen have become macrobiotic neopagans; conservative, assimilationist propagandists have become antimainstream radicals. Changes have occurred, not only in the most conspicuous aspects of gay culture, but in the least visible and, at first sight, insignificant ones, from the facial expressions of cross-dressers and the way actors kiss in porn films to the coverage of opera in our newspapers and our attitudes toward the desirability of chest hair and tan lines; from the language we use to describe our preferences in bed ("butch/fem" vs. "top/bottom") and the expressions we use to identify our lovers ("special friend" vs. "husband") to the literary circumlocutions pornographers have created for the rectum ("musky cock blossom" vs. "hot hungry hole") and the arsenal of words with which they poeticize erections ("temple of priapus" vs. "prick" and "pecker").

The force behind these changes is the accelerating pace of our assimilation into mainstream society. What is happening to gay culture parallels what has been happening to popular culture on a much larger scale ever since the invention of a metaphor central to our understanding of the historical mission of America: the melting pot. Although this image is meant to suggest everything that is hospitable, tolerant, and welcoming about our society, it inadvertently conjures up a picture, not of a lively community of separate cultures, each of which makes a distinctive contribution to an inclusive and well-functioning democracy, but of an inedible ethnic goulash spoiled by too many ingredients, a sludgelike stew of racial and national differences. By looking closely at the changes that have occurred in gay culture in the past few decades, I attempt to represent the process through which a culture with unique traditions and rituals is submerged into the melting pot, its distinguishing characteristics dissolving into this grey, flavorless gruel as its members are accepted by society at large.

Despite the role that immigrants and minorities have played in American history, our country has never exhibited an exceptional degree of tolerance for racial idiosyncrasies. Nor is the homogenization of American culture the consequence of sheer bigotry and xenophobia, of our inability to accept in our midst the unsettling presence of strangers. Another reason for the growing sameness of our society is that the physical and psychological conditions necessary for the preservation of ethnic differences have all but disappeared. A diverse culture presupposes a nation fractured by the religious and ideological differences that have now given way to a tolerant ecumenicalism and, moreover, one that is splintered into distinct regions, divided by insurmountable geographic distances now easily overcome through high-speed travel—through automobiles, Amtrak, and airplanes. The rise of the telephone, the Internet, and the mass media have all contributed to America's homogenization and made it more and more difficult to maintain a separate and distinct ethnic identity that can withstand the demoralizing effects of watching, reading, and consuming the same sitcoms, comic strips, and mass-produced commodities, from Tide to Coke, from Sunbeam bread to Kellogg's cornflakes. *The Rise and Fall of Gay Culture* traces the circuitous route of assimilation, following the long trail of debris jettisoned by a decaying civilization as it levels the features of the various tribes it comprises in order to create out of a racially pluralistic society a single monolithic culture. By focusing as a test case on the changes that have occurred in the gay community, I describe the gradual dissolution of the ethnic diversity of a country that demands from its minorities nothing less than a voluntary act of subcultural suicide performed to avoid both social ostracism and economic disenfranchisement.

Some minorities have proven to be more resistant to assimilation than homosexuals. Blacks, for instance, have stubbornly refused to relinquish the characteristics that the mainstream finds unacceptable about their culture. They have even gone so far as to invent their own language, a colorful form of street slang that is rapidly evolving into an indecipherably distinct dialect in its own right, a folk idiom that, if it succeeds in divorcing itself from American English altogether, will only reinforce the oppression of black people.

Gay culture, by contrast, has behaved in the exact opposite manner, in part because of the business world's growing recognition of our appeal as a market. Unlike the customs and rituals of African Americans, our own traditions have been uniquely jeopardized by assimilation. Homosexuals are being accepted so quickly by the general public that two of the most valuable features of our culture, our involvement with the arts and camp, our highly mannered style of humor, are disappearing. *The Rise and Fall of Gay Culture* identifies and describes those features of the gay sensibility that have made homosexuals the ideal victims of a process of cultural erosion that has made further inroads into the gay community than it has into the communities of other marginalized groups, whom manufacturers have neglected even as they lay siege to gays as America's paradigmatic shoppers. The gay sensibility, which I define strictly as a political response to oppression, and not as an innate characterological predisposition for the arts and aestheticism, as the so-called essentialists mistakenly define it, has paved the way for our acceptance into society and made us far more defenseless as a target for takeover than other ethnic groups whose cultures are less economically attractive than the affluent lifestyles of many gay men.

While the commercial exploitation of homosexuals has played a key role in our assimilation, naive leftist conspiracy theories about the pillaging of gay culture by corporate America completely misrepresent the complexities of the whole process of our acceptance by mainstream society. They reduce it to a simplistic Marxist fairy tale about rapacious CEOs sitting around boardrooms studying graphs and dissecting pie charts as they hatch invidious schemes to rob us of our hard-earned dollars. The commercialization of gay culture was not an act of rape, of colonialist expansionism, of an unprincipled oppressor preying upon the defenseless minority that groveled at its feet, cowering before the lash of its whip. We invited corporate America into our lives, begged and pleaded with it to recognize our economic potential, to harness our tremendous buying power and pay homage to our political strength. The selling of gay culture was a synergistic arrangement, a marriage of convenience, a profitable intersection of interests, one that, far from resisting, homosexuals have fought long and hard to bring about, doing everything possible to make themselves more appealing in the eyes of advertisers.

The eventual disappearance of gay culture constitutes a significant loss, not just for gay people, but for American culture in general. This is not only because the elimination of ethnic differences will inevitably diminish us as a nation, turning us into a drab and homogeneous mass of identical citizens, but because homosexuals have always played a vital role in the American cultural scene, an arena dominated by armies of gay composers, writers, directors, architects, dancers, choreographers, and curators. Because we have traditionally alleviated the emotional frustration caused by homophobia through the pursuit of culture, the safety valve that our creativity provided us will become superfluous as oppression decreases. The unfortunate consequence will be that our need to produce art will begin to wane, and we will feel less inclined to assert ourselves as the proverbial tastemakers of our society. Assimilation is not just an isolated act of subcultural self-forfeiture. It has profound ramifications for the country's cultural life, which will be deprived of a major source of artistic and intellectual energy as homosexuals are finally integrated into a society they once judged, belittled, and ridiculed by lording over it their good taste and assuming the smugly incontestable airs of impeccable connoisseurs.

The assimilation of the gay community can be measured in the dramatic changes that have occurred in our attitudes toward popular culture, specifically, toward the new breed of internationally acclaimed celebrities who once served as the universal bonding agent that brought homosexuals together as a minority. One of the major ironies of the history of gay men in America is that the forces of centralization now leveling the differences between other minorities first enhanced rather than weakened our feelings of solidarity. Only over time, as we shall see, did the increasing regimentation and uniformity of American life begin to sap the foundations of the very subculture that this decimating process of homogenization originally helped to create.

The Death of Camp:

Gay Men and Hollywood

Diva Worship, from

Reverence to Ridicule

"If all the time the manager of the theater holds back the good roles
from us, may we not insist upon understudying the stars?"

Isak Dinesen,
"The Deluge at Norderney"[1]

SOMETIME IN MY VERY early adolescence, I acquired,
while living in the very heart of Appalachia, a land of
lazy southern drawls, a British accent. No one around me had a
British accent; my father was from Chicago Heights, my mother
from Braggadocio, Missouri, and my peers were budding good old
boys whose fathers drove tractors and pickup trucks and spoke in
an unmusical twang that I, a pompous fop in my teens, found distinctly undignified.

Given the hearty, blue-collar community in which I grew up, the
origin of my stilted style of delivery remained a complete mystery to
me until, as an adult, I began to watch old movies again. Over and
over in the voices of film stars as different as Joan Crawford in
Mildred Pierce and Katharine Hepburn in *Suddenly, Last Summer*, I
heard the echoes of my own voice, the patrician inflections of char-

---

[1]*Seven Gothic Tales* (New York: Vintage, 1972), p. 74.

acters who conversed in a manufactured Hollywood idiom meant to suggest refinement and good breeding, the lilting tones of Grace Kelly in *Rear Window*, Bette Davis in *Mr. Skeffington*, Tallulah Bankhead in *Lifeboat*, or even Glinda the Good Witch in *The Wizard of Oz*.

In that tour de force of bitchy camp, *The Women*, the all-female cast speaks in two distinct accents: the harsh American cockney of the kitchen help, who squabble about the muddled affairs of their wealthy mistresses, and the high-society, charm-school intonations of the Park Avenue matrons who rip each other to shreds in the gracious accents of an Anglophilic argot concocted by the elocutionists at the major studios. Only Joan Crawford, the inimitable Crystal Allen, a social-climbing shopgirl who claws her way up to the top, can speak in both accents as the occasion requires, one for when she is at her most deceitful, hiding her common upbringing beneath the Queen's English of the New York aristocracy, and the other for when she is being her true self, a crass, money-grubbing tart who gossips viciously with her equally low-class cohorts at the perfume counter.

To an insecure gay teenager stranded in the uncivilized hinterlands of North Carolina, the gracious ladies of Park Avenue and Sutton Place embodied a way of life more glamorous and less provincial than his own. The influence of Hollywood films was so pervasive among young homosexuals that it insinuated itself into our voices, weakening the grip of our regional accents, which were gradually overridden by the artificial language of this imaginary elite. Even today I have never succeeded in exorcising Joan, Bette, Grace, and Kate from my vocal cords, where they are still speaking, having left the indelible mark of Hollywood's spurious interpretation of classiness, culture, and gentility branded into my personality. This strange act of ventriloquism represents the highest form of diva worship and is the indirect outcome of my perception in my youth that, as a homosexual, I did not belong in the community in which I lived, that I was different, a castaway from somewhere else, somewhere better, more elegant, more refined, a little Lord Fauntleroy marooned in the wilderness. In my unconscious imitation of the voices of the great film stars, I was seeking to demonstrate my separateness, to show others how out of place I felt, and, moreover, to fight back against the hostility I sensed from homophobic rednecks by belittling their crudeness through unremitting displays of my own polish and sophistication. I was not attracted to Hollywood stars because of their femininity, nor did my admiration of them reflect any burning desire to be a woman, as the homosexual's fascination with actresses is usually explained, as if diva worship were simply a ridiculous side effect of gender conflicts. Instead, it was their *world*, not their femininity, that appealed to me, the irrepressibly madcap in-crowd of *Auntie Mame*, of high spirits and unconventional "characters," of nudists and Freudians, symphony conductors and Broadway prima donnas, who lived in a protective enclave that promised immunity from shame and judgment, beckoning me with its broadmindedness and indulgence of sexual eccentricities.

For me and countless other gay men growing up in small-town America, film provided a vehicle for expressing alienation from our surroundings and linking up with the utopic homosexual community of our dreams, a sophisticated "artistic" demimonde inhabited by Norma Desmonds and Holly Golightlys. Homosexuals' involvement with Hollywood movies was not only more intense but fundamentally different from that of the rest of the American public. For us, film served a deeply psychological and political function. At the very heart of gay diva worship is not the diva herself but the almost universal homosexual experience of ostracism and insecurity, which ultimately led to what might be called the aestheticism of maladjustment, the gay man's exploitation of cinematic visions of Hollywood grandeur to elevate himself above his antagonistic surroundings and simultaneously express membership in a secret society of upper-class aesthetes.

Richard Friedel's novel *The Movie Lover* (1981) provides a telling illustration of how gay men used cinema for the defensive purposes of dramatizing their alienation. Burton Raider, its gay protagonist, is such a precocious coxcomb that he reads *Vogue* in his crib and refuses to wear the insipid teddy-bear bibs and Day-Glo overalls his parents buy for him, spurning sweaters with choo-choo-train prints and opting instead for kimonos and capes. In this affectionate caricature of the gay sensibility, Burton searches for some way to underscore his difference from his untidy, proletarian cousins, who despise him for his effeminacy and are content to catch frogs and throw stones at tin cans while he sobs on the sofa over Rita Hayworth movies or swoons over "the vertiginous Ann Miller and the noble Norma Shearer."[2] One Christmas, he even asks a bewildered Santa Claus to bring him a lavish photo album of MGM stars, a present ideally suited for a young homosexual who "never quite belonged, never quite fit in"[3] with the other children on his block.

It is this feeling of estrangement that leads him to flaunt, through the imitation of film, what he modestly refers to as his "singularity." When both he and his cousins unwrap dump trucks, he imperiously sends Santa scurrying back to the North Pole to retrieve the forgotten book, sputtering at the bewildered saint's retreating figure, dashing for his sled, "what [am] I supposed to do now . . . go over and play blue-collar worker"[4] with his cousins, whom he watches contemptuously as they excavate a construction site by the Christmas tree. As my own voice and Burton's affectations reveal, the preciousness of the aesthete, our love of Japanese screens, Persian carpets, kimonos, capes, MGM stars, and British accents, reflects less the homosexual's innate affinity for lovely things, for beauty and sensuality, than his profound social discontent, which we attempt to overcome by creating flattering images of ourselves as connoisseurs and epicureans.

The hard-bitten personalities of such Machiavellian careerists as Joan Crawford and Marlene Dietrich were, of course, not irrelevant to gay men's fascination with them. In fact, we related so intensely to the steeliness of characters like the murderous Bette Davis in *The Little Foxes*, who, with chilling equanimity, stands by as her choking husband writhes in convulsions before her, clutching his heart and helplessly groping for his missing blood pressure medication, that we used them as substitutes for ourselves, refashioning them in our own

---

[2]*The Movie Lover* (New York: Coward, McCann & Geogegen, 1981), p. 17.
[3]*The Movie Lover*, p. 23.
[4]*The Movie Lover*, p. 19.

images. In the homosexual's imagination, Hollywood divas were transformed into gay men, undergoing a strange sort of sex change operation from which they emerged as drag queens, as men in women's clothing, honorary butch homosexuals as fearless as Joan Crawford in *Johnny Guitar* playing Vienna, a hard-boiled saloon keeper who guns down her rival, Mercedes McCambridge, or as Tallulah Bankhead in *Lifeboat* playing a shipwrecked reporter, adrift in the Atlantic, who uses her diamond Cartier bracelet as bait to catch fish. Drag queen imagery has, in fact, always pervaded gay men's discussion of the legendary Hollywood actresses, of Gloria Swanson, whose "acting has more than a whiff of the drag queen about it";[5] of Vivien Leigh, whom gay author Paul Roen identifies with "for the simple reason that I know she's really not a woman";[6] or of Mae West, who was "Mt. Rushmore in drag," as well as "the first woman to function as a leading man."[7] (For decades, the latter was even suspected of literally *being* a biological male until her post-mortem finally convinced her skeptical gay fans that her curvaceous hips and imposing bosom were the real thing and not prosthetic foam rubber devices.)

Because of our fiercely fetishistic involvement with diva worship, the star even in a sense traded places with her gay audience, who used her as a naked projection of their frustrated romantic desires, of their inability to express their sexual impulses openly in a homophobic society, and to seduce and manipulate the elusive heterosexual men for whom many homosexuals once nursed bitterly unrequited passions. In the process of this transference, the diva was voided of both her gender and her femininity and became the homosexual's proxy, a transvestite figure, a vampish surrogate through whom gay men lived out unattainable longings to ensnare such dashing heartthrobs as Clark Gable, Humphrey Bogart, and Gene Kelly.

Although at first sight gay diva worship seems to have been as giddy as an adolescent girl's moonstruck infatuation with her teen

---

[5]Paul Roen, *High Camp* (San Francisco: Leyland, 1994), p. 212.
[6]*High Camp*, p. 173.
[7]Toni Lee, *Advocate*, Sept. 1969, p. 36; Freeman Gunter, *Mandate*, July 1992, p. 17.

idols, the homosexual's love of Hollywood was not an expression
of flamboyant effeminacy but, rather, in a very literal sense, of
swaggering machismo. For all of the lush sensuality of Greta
Garbo melting limply into the arms of John Barrymore in *Grand
Hotel* or Elizabeth Taylor batting her eyes at the impotent Paul
Newman in *Cat on a Hot Tin Roof*, diva worship provided effeminate men with a paradoxical way of getting in touch with their
masculinity, much as football provides a vicarious way for sedentary straight men to get in touch with *their* masculinity. Despite
appearances to the contrary, diva worship is in every respect as un-
feminine as football. It is a bone-crushing spectator sport in which
one watches the triumph of feminine wiles over masculine wills, of
a voluptuous and presumably helpless damsel in distress single-
handedly mowing down a lineup of hulking quarterbacks who fall
dead at her feet, as in *Double Indemnity*, where Barbara Stanwyck
plays a scheming femme fatale who brutally murders her husband
and then assists in dumping his lifeless body from a moving train
in order to collect his insurance policy, or in *Dead Ringer*, where
Bette Davis watches calmly as her dog lunges for the throat of her
gigolo boyfriend. As one gay writer wrote about his attraction to
the classic cinematic vamp, "as any drag queen can tell you: beneath all those layers of cosmetic beauty lies the kind of true grit
John Wayne never knew."[8] Before Stonewall, homosexuals exploited these coldblooded, manipulative figures as a therapeutic
corrective of their own highly compromised masculinity. To counteract their own sense of powerlessness as a vilified minority, they
modeled themselves on the appealing image of this thick-skinned
androgyne-cum-drag-queen, a distinctly militaristic figure who,
with a suggestive leer and a deflating wisecrack, triumphed over
the daily indignities of being gay. Even today, gay men still allude
to the star's usefulness in enabling them to "cope," in offering
them a tough-as-nails persona that they can assume like a mask
during emotionally trying experiences in which they imagine themselves to be Joan Crawford in *Mildred Pierce* building her restau-

---

[8]George Heymont, *Bay Area Reporter*, Jan. 25, 1990, p. 33.

rant empire or Bette Davis in *Dark Victory* nobly ascending the
stairs to die alone in her bedroom, struck down in the prime of
her life by a mysterious brain tumor. In an article on Ruby Rims,
a female impersonator so immersed in celebrity culture that he has
even named his cats "Eve" and "Channing," the *New York Native*
describes how homosexuals fight back through imitation, through
the often unconscious reenactment of Hollywood scenarios in the
course of real-life experiences:

> [Rims] finds that if he is angered or frustrated by something or someone, he
> can usually give vent to his feelings by becoming Bette Davis. . . . "She's a
> release for me," he said, his face brightening. "I can walk right up to someone
> and say"—*gasp*—" 'You're an asshole,' and blow cigarette smoke in their
> face."[9]

Quite by accident, by pure serendipity, the diva provided the psychological models for gay militancy and helped radicalize the subculture. The homosexual's inveterate habit of projecting himself into the
invincible personas of Scarlett O'Hara in *Gone with the Wind* or Al-
exandra del Lago in *The Sweet Bird of Youth* prepared the ground
psychologically for the political resistance that was to come in the 1960s
and 1970s when the gay man's internal diva was at last released from
the subjective prison of his fantasy world to take the streets by storm.
When drag queens fought back at Stonewall, chances are that what
they had on their minds was the shameless chutzpah of their film
icons, whose bravura displays of gutsiness they were reenacting. We
consumed, assimilated, and recycled Hollywood images in such vast
quantities and with such intense passion that it is interesting to spec-
ulate whether gay liberation would have been delayed had gay men
not found inspiration in these militant paradigms. Something as retrograde and conformist as popular culture, with its uncritical advocacy
of materialism, success, and blissfully domestic heterosexual relationships, was actually used for radical purposes, enabling a despised subculture to defend itself from the very America Hollywood celebrated.

---

[9]Donna Nowak, *New York Native*, Sept. 28, 1987, p. 31.

In the absence of the gay-positive propaganda in which contemporary gay culture is saturated, film became a form of "found" propaganda that the homosexual ransacked for inspiring messages, reconstituting the refuse of popular culture into an energizing force.

As Rims's comments reveal, one aspect in particular of the Hollywood actress's persona appealed to gay men: her bitchiness, her limitless satiric powers, as in *The Women* where the characters taunt each other with such venomous comments as "where I spit no grass grows," "your skin makes the Rocky Mountains look like chiffon velvet," and "chin up—that's right, both of them," or in *All About Eve* in which Bette Davis toasts the slanderous critic who raises his wine glass to her across a restaurant by taking a ferocious bite out of a stalk of celery.

Homosexuals were drawn to the image of the bitch in part because of her wicked tongue, her ability to achieve through conversation, through her verbal acuity, her snappy comebacks, the control over others that gay men were often unable to achieve in their own lives. The fantasy of the vicious, back-stabbing *vagina dentata*, always quick on her feet, always ready to demolish her opponent with a stunning rejoinder, is the fantasy of a powerless minority that asserts itself through language, not physical violence. Straight men express aggression through fistfights and sports; gay men through quick-witted repartee and caustic remarks. Straight men punch; gay men quip. Straight men are barroom brawlers; gay men, bitches. By providing the models for the beautiful shrew who, in film after film, attained a kind of conversational omnipotence, Hollywood fueled the homosexual's love of archness, of withering irony, which became the deadliest weapon of all in the arsenal of the pre-Stonewall homosexual. If shit-kicking amazons in sequins, ermine, and lamé inadvertently helped each gay man nurture, like his own inner child, his own inner diva, and thus strengthened his will to resist his degradation at the hands of a homophobic society, wittiness was the primary element of his revenge, the method by which he gained the upper hand over his enemies, remaining in possession of the battlefield long after the victims of the winged barbs he hurled had beat a hasty retreat. Given the centrality to the subculture of the image of the arch queen, it is not an exaggeration to say that gay politics grew out of gay wittiness, whose acerbic muse was the mordant Hollywood goddess. Wittiness was the first very tentative step toward gay liberation, a vitriolic expression of discontent, of our disdain for American prudery, which we reviled through verbal protest, a compulsion to denigrate, to engage in cutthroat bickering, which eventually reached critical mass and led to concrete political action. Bitching, in other words, was a form of protopolitics. It channeled the bitter frustrations of homosexuals' lives into a pronounced conversational mannerism that marked an important symbolic stage in the gay man's effort to translate his otherwise impotent rage into practical measures for social reform.

Hollywood suffused the gay sensibility during the first half of the twentieth century, not only because of its usefulness as "found" propaganda, but also because of the power of the new medium to build group solidarity. Given that homosexuals are an invisible minority whose members are not united by obvious physical characteristics and who are indeed often unrecognizable even to each other, they had to invent some method of identifying themselves as a group or risk remaining in the politically crippling state of fragmentation that for decades kept them from organizing to protect their basic civil rights. Blacks are united by their skin color, Chicanos by their language and place of origin, and the disabled by their infirmities. Homosexuals, however, are bound together by something less tangible: by their tastes, their sensibility, by the books they read, the clothes they wear, and the movies they watch.

Before the gay sensibility developed, homosexuals constituted an alienated diaspora of scattered individuals who lived a splintered existence in localized pockets where they strove to efface every identifying mark that might compromise them in the eyes of outsiders, breaking their cover and thus leading to their professional downfall and personal humiliation. For a minority trying so vigorously to erase itself, political unity was a contradiction in terms. With the codification of the gay sensibility and the liberation of men trapped in the solipsistic isolation of intense shame, the homosexual suddenly recognized that he belonged to a group, an elaborate network of fellow solipsists who began to establish connections with each other. Bridges were built partly through the cultivation of shared tastes in popular culture, through a reverence for a group of cinematic heroes whose glamor lent an unprecedented centrality to the previously disjointed and atomized nature of gay life. Hollywood divas were drafted, naturally without their knowledge, into the role of quasi-gay-liberation leaders, their charismatic presence unifying a body of followers who flocked together, not necessarily because of their idol's peculiar talents as an actress, but simply because she provided a kind of magnet. Large numbers of gay men established around these stars a new type of esprit de corps as the votaries of a particular pantheon of goddesses. Fandom, in other words, was an emphatic political assertion of ethnic camaraderie, as was the gay sensibility itself, which did not emanate from some sort of deeply embedded homosexual "soul," but arose as a way of achieving a collective subcultural identity.

Up until the 1960s, the performer served as a bellwether, a prophet without a religion, a platform, a cause, a messiah whose disciples were more in love with themselves than they were with their star. The priority of audience over artist becomes particularly clear in the case of the ultimate idol of the gay masses, Judy Garland. Her concerts during the 1950s and 1960s were so popular among homosexuals that, in each city in which she appeared, local gay bars emptied as their patrons came out en masse to hear a dazed and disoriented performer, slumped over the microphone, croak out the broken lyrics of songs that, in her final days, she had difficulty remembering.

Garland's force as a lodestone, an excuse for a public gathering of homosexuals, emerges in the existing accounts of her concerts, which witnesses describe as orgiastic rites of blind idolatry during which screaming multitudes of homosexuals, whipped up into a frenzy by such plaintive songs as "Over the Rainbow" and "The Man That Got Away," wept out loud, laying on the stage at their divinity's feet mountains of flowers. "It was as if the fact that we had gathered to see Garland gave us permission to be gay in public for once,"[10] one

---

[10]Richard Dyer, "Judy Garland and Gay Men," p. 145. From *Heavenly Bodies: Film Stars and Society* (New York: St. Martin's Press, 1986).

older gay man wrote of a 1960 concert, while another recalled a performance he attended as "more a love-in than a concert":

> When Judy came onto the stage, we were the loudest and most exuberant part of that audience. We not only listened, we felt all the lyrics of all the songs. Judy Garland was all ours; she belonged to every gay guy and girl in the theatre. I like to think that we were the greatest part of that audience; the part that Judy liked best.[11]

Although Garland was in many ways a brilliant performer, homosexuals came to regard her simply as the catalyst for the raucous, gay pride "love-ins" that erupted spontaneously during her concerts. Her uncritical mass appeal helped overcome our fragmentation to create for only a few hours, within the safe confines of an auditorium, an ephemeral, transitory "community" that lured us out of the closets in order to experience the unforgettable thrill of a public celebration of homosexuality. Those commentators who insist on trying to explain gay diva worship exclusively on the basis of the intrinsic appeal of a particular star—as a result of her pathos, suffering, vulnerability, glamor, or sexiness, to give only a few of the reasons that have been offered—have in many ways chosen as their starting point a mistaken premise. The answer to the proverbial question "why did gay men like Judy Garland so much?" is that they liked, not her, so much as her audience, the hordes of other gay men who gathered in her name to hear her poignant renditions of old torch songs that reduced sniffling queens to floods of self-pitying tears. The hysterical ovations her audiences gave her were in some sense applause for themselves. Garland was simply the hostess, a performer who good-naturedly rented out her immense reputation as an occasion for a huge gay party, a dry run for Stonewall, a dress rehearsal for the birthday bash of the burgeoning gay rights movement, which her last and most important concert, her funeral, was to inspire only a few years later.

It was this shared knowledge of popular music and film that cre-

---

[11]Toni Lee, obituary of Judy Garland, *Advocate*, Sept. 1969, p. 35.

ated the very foundations of camp. Homosexuals quickly incorporated into their conversations and style of humor a body of
subcultural allusions, ranging from Carmen Miranda in *The Gang's
All Here* singing "The Lady in the Tutti-Frutti Hat" in eight-inch
platform heels on a runway framed by giant strawberries, to Marlene
Dietrich wearing a blond Afro crooning "Hot Voodoo" in *Blonde
Venus* while chorus lines of cavorting Negresses wearing war paint
do the cakewalk behind her, to Maria Montez in *Cobra Woman*,
dancing a kootch dance in a slinky, sequined snake dress as she
selects terrified subjects for blood sacrifices, who are borne off shrieking to their unhappy fate.

Through constant quotation of the scripts of Hollywood movies
in our private conversations, we created a collage of famous lines
and quips, which, after frequent repetition, achieved the status of
passwords to a privileged world of the initiated, who communicated
through innuendo, through quoted dialogue pregnant with subtext.
A miscellaneous body of canonic lines was lifted straight out of the
masterpieces of popular culture and exploited as a way of declaring
our membership in the forbidden ranks of a secret society:

Toto, I don't think we're in Kansas anymore.

But you are, Blanche, you are in that chair.

I have always depended on the kindness of strangers.

Buckle your seatbelts, it's going to be a bumpy night.

What is the scene? Where am I?

What a dump!

Jungle red!

When gay people engaged in camp before Stonewall, they often
did so as a way of laughing at their appropriation of popular culture
for a purpose it had never been intended to serve: that of identifying
themselves to other homosexuals and triggering in their audience
instantaneous recognition of stock expressions, gestures, and double-

entendres that strengthened the bonds that held them together. Even today, a performer as gifted as Lypsinka, whose acts consist entirely of an intricate series of quotations from films, succeeds as a brilliant comic by virtue of her uncanny ability to play on her audience's gleeful sense of unity as a minority, an ethnic group that relives, long after we have established other channels of communication, the power of allusion to increase solidarity. Lypsinka simply mouths the words "no wire hangers" or "Barbara, pleeeeeease!" and her audience howls with laughter caused, not by the intrinsic hilariousness of the lines, but by the delight we take in the unanimity of our response, in our virtually reflexive recognition of the source of the allusions. This esoteric knowledge contributes to the elitist pleasure of a coterie sealed off from the rest of the uninitiated American public.

Camp and diva worship also served a more narrowly personal function than just providing us with a repository of subcultural narratives that became our own private language. Before Stonewall, allusions to such films as *The Women*, *Mildred Pierce*, *Now, Voyager*, *A Streetcar Named Desire*, or *Gilda* were ingeniously incorporated into the extremely delicate business of cruising for friends and sex partners, many of whom would undoubtedly have been far too timid to state their preferences openly. How much simpler it was to encode one's sexual orientation into something as elusive and uncompromising as a taste for a particular actress, whose name could be dropped casually in the course of a conversation in hopes that one's partner would pick up the gambit and agree that he did indeed like Judy Garland, that Mae West was outrageously funny, and that Tallulah Bankhead was, as she herself once said, "as pure as the driven slush." As exemplified by that time-honored expression "a friend of Dorothy," a particular taste in film provided a useful come-on for cautious gay men, who could reveal themselves to others without risking exposure, since only a fellow insider would recognize the allusion, thus allowing the homosexual to circumvent the potential embarrassment of a dismayed or even hostile reaction to a flat declaration. Over the decades gay men became so adept at communicating their forbidden desires through camp allusions that a sort of collective amnesia has descended over the whole process, and we have lost sight of the fact that our love for performers like Judy Garland was actually a learned behavior, part of our socialization as homosexuals. Many gay men still mistake their cultish admiration for the likes of Tippi Hedren, Kim Novak, or Barbara Stanwyck as an expression of an innate gay predisposition, as if the love of actresses was the result of a physiological imbalance in our smaller hypothalamuses, of a diva chromosome in our DNA which produced a camp sensibility that somehow preceded our awareness of our homosexuality.

As early as the 1950s, our use of camp as a method of cruising began to change. Irony was always present in the subculture's involvement with celebrities, partly because of the homosexual's sly awareness that he was misusing something as naive and wholesome as popular culture, with its golly-gee-whiz, Kansas-bred Dorothys and its Norman Rockwell happy endings, to reinforce something as illicit and underground as his solidarity with other homosexuals. As time went on, however, the note of facetiousness implicit in many gay men's treatment of Hollywood became louder and louder, until the wry smile of camp became the cackling shriek of the man who could no longer take seriously the divas he once adored.

By the early 1960s, some gay men had begun to express repulsion for our obsequious fawning over celebrities. Patrick Dennis's 1961 camp masterpiece *Little Me* provides a clear instance of the increasing skepticism homosexuals were bringing to their involvement with Hollywood. The novel purports to be the memoir of Belle Schlumpfert, aka Belle Poitrine, a great film actress, but in fact this imaginary autobiography, complete with hilarious photographs documenting Belle's meteoric rise to fame from her humble beginnings as the daughter of a scarlet woman, is an irresistibly scathing satire of a megalomaniac piece of trailer trash who uses the casting couch as a trampoline to catapult herself into stardom. By the 1980s and 1990s, the pantheon of immortals, while still treated reverently by many gay men, had become fair game for ridicule, as when New York drag queens commemorated the 1981 release of *Mommie Dearest* by dressing up as Joan Crawford and kicking life-size effigies of her daughter Christina up and down Christopher Street. Similarly, in 1987, *New York Native* columnist Dee Sushi imagined a hypothetical Broadway musical based on *Whatever Happened to Baby Jane?* in which a chorus line of spinning wheelchairs would whirl across the stage like dervishes to the accompaniment of a song entitled "But Cha *Are!*"[12]

One of the reasons for the change from reverence to ridicule, from Joan Crawford as the bewitching siren to Joan Crawford as the ax-wielding, child-beating, lesbian drunk, is that, in the minds of younger homosexuals, the diva had come to be perceived as the emotional crutch of the pathetic old queen. Surrounded by his antiques and registered crockery, this geriatric spinster compensates for the loneliness of his thwarted life by projecting himself into the tantalizing hourglass figures and haute couture ball gowns of his favorite actresses. For gay men under the age of 40, the classic film star has become the symbolic icon of an oppressed early stage in gay culture in which homosexuals sat glued to their television sets feasting their eyes on reruns, achieving through their imaginations the sense of self-worth that gay men now attain by consuming the propaganda our political leaders disseminate in such vast quantities. For the contemporary homosexual, who prides himself on his emotional maturity and healthiness, the use of the diva to achieve romantic fulfillment through displacement is the politically repugnant fantasy of the self-loathing pansy whose dependence on the escapism of cinema must be ritually purged from his system. We accomplish this catharsis by creating through conversations, theater, and even cabaret acts images of the vulgarity and psychological desperation of glamorous actresses, of Joan Crawford clobbering Christina with a can of bathroom cleanser or chopping off the head of her faithless husband in *Strait-Jacket*.

John Weir's novel about AIDS, *The Irreversible Decline of Eddie Socket* (1989), revolves around this act of purgation. Like Rims, its dying protagonist attempts to face his bleak future by staging what he calls "Barbara Stanwyck moment[s]." With his inspired sense of melodrama, he appears to be a typical example of a gay man with a

---

[12]*New York Native*, Jan. 26, 1987, p. 33.

relentlessly active internal diva, but, far from offering "empowerment," she becomes a vampire that feeds on his vitality, an incubus that saps his life of its reality and makes him feel that "the whole fucking world was in quotes. Was death going to be in quotes, too?"[13] Lying in his excrement in his hospital bed, abandoned by the nurses and orderlies who are too afraid to touch him, he wonders out loud to a friend:

> Who's the main character in my life? . . . Who is starring in my life? It can't be me . . . I'm just a walk-on. . . . Not even a supporting player. Not even a cameo appearance by a long-forgotten star. I'm just an extra. No one else is starring in my life. That's why they're halting production. It's a bad investment for the studio.[14]

Returning from the hospital, his friend has an hallucination that can be interpreted as a diatribe against the gay escapist whose obsession with actresses diminishes the reality of his life, starving it of its meaning and providing a safe emotional haven from the difficulties of being a homosexual. As he sits on a crosstown bus, Elizabeth Taylor appears out of the blue and proceeds, before his very eyes, to pull herself apart like Lego blocks in order to disabuse him of his adoration, first removing her contact lenses, then her chin, cheeks, breasts, left buttock, and right kneecap, until he realizes that, despite all of her glamor, "she's a walking prosthesis," "a pile of rubber parts on the floor between us, . . . all diminished."[15] Stuffing herself into a shopping bag, she hobbles off the bus, no longer the alluring emblem of the life the homosexual cannot live, but a Mr. Potato Head. This apocalyptic image of Taylor's self-destruction is pivotal to a book that is, in many ways, an anticamp requiem, an expression of the young homosexual's mounting impatience with the retrograde use of Hollywood as a security blanket.

---

[13]John Weir, *The Irreversible Decline of Eddie Socket* (New York: Harper & Row, 1989), p. 106.
[14]*The Irreversible Decline*, p. 240.
[15]*The Irreversible Decline*, p. 242.

The sacrosanct image of the Hollywood deity was also tarnished by the fact that, in the late 1960s and 1970s, gay men began holding their proto-gay-liberation leaders to a higher political standard. Because of the role actresses played in bringing gay men together as fans and instilling in them a sense of national identity that transcended the fragmented world that existed before Stonewall, homosexuals were at first unswervingly loyal to their patron saints and remained largely blind to their glaring deficiencies as the subculture's unofficial envoys to mainstream society. As we became more politically aware, however, and more conscious of our clout as a unified minority, we became impatient with the patronizing maternalism of early gay politics, which had produced the great matriarchy of mother hens who hovered protectively over their broods of gay fans. After Stonewall, we were no longer satisfied with the crumbs of celebrities' halfhearted comfort and support, with the meager consolation they offered for the humiliation of our social ostracism, which rarely amounted to more than such statements as "you poor little darlings" or "leave them alone, you bullies, they're so harmless."

In a 1971 issue of the *Advocate*, an interesting flurry of letters shows how uncomfortable gay men were beginning to feel with the tepid politics of maternalism. An outraged fan of Mae West wrote in to express his amazement at a passage he discovered in her autobiography, which read as follows:

> In many ways homosexuality is a danger to the entire social system of western civilization. Certainly a nation should be made aware of its . . . effects on children recruited to it in their innocence. . . . As a private pressure group it could, and has, infected whole nations. The old Arab world rotted away from it.[16]

In the weeks that followed, hard-core gay fans, unshaken in their devotion to their idol, leapt to her defense, trying to exculpate her from such damning evidence and blasting her accuser as a

---

[16]*Advocate*, Oct. 31, 1971, p. 29.

turncoat ("some fan!" one admirer complained). Even West's personal secretary, Robert Duran, wrote in to offer the feeble excuse that the quotation had been taken out of context and, far from being homophobic, "Miss West has always glorified gay people."[17]

Gay men must have been just as dismayed by Bette Davis's statement in 1964 that most of her fans were not "normal" but were "pansies." She singled out one particularly repulsive member of her perverted entourage, a doting 12-year-old boy who worshipped the ground she walked on: "his mother warped him somewhere down the line. He's a *pansy* at twelve! . . . If I had a son [like him], I'd *kill* myself!"[18] Even one of the biggest fag hags of all time, Marlene Dietrich, who, in the 1920s, at the height of the Weimar Republic, had coached drag queens on how to entwine themselves seductively in their feather boas and gesture with their vampish cigarette holders, maintained an at best ambivalent relationship with her gay fans. In her extreme old age, lying in squalor in her Paris apartment, she became convinced she would get AIDS from opening the fan mail sent by her largely gay following, a fear that inspired her to write a poem in illiterate doggerel which she requested her daughter to publish posthumously: "My Mother/Died of AIDS/She got it/From/the Mails . . . /She was hard/As nails/But AIDS/Was harder."[19]

Throughout the 1960s and 1970s, gay men defected from the once swollen ranks of their proto-gay-liberation leaders, who were retired as obsolete political vehicles and consigned to a museum of gay kitsch. Younger homosexuals picked up the discarded costumes and exaggerated mannerisms of these fading reputations and turned them into a communal grab bag for Halloween pranks, using the graven images of the old religion as satiric playthings for quaint camp pastimes. The temple of celebrity worship was pillaged and defiled, and the sacred vestments became dresses for drag shows, with gay men

---

[17]*Advocate*, Nov. 24, 1971, p. 24.
[18]James Spada, *More Than a Woman: An Intimate Biography of Bette Davis* (New York: Bantam, 1993), p. 387.
[19]Maria Riva, *Marlene Dietrich* (New York: Knopf, 1993), p. 773.

wearing the girlish ponytails and clown-white makeup of the ravaged Bette Davis in *Whatever Happened to Baby Jane?* or impersonating a cadaverous Marilyn Monroe exhumed from her crypt, her body scarred with the bloody gashes of her autopsy.

The homosexual's rebound from popular culture was also inspired by the ambivalence toward low-brow entertainment that lies at the very heart of the gay sensibility itself. In the years before Stonewall, Hollywood enabled the homosexual to express his alienation from the uneducated American public by cultivating the aestheticism of maladjustment. And yet aestheticism was an extremely problematic solution to the often harrowing challenges facing the effeminate homosexual. Most gay men had neither the means nor the education to avenge themselves against the contempt of their oppressors by cultivating the invulnerable persona of the aristocratic dandy, who filled his rooms with Oriental objets d'art and decadent Aubrey Beardsley prints. The ideal of the aesthete, of the tasteful devotee of the religion of beauty, is one that requires considerable leisure, as well as financial resources, and that posed a particularly punitive economic burden on men who were themselves, more often than not, as ignorant of high culture as the plebeians whose tastelessness they sought to denigrate by exhibiting their own savoir faire.

The movies, therefore, provided a poor man's aestheticism, a cheap method of satisfying the frustrated aesthetic sensibility of florists, hair stylists, waiters, and bank clerks who would otherwise not have been able to erect such protective divisions of elegance. One of the primary elements of camp, the obsession with popular cinema, became an integral part of gay life as a result of its psychological utility to a group of men pathetically striving to step out of their class entirely and take refuge in the sumptuous lives of the well-to-do. Using the only materials they could afford, the images of extravagant wealth available in film—the fabulous gowns, palatial estates, penthouse love nests, mink stoles, and Rolls-Royces—they devised a clever technique of shielding themselves from bigotry through the vicarious experience of unattainable affluence.

As Susan Sontag makes clear in "Notes on Camp,"[20] however, the sensibility of the overbred dandy, who carries *Les Fleurs du Mal* in one hand and *À Rebours* in the other, is a "snob" sensibility, one that reviles the very medium that fueled the lower-middle-class homosexual's fiction of superiority. The gay sensibility is thus at war with itself, at once feeding on the accessible glamor of Hollywood and convinced that it is debasing itself through its obsessive contact with Tinsel Town's cheapness. The same cinematic images that sustain the homosexual's aestheticism are tainted with the chintziness and mediocrity he is seeking to escape. Because of the dilemma facing the would-be dandy, reverence and ridicule go hand in hand. Implicit in the homosexual's adoration of the star is his revulsion from her, a repugnance that stems from his conviction that she is the incarnation of the low-brow culture from which he is attempting to disassociate himself. This contradiction erupts in such iconoclastic acts of celebrity desecration as the San Francisco Yuletide performance of "Christmas at the Crawfords," an annual burlesque of the famous 1949 radio broadcast in which Joan Crawford, rather than cooing graciously into the microphone in an effort to convey the impression to her listeners of being the perfect, selfless mother, whips out a coat hanger and, bellowing homicidal threats, thrashes her negligent daughter right on the spot. Similarly, in the New York drag festival Wigstock, celebrity desecration figures so prominently that the whole spectacle often degenerates into a funeral in honor of the dead diva, who is paraded around by ghoulish drag queen pallbearers, by men dressed up as Agnes Moorehead after she breaks her neck in *Hush, Hush, Sweet Charlotte* or *Psycho*'s Janet Leigh mauled by "Mother."

The new fascination with the diva as kitsch, a laughingstock, a reptile in a dress who cussed like a trooper and threw drunken tantrums in public places, was the result, not only of a contradiction intrinsic to the gay sensibility, but of a contradiction intrinsic to two extremely important things, to the very nature of glamor and the medium of film itself. A key aspect of homosexual camp stems from

---

[20]*Against Interpretation* (New York: Dell, 1966), p. 289.

factors that, while having nothing specifically to do with the gay sensibility, have nonetheless given it its distinctive shape. They provided the impetus for a form of gay mockery that originated in our disillusionment with our once "empowering" role models who, as they became older and lost their position of preeminence in American society, could not sustain their prestige in the eyes of their gay fans. Changes that occurred in the careers of the women behind the legends also occurred in the gay man's attitude toward himself and in the uses he was able to make of Hollywood glamor. What happened to the real diva also happened to the imaginary one, so that the fate of these two mythical beings was closely linked. They had become part of us; we had incorporated their style into our own. When they declined, we declined; when they were discredited, we were discredited.

The waning of the gay man's fascination with Hollywood derives partly from the untenability of the star's aloof demeanor. As embodied in the unapproachable style of the great actresses, glamor was meant to seem immortal and unchanging, a state of effortless perfection that was permanently fresh and immaculate. In the course of the most catastrophic film events, the celebrity's makeup and coiffure remained as stunning as if she had just stepped out of a beauty parlor, no matter how many natural disasters she rode through unscathed, how many burning buildings collapsed around her as she fled, or how many hired hitmen chased her breathlessly through the streets as she skipped along like a triathlete on the daintiest of stiletto heels.[21] It was the actress's superciliousness, her indifference to what was

---

[21]A magnificent and decidedly campy image of the insularity of glamor, of its refusal to interact with its environment, to change in any way, for the mascara to run or the dress to rip, comes in Hitchcock's *Lifeboat*, which opens with a shot of a ship going down, its smokestack slowly sinking into the sea. The camera then sweeps across the water, panning the floating wreckage—dead bodies, a *New Yorker* magazine, a trunk, a chess set, a child's doll—until it comes to rest upon the image of a single lifeboat rocking calmly on the waves. Sitting alone like a queen on her throne is Tallulah Bankhead, who appears wrapped in a mink stole, perfectly dry, perfectly coiffed, her lipstick perfect, her face perfect, her dress a marvel to behold, the only flaw being an unsightly run in her silk stocking, which she examines despairingly while corpses bob around her and the muffled screams of the drowning survivors echo through the fog.

happening around her, that appealed so strongly to the members of a minority who were constantly being challenged by their contemptuous peers, derided and belittled by a society whose disdain encouraged fantasies of invincibility in even the most effeminate men.

In real life, however, the thick-skinned androgynes on whom gay men modeled their internal divas were unable to live up to these cruel standards of perfection, with the result that the homosexual's adolescent belief in their unassailable divinity was challenged in ways that had far-reaching consequences for his involvement with them. Because glamorous actresses attempted to seem as indestructible in their own lives as they were in their film roles, they were plagued by bathos, by the ever-present danger of mess, by the threat of accidents—the slip of a foot, the split of a seam, spills, stains, but, most importantly, by the inevitability of old age. The classic Hollywood stars sought to embalm themselves, through a form of self-taxidermy, in an inhuman aura of agelessness, even as the passage of time began subtly eroding their legendary immortality, destroying their godlike illusion of eternal youth, and simultaneously inflicting mortal wounds on the gay man's role models. As the decades went by, fissures began to appear in the flawless facade of actresses' impenetrable elegance, and their humanity, despite their efforts to suppress it, emerged in all of its comic fallibility. They not only aged, they had breakdowns, developed drug addictions, became compulsive shoplifters, shook like aspen leaves from Parkinson's disease, and sank into the early senility of Alzheimer's. The drunken Dietrich, tottering on high heels, fell face first into the orchestra pit during at least two of her concerts, while Bette Davis's wig fell off after she was carted away plastered from a ceremony at which she was accepting an award. At the age of 60, the alcoholic Joan Crawford appeared drunk on television in the unconvincing role of a 28-year-old nymphomaniac in a soap opera, while Judy Garland, stoned out of her mind during one of her concerts, belted out "San Francisco" while the orchestra played "Chicago."

In addition to old age, a second factor led to the actress's devastating loss of credibility. If glamor is a hoax just waiting to be exposed, the very camera that exalted these women was also the agent of their downfall, the instrument of their torture, the divinely sanctioned method of punishment for their pride. A capacity intrinsic to the medium of film—its ability to record for all posterity the effects of age on the divas' bodies—created an essential element of modern camp: its obsession with decay, decomposition, and decrepitude, with a 63-year-old Joan Crawford in black fishnet tights playing a circus ringmistress in *Berserk* or an unsteady Dietrich clinging for support to the stage curtain, her wig askew, her lipstick smeared, her voice no more than a hoarse whisper as she wailed out a drunken rendition of "Where Have All the Flowers Gone?"

By the 1950s, the careers of Dietrich, Crawford, Davis, and Hayworth were essentially over. But—and herein lies the secret ingredient of gay men's recipe for camp—long after their idols' reputations had begun to decline, the cameras kept rolling even as these sex goddesses turned into withered hags before our very eyes, fighting to revive their waning careers, finally sinking into the unfathomable depths of B-grade horror flicks, playing ax murderesses and psychotic forgotten stars.

With the advent of television, the nightly broadcast of reruns drove the final nails into their coffins: for the first time in history, gay men were allowed to see, virtually side by side, what these women once were and what they had become, watching one night a glamorous Bette Davis in *The Letter* at the height of her career and the next a battered old crone starring in *Whatever Happened to Baby Jane?* glaring bewildered at her gruesome reflection in the mirror where she stood in pigtails and pinafores, her ancient face caked with the makeup she troweled on for her part at her own insistence.

Without reruns, there is no camp, for camp is about the death of glamor, about the shattering of the sacrosanct illusion of the actress's inimitable aura of youth and invulnerability, about knocking the idol off her pedestal and dragging her through the mud, subjecting her decrepitude to the same minute scrutiny to which the medium of film once subjected her beauty. Camp is rooted in the gay man's profound disillusionment with celebrity culture. It expresses betrayal. It is the gleeful sadism of the fan who has been tricked, who discovers he has been complicit in an elaborate swindle, a monstrous lie, who realizes that his youthful cinematic fantasies are false, that his role models are marionettes, puppets whose talent and glamor were all smoke and mirrors. Out of this loss of innocence, homosexuals have created a macabre form of ethnic humor in which they dance upon their former role models' graves, reliving again and again the hilarious realization that the diva was *not* a goddess, that she was flesh and blood, that she got fat just like they did, that she got wrinkled just like they did, that she had a miserable life and horrid children and crippling diseases and financial crises and even died just like they did, but with one major difference: in the case of the diva, the press was there to get it all down, to record every pratfall and black eye and lesbian affair and drug overdose and nose job and trip to the fat farm and convalescence in the Betty Ford Center.

While camp is fueled by the ability of film to record the ravages of time, to document the process of aging as homosexuals had never seen it before, it has also been shaped by the rise of investigative journalism and the invasiveness in modern life of the media, which suddenly brought gay men in closer proximity, not only to the divas' deteriorating bodies, but to their chaotic private lives. Within the last 25 years, a rash of tell-all biographies has catered to the public's insatiable desire for information, including three poison pen memoirs of Crawford, Davis, and Dietrich by their ungrateful daughters, who, to the delight of millions, committed immensely entertaining acts of literary matricide.[22] The press changed the entire psychology of diva

---

[22]In these and other best-selling biographies, we learn such compromising details about the stars as the fact that the drunken Joan Crawford propositioned her children's nurses, pounding furiously on their locked doors at night, begging to be let in; and that Marlene Dietrich, in her eighties, fell in love with Baryshnikov, telling her scandalized daughter that, "after all the years of nothing, I should be nice and tight again 'down there,' don't you think?" She also carried on a long-distance epistolary love affair with a California doctor to whom she sent a pair of "tweensy-weensy" chorus-girl panties that she sprinkled with perfume and then rubbed on her crotch. Even Judy Garland, who self-destructed in public and whose private life was therefore an open book, has been mined as a rich source of gossip. In David Shipman's *Judy Garland: The Secret Life of an American Legend*, we learn that by the 1950s "Amphetamine Annie," whose death by overdose the *New York Daily News* was said to have already set in type in preparation for what its editors perceived as a foregone conclusion, had become such an inveterate

worship, altering it so radically that celebrities could no longer serve the same invigorating function of inspiring gay men with pride and determination. As a result, homosexuals were left with an unburied corpse festering in their imaginations, the lifeless remains of a public figure who did not carry the same weight of authority and who was therefore subject to the necrophilic depredations of camp. The homosexual's mockery of his heroines is something he is also doing to himself, using the humor of celebrity desecration as an anesthetic for the amputation of an obsolete part of the gay psyche.

The evolution of our attitudes toward divas can be explained by a simple fact: devotion always ends up consuming its object, demanding ever greater intimacy with the source of its obsession. And yet intimacy is the very thing that destroys reverence, that turns reverence into ridicule, for idolatry can be maintained only through distance, through aloofness, through the celebrity's ability to keep her gay public at bay, always wondering, always guessing at what lies behind her magisterial facade, at the mysterious goings-on in the heart of the inner sanctum behind the electric fences and the body guards. While remoteness and ignorance are the primary requirements of the primitive folk religion of homosexual celebrity worship, everything in modern secular society conspires to eliminate this distance, to close in on the immediate cause of the gay man's fascination, to hunt it down like game and force it out into the open. Obsessed with our need to know more about the people we fetishize, we sic the press on them like dogs to get the scoop, to snap the photograph of the adulterous rendezvous at the secret hideaway, to record every gaffe, every candid moment of the frazzled star without her makeup, looking hideous in a T-shirt and sweatpants as she slips out the back door of the drug rehabilitation clinic.

In a society based on an unrestricted free press and accustomed

---

pill popper that she sewed Darvon and bennies into the hems of her dresses, a habit that led her friends to take the precaution of emptying their medicine cabinets before she swooped down on them for a visit to replenish her supplies. Once, when a gay acquaintance loaned her his house for a month, he hid every pill he owned except for a full bottle of mange tablets for his dog, only to discover when he returned that, much to his horror, this walking pharmacopoeia had scarfed them all down.

to the high standards of truth that a free press instills in us, it is impossible to maintain the conditions of mystery and remoteness that make something as superstitious and old-fashioned as Hollywood idolatry possible in the first place. Gay diva worship is a cult that requires the blind faith of credulous fans who are content to kowtow and genuflect and never to even think of peeking behind the curtain. Camp is what happens when the curtain is lifted. The irreverent humor of the drag queen dressed up as a trembling Katharine Hepburn, a dazed Peggy Lee in a scarf and black shades, or a haggard Tippi Hedren in *The Birds*, represents the last gasp of idol worship in a secular age, the passing of a mode of religious experience, whose funeral gay men celebrate with delightfully deranged fervor. Camp is the final rite of the religion that failed, the satirical requiem of the heathen fetishist who has lost faith in his god, who has watched too many reruns and seen too many incriminating photographs and read too many kiss-and-tell biographies to believe in the myth of glamor. Gay men have created a school of humor out of what amounts to the fundamental religious crisis of twentieth-century popular culture.

But camp has always been something more than just the death throes of pagan idolatry in a secular age. It has also served, as we have seen, to consolidate group identity. Because gay culture is becoming less closeted, however, the need to seal our furtive communal bond through the secret handshake of Hollywood trivia is disappearing, and with this disappearance, a crucial element of the gay sensibility has been thrown into jeopardy. Liberation is destroying the need for celebrity culture as a group marker, as a way of expressing tribal inclusion in a private membership club of the cognoscenti. Gay men have other, less circuitous ways of meeting and socializing, now that the whole purpose of communicating in code has disappeared with the explosion of mega dance clubs, gay men's choruses, computer bulletin boards, phone chat lines, bowling leagues, Gay and Lesbian Sierra Clubs, and self-help Bible study groups for gay Mormons in recovery. Many homosexuals under the age of 30 have never even seen a film starring Joan Crawford, let alone relished the magnificent biographical ironies of *A Star Is Born* or seen Bette Davis's hair fall out in *Mr. Skeffington* or Rita Hayworth dance in *Gilda* or Marlene Dietrich play a melancholy and infinitely wise courtesan in *Shanghai Express* who turns sadly to an old suitor and laments, "it took more than one man to change my name to Shanghai Lily."

While gay culture is still obsessed with celebrities (although primarily as a political force, a PR tool for promoting "visibility"), young gay men no longer have the same involvement with popular culture that they had when the movies served almost as a social intermediary, a matchmaker, a badge to identify oneself to other members of the clan, other "friends of Dorothy." As the forces of social stigma and oppression dissipate and the factors that contributed to the making of the gay sensibility disappear, one of homosexuals' most significant contributions to American culture, camp, begins to lose its shape. The grain of sand, our oppression, that irritated the gay imagination to produce the pearl of camp, has been rinsed away, and with it, there has been a profound dilution of the once concentrated gay sensibility. Camp cannot survive our ultimate and inevitable release from the social burden of our homosexuality. Oppression and camp are inextricably linked, and the waning of the one necessitates the death of the other.

Stereotypes often contain a grain of truth even though we are forbidden to say so in polite society. The stresses and strains of living in a country fractured by ethnic pluralism require that we never openly mention the widely held but easily misunderstood beliefs that many Jews are high strung and intellectual, that many WASPs are rich and uptight, that many Koreans are thrifty and reserved, and that many homosexuals are witty and "creative." All too often, however, these putative group characteristics, while in fact representative of a distorted and vastly oversimplified truth, are said to reflect some sort of intrinsic "soul," as if Jews were intellectual out of biological necessity, as if WASPs were born to eat bland food and shop at L.L. Bean, as if Koreans were ordained by fate to become grocers, or as if homosexuals were drawn to such professions as floristry and interior decoration out of a compelling physiological urge. In the case of gay men, our seemingly hereditary predisposition for tastefulness and the arts, for belting out show tunes in piano bars and swooning over *La Traviata*, is not an innate character trait but a pragmatic response to the conditions of a hostile environment. We are aesthetes by need, not by nature. The gay sensibility is as efficient and practical as a household appliance, a labor-saving device that streamlines the complicated business of adapting to the pressures of our marginality as well as to the unusual psychology of homophobic oppression.

What sets us apart from all other minorities is that we have neither a geographical place of origin (along with the shared cultural traditions that a common national heritage produces) nor physical characteristics—no skin color, no distinctive facial features, no prominent Semitic noses, fair Aryan complexions, or Asiatic eyes. We are, by definition, an utterly nondescript diaspora, dispersed through every social class and region of the country, a hidden fraternity united solely by something as subjective as our erotic fantasies. Because we are the only invisible minority, we must invent from scratch those missing physical features that enable us to spot our imperceptible compatriots, who would remain unseen and anonymous if they did not prominently display on their own bodies, in their sibilant voices and shuffling gaits, in their immaculate grooming and debonair style of deportment, the caste mark that constitutes the essence of the gay sensibility.

And yet if these subtle, understated signs and telltale gestures are to unite us without at the same time incriminating us, revealing our presence without subjecting us to the humiliation of exposure, they must remain indiscernible to those for whom they are not intended, the masses of heterosexuals who are deaf to their silent appeal. While in the earlier part of the century the uninformed majority saw nothing but a man with a floppy red bow tie and white kid gloves, the chosen few saw something infinitely less prosaic: a kindred spirit eagerly waving to them across the yawning abyss of disgrace and social ostracism that kept homosexuals from meeting. The gay sensibility comprises the reflective surfaces off of which our radar echoes as we transmit an incessant pulse of undetectable signals, constantly scanning the public domain for distant transmissions. Because of our transparency, we define ourselves as a group through our shared tastes, styles in clothing, preferences in movie stars, types of catty humor, distinctive choices in interior decoration, and even affected British accents, the instantly recognizable clues that we have scrambled into what is perhaps the most elaborate code in human history. This illegible language has been encrypted into our gestures like invisible ink, the incriminating evidence of our treasonable misconduct, the stylistic fingerprint that we leave at the scene of the crime, giving a physical presence to something as slippery and intangible as desire. The gay sensibility is composed of the remnants of the billions of hints and insinuations that gay men have dropped in the course of the last hundred years, the fossilized residue of innuendo and double-entendres that gives the conversations we have in public a subregister, an inaudible undertow of suggestiveness that only the initiated can perceive. The outsider remains oblivious to these subterranean semantics, to the articles of clothing, passwords, and lines of film script with which we utter the unutterable, saluting each other through the rents we tear in the veil of secrecy.

If the gay sensibility provides an oblique method of communication with other homosexuals, it also provides a means of compensating for social disenfranchisement, a problem we solve through what I have called the aestheticism of maladjustment. When the early twentieth-century art collector Isabella Steward Gardner was cruelly spurned by the Boston Brahmins who excluded her from their ranks as a social-climbing, nouveau riche upstart, she took revenge by amassing one of the largest private art collections in the country, a vainglorious monument to the frustrated ambitions of a megalomaniac socialite. The homosexual sensibility is simply this excluded parvenu's symbolic triumph writ large. Aestheticism became a substitute for moral respectability, a righteous surrogate for the acceptance and social standing that we were unable to achieve in more conventional ways.

While the need for retaliation would seem to be too petty and mean spirited a motive for the creation of significant art, the aestheticism of maladjustment is the source of some of the most valuable contributions that homosexuals have made to American society. It is this unconscious act of revenge and not a gay soul that is the secret to our creativity, the reason so many of us flock to the arts, why we become choreographers, playwrights, actors, and writers, why we are so disproportionately represented at musical conservatories, why we staff the major theater companies, why we design the most famous lines of fashion, why we are antique collectors, opera queens, and gallery directors. Without the aestheticism of maladjustment, the American cultural landscape would be, if not altogether barren, at least considerably less interesting, with far fewer ballet companies, more bad films, tackier styles of clothing, and uglier inner-city neighborhoods full of the crumbling tenements that homosexuals gentrify, turning dilapidated fixer-uppers into richly appointed condos, the architectural embodiment of our need to achieve social status through our tastes, our sensibility.

As we have seen, however, our self-conscious attempts to demonstrate our tastefulness ultimately become a subcultural millstone, since only those gay men who can afford the appurtenances of culture and who have the education to flaunt their powers of discrimination can pass themselves off as credible connoisseurs. Most homosexuals are thus caught in an impossible bind, forced to live according to a standard of elegance and refinement well beyond their means, outclassed by the aristocratic ideals they employ as a corrective to their victimization by sexual apartheid. To alleviate this situation, we have devised an ersatz aestheticism that we cultivate, not only through our involvement with the arts, but through our involvement with department stores, through shopping, the purchase of expensive toiletries, vintage wines, fashionable clothing, and designer accessories like Rolex watches and Ralph Lauren eyewear. The display of our refinement as consumers, as resourceful bargain hunters who ferret out the best deals on Armani suits and damask slipcovers, on Oriental throw rugs and antique armoires, easily replaces the display of our refinement as art lovers. In the course of the twentieth century, homosexuals have turned the aestheticism of art and culture into the aestheticism of products, the commodities that spill out of the Macy's bags constantly swinging from the arms of the urban homosexual, a figure laden with the spoils of his spending sprees, an image that has largely replaced that of the monocled fop twirling his cane and sniffing the carnation in his lapel.

In the vulgarization of aestheticism in the last hundred years, one sees the fatal link between the gay sensibility and consumerism. The use of aestheticism as a form of civil disobedience, of sublimated rage against an artless society, has made us psychologically dependent on shopping as a way of redressing our sense of inferiority and has thus transformed us into a potential gold mine for manufacturers who recognize the untapped economic potential of this upscale and yet insecure market. The snobbish sensibility we used to rebel against our status as second-class citizens has become the very thing that has made us so appealing to corporate America, the selling point that provides the key to our social reintegration, which has been accelerated as companies supply the ammunition of expensive goods, the Gucci shoulder bags and the designer fragrances, that we use in our war against philistinism. There is no little irony in the fact that a feature intrinsic to the gay sensibility has led to the extreme commercialization of the subculture. The old-fashioned vehicle of our rebellion against our exclusion, our aesthetic repudiation of the judgments of homophobes, has paradoxically become the secret of our acceptance by society. As homosexuals are courted by Fortune 500 companies, we will be granted the respectability we were once denied and experience a gradual social rehabilitation. This improvement in our public image will in turn mitigate the oppressive conditions in which we live and thus undermine the whole purpose of the gay sensibility. It is only a matter of time before our distinctive characteristics as a minority begin to dissolve as they are rendered superfluous by our new sense of pride as an elite sector of the consumeristic society that is absorbing us into a featureless mainstream market. Our moral redemption is directly correlated to our financial value to a society destined to find us too commercially useful to prevent us from participating in its economic prosperity.

Just as our attitudes toward divas have evolved over time as gay culture has become more open, so, too, have our personal ads changed significantly in the last 50 years. If our capricious relation to cinema shows the dissolution of a sharply defined gay identity, the language we use to describe ourselves to our potential partners has also been shaped by our conscientious efforts to blend into the mainstream, imitate heterosexuals, and rid ourselves of an increasingly archaic subculture, which many gay men are now actively seeking to nullify.

The evolution of gay personal ads and of our worship of divas is similar in another respect as well: mass culture—this time in the form of the print media, the U.S. Postal Service, and the telephone—has again provided a vehicle for establishing links with other homosexuals. Ironically, gay men have used the most public and accessible features of popular culture to satisfy this most private and secretive of sins, which, far from remaining undercover, has found effective outlets in open and unrestricted forums, from rest rooms and parks to celebrities and daily newspapers.

The Evolution of

the Personals and

Gay Romance

S OME OF THE FIRST gay personal ads to be published in America appeared, not in the clandestine newsletter of a secret fraternal society of sex radicals, but in a wholesome family magazine that was not only freely distributed but available even to young children, who were allowed—indeed, encouraged—to advertise in its pages. In 1946, F.W. Ewing brought out the inaugural issue of one of the most outrageous scams ever perpetrated in modern journalism, *The Hobby Directory*, the house organ of the National Association of Hobbyists for Men and Boys. The publication's exalted ideals of ostensibly platonic camaraderie can be summed up in a poem the magazine printed by a subscriber, the notorious homosexual Bois Burk, who expressed his debt to the *Directory* in a couplet: "A truly beautiful experience I think/When true friends are made by pen and ink."[1]

Consisting solely of personal ads, the magazine claimed that its mission was "to help its members find hobby friends,"[2] but in fact it really amounted to little more than a bizarre dating service. While many of the ads in the first few issues appear to have been placed by straight men filled with a legitimately burning passion for spelling

---

[1]The copies of *The Hobby Directory* I used were Burk's own copies and were filled with his annotations about which men he had contacted. June 1951, p. 6.
[2]*Hobby Directory*, Mar. 1951, p. 1.

reform and mineralogy or for collecting whiskey labels, match covers, or even cocktail stirrers, legions of gay men quickly infiltrated the *Directory*. Homosexuals soon requisitioned the entire magazine as a vehicle for ferreting out other members of their persuasion, their ads ultimately shoving aside those of philatelists, boys into model train sets, and devotees of bottle caps and cigar bands. Advertisers didn't openly state their sexual preferences, of course, but communicated with each other in code, leaving a coquettish trail of self-incriminating clues. For instance, they expressed a desire to meet other "bachelors," "single hobbyists," "servicemen," "ex-marines and sea-going swabbies" who could appreciate the exquisite handicrafts of nimble-fingered artisans, especially those who engaged in the manly arts of crocheting, needlework, knitting, embroidery, ballet, nude sunbathing, and—the most enigmatic hobby of all—"adventure." In 1949, one man dispensed with the sophomoric ruse of hobbies altogether and wrote that he hoped the *Directory* would enable him to broaden his acquaintance with an idiosyncratic spectrum of hobbyists, from "cowboys, sheepherders, miners, [and] lumberjacks" to "ranch hands, sailors, and guys who wear levis, cords, [and] leather jackets, with pep in their step and a sparkle in their eyes." Another man made his proclivities known by adopting the foppish mask of a nineteenth-century aesthete, a high priest in the religion of beauty: "I'm a patron of the arts, who solely doth to beauty rally.... Like a sorcerer I dabble with many crafts... my specialty is collecting portraits of characters strange." By 1951, the well-kept secret of this extraordinary hoax was all but betrayed by Ewing himself who took to task those members who "do not give their correct ages"[3] but shave off years and even decades, thus misleading hobbyists who had hoped to share only with men of their own generation such pastimes as collecting drawings of naked adolescents, "memorabilia related to boys famous in history," or "photos of young men in service uniforms."

Aside from *The Hobby Directory*, which was sold quite openly and was even supported by a number of crafts stores, early gay personal

---

[3]*Hobby Directory*, Sept. 1951, p. 6.

ads were usually published in short-lived, fly-by-night pamphlets distributed on the sly through a kind of sexual samizdat. In such proto-"zines" as *Communique* or *Trans-World Classified*, both of which were published in the early 1960s and smuggled from reader to reader like contraband, the ads of homosexuals appeared right next to those of heterosexuals. One of the first exclusively gay forums for personal ads was the Los Angeles publication *Romans*, whose maiden issue in 1964 featured on its cover an image resonant with misgivings about the propriety of homosexuals advertising for partners: a bas-relief of Judgment Day in which a hellish host of fiends jab the prongs of their pitchforks into the rear ends of a demoralized procession of lost souls, whom they proceed to scald in a caldron of boiling oil and then hurl into a smoldering pit of fire and brimstone. While a smattering of gay ads were published throughout the mid-1960s in such trailblazing publications as *Cruise News & World Report* or the *Haight Ashbury Maverick*, it wasn't until January 1969 that the *Advocate*'s scandalous "Trader Dick's" classified section emerged as the raunchiest forum for gay personals, a position it would maintain throughout the 1970s. Here, advertisements placed by "gay bachelors," "groovy models," and "hep guys" were nestled among notices placed by men seeking roommates, prostitutes offering their services as "chauffeurs," and entrepreneurs selling such de rigueur health-and-beauty products as "custom-made hairpieces," "makeup that will make you look 10 yrs. younger and last for 3 days," and "sensuous enemas including the famous Mae West health enema."

The long and venerable tradition of cruising for "pen pals" through contact ads became entrenched in gay culture at such an early stage in its development because the U.S. Postal Service offered a relatively safe method of communication for closeted homosexuals unwilling to take the professional gamble of being hauled out of bars and tossed into paddy wagons. The personals were thus perfectly adapted to an atomized culture of isolated individuals whose only sense of community came from responding to the anguished cries of other gay men strewn across the entire continent, pining away in hick towns where gay life consisted of a truck stop on a turnpike and a Greyhound Bus depot. Not surprisingly, the authors of early personal ads did not have the luxury to be as finicky and selective as modern advertisers (who lust after busty blond boy toys who are "hot, horny, and hung") but were recklessly indiscriminate about the sort of man they were seeking. Personal ads from the 1940s, 1950s, and even the 1960s provide a perfect snapshot of gay life before the rise of the commercialized subculture, a world of bewildered inverts marooned in the boondocks, starving for companionship in Elyria, Ohio, and Butte, Montana, aimlessly groping about in the dark in hopes of stumbling upon another homosexual.

Even as late as 1968, in an issue of the gay publication *The Male Swinger*, the writers were so unspecific about their own characteristics, let alone those of the men they were seeking, that readers were forced to winnow through ads that presented a generic figure, a Man Without Qualities, a featureless cipher often identified solely by a box number or the region of the country in which he lived:

Will welcome all letters from anyone who cares to write.

Would like to hear from anyone, anywhere.

Would like to hear from all.

Will write anyone who writes me.

Will reply to all male mail, any age or race.

Will respond to males within a radius of 100 miles.

Wishes correspondence with other gay men.

The brevity and inclusiveness of these undescriptive notes, like the messages placed in bottles by shipwrecked castaways, contrast dramatically with the lengthy wish lists of unreasonable specifications and inflated prerequisites found in contemporary ads. One has only to look at the classified section of virtually any contemporary gay newspaper to see how far we have advanced from the Balkanized world of lonely shut-ins begging for pen pals to a highly organized subculture in which arcane fetishists communicate with each other about everything from water sports and bootlicking to musical comedies and competitive bridge. By means of the telephone and the computer, advertisers can now make instantaneous contact with other men who practice their abstruse "hobbies," the diversity of which is reflected in such rubrics as "Relationships," "Shared Interests," "Just Plain Sex," "Vanilla Sex," "Pig Sex," "Raunch," "Hardcore," "The Unusual," "Daddies & Daddies Boys," "Bears," "Asians, Latins & Blacks," and "None of the Above."

In the late 1960s and early 1970s, a new character emerges in gay personal ads: Mr. Right, a sentimental figure who, over the next decade, slowly edges out the Man Without Qualities, the bafflingly nondescript representative of an increasingly obsolete period of desperation and anonymity. The sweeping generality of an advertiser from Davenport, whose sole criterion for the man he is seeking is that he reside in the vicinity of Omaha or Dubuque, makes an interesting comparison with the selectivity of the advertisers in recent gay newspapers who use such beseeching, love-sick headlines as "Looking for Mr. Perfect," "The Man of My Dreams," "The One and Only," "Please Help Me Find You," "I Want a Dream Lover!," "My Fantasy Man," and "I Know You're Out There." As gay liberation widened the pool of our potential partners, we became more and more fastidious and harder to please until personal ads were transformed from open-ended cattle calls (as in ads that read "DESPERATE!," "Help!," and "lonely male!") into quixotic quests for the ideal partner, the one-in-a-million man who can satisfy our stringent new requirements for sexual and emotional compatibility. A fairy-tale notion of fate lies behind many contemporary gay personal ads, which are haunted by the illusory figure of Prince Charming, by a knight in shining armor who will sweep us off our feet, thereby fulfilling the romantic daydream of a culture paralyzed by choice and spoiled by the privileges of open communication.

The shift from the Man Without Qualities to the perfect mate represents a revolutionary development in gay men's understanding of their relationships. The unrealistic standards that lie behind the primary sexual mirage of the assimilated gay imagination are premised on the very modern assumption that the homosexual searching for Mr. Right is awash in Mr. Wrongs, in hordes of panting suitors whom he can scornfully disqualify on the basis of a single defect in hopes of meeting his soul mate, his preordained destiny. The notion of Mr. Right would have been unthinkable to the geographically isolated hobbyists of the first half of the twentieth century who, far from having the luxury to squander their energies scouring the planet for an ideal lover, had to devote themselves to the onerous task of finding even a handful of gay friends, who existed in a "subculture" that extended no further than each other's living rooms. When gay liberation increased contact among homosexuals, it inadvertently contributed to the state of romantic dissatisfaction in which many of us now flounder, nursing our blighted hopes and infeasible dreams, convinced that we must patiently await the arrival of our own personal messiah, an unattainable mystery man who makes many men as discontented as the secluded outcasts who lived in the fragmented world that preceded the subculture. Gay liberation has thus made us simultaneously more romantic and less tolerant of the imperfections of our potential lovers, any one of whom would probably have satisfied the more modest expectations of those whose first requirement in a man was that he live within "a radius of 100 miles."

After Stonewall, writers of personal ads also began to manipulate grammar and syntax in ways made possible only by the emergence of a collective homosexual identity. Men who published ads before 1970 usually wrote in a strangely detached and objectified third person in which they rattled off a mechanical list of their credentials, a résumé of their attributes and qualifications, as if they were describing, not themselves, but a friend, a "congenial white bachelor in his mid 40s" or "a male gay teenager with a groovy bod." During the 1970s, however, many men not only abandoned the third person for the first, but also stopped addressing their readers as amorphous entities identified by the inappropriately clinical noun "male" or by such drab and dehumanizingly broad expressions as "sincere type," "rugged husky type," "hairy he-man type," or "broadminded butch type." Instead, they spoke to their audience in distinctly chummy terms as members of the same sexual clan, the same coterie, as a "you," as in "after I spank you good & long for being such an adorable, naughty guy . . . , [I] will console you and your red, bare bottom!" Writers also started to fashion their ads as dialogues or fragments of scripts, chatty, intimate tête-à-têtes filled with rhetorical questions ("Want true love?" or "Tired of the merry-go-round of turn-offs and inconsiderates one meets thru these ads?"), cheerful greetings ("Hi!" or "hey you big, heavy-hung black dudes!"), and even commands ("titillate me! drive me wild!" or "bend over and show dad what you've got"). These subtle syntactical shifts reveal that the writer is no longer a frightened and lonely individual conducting blind fishing expeditions among an anonymous mass of gay men who constitute an unknown quantity, a nameless, faceless riddle. Rather, he considers himself a card-carrying member of a distinct sect whose habits and aspirations he shares and whom he is therefore able to address in a confidential new spirit of camaraderie that would have been impossible in an era in which homosexuals did not share any common culture, dispersed as they were in isolated pockets across the country.

If the evolution of the subculture can be measured in the radical differences between the pre-subcultural homosexual's plaintive cry "would like to hear from anyone, anywhere" and the assimilated gay man's ultimatum "I Want a Dream Lover!," it can also be charted in the dramatic changes that have occurred in the quaintly chivalrous euphemisms that gay men once used to sidestep the sexual implications of the relationships they were seeking. Well into the 1970s, advertisers often took refuge in an anachronistic set of vague and noncommittal terms that refer, not to the "deep-throat oral sluts," "sperm sponges," and "headboard bangers" of the 1980s and 1990s, but rather to two chastely classical lovers who seemed to be seeking each other's companionship solely for the privilege of celebrating together an entirely idealized form of "male friendship." Before Stonewall, men never specified that they were seeking a "boyfriend" but chose instead such passionless subterfuges as "a lasting companionship," "a permanent tie," "an intimate fellowship," "a loving partnership," or "a special friendship." These expressions suggest a degree of irresolution about what gay men were to call their long-standing sexual relationships, which were so far beyond the pale of

respectability that no vocabulary had been developed to describe
them other than tepid circumlocutions that evoked a cold and virginal type of unconsummated brotherly love.

Compare, for instance, the austere language of an ad from 1964—
"bachelor seeks honest male friendship"—with the rhetoric of an ad
from 1992:

MARRIAGE MATERIAL, BUT . . .

Long courtships are more my style. How about evenings at the opera, spicy
ethnic dives, sunspot weekends, a big Christmas tree, a good bottle of wine,
homemade pasta for a few friends, and lovemaking beside a crackling fire.
Winter is coming and I'd like to settle in.

Spelling out all of the connubial activities that the reader is forced
to infer in the first ad, the second plagiarizes the language with
which mainstream America describes heterosexual marriages. Conjugal terminology is now commonplace in gay newspapers, as in ads
that exclaim "marry me!," "are you a husband looking for a husband?," or "[let's] go straight to the shotgun wedding. . . . But before
we pick out the china pattern, [let's] get . . . acquainted." Throughout
the 1970s, the terminology that gay men used to describe their relationships was gradually heterosexualized until by the mid- to late
1980s we felt no qualms whatsoever about bandying around such
terms as "dates," "boyfriends," "husbands," "spouses," and "better
halves." Prior to this time, gay relationships were less colored by
heterosexual rhetoric because they were still emerging from a period
in which two men came together without the benefit of clear labels
to categorize their feelings for each other, cut off as they were from
the supporting structure of a sophisticated subculture that was only
later to invent a language for gay love by pirating it from the language of heterosexual romance.

At times, this heterosexualizing rhetoric transforms the relationships that advertisers describe into literal travesties of straight marriages, crude forgeries that conjure up images of fittings for the bridal
gown and anxious arrangements for all of the nuptial rites, which
are paraded around on the page with a kind of giddy pride. "A band

of gold would be great," one man effuses, while another outdoes the most soulful of lovelorn heterosexual lonely hearts:

I'm a sweet, masculine lover, the marrying kind so honey, cuddle up and melt in my warm, loving arms, passionate kisses and my manly ways and charms. This . . . country boy sure is a happy camper! I got a heart full of soul and a lot of love to give. And I ask, kindly with sincere affections, darlin', will you be my sweetheart and I'll be your loverman. I will adore, cherish and love you inside and out with a whole lot of hugging and a-lovin'. I only ask that you . . . commit at creating a beautiful relationship/marriage. . . . Seeking Caucasian male, 25–39, to be my dear, devoted husband, a honey that I can be sweet on. I love . . . keeping home and my darling husband warm, cozy and well loved.

The exasperating conventionality of this advertisement, which even alludes to an exchange of vows in the words "adore, cherish and love you," is not just the product of this particular writer's emotionalism. Rather, its mawkishness stems in part from a propagandistic campaign that homosexuals have been waging since gay liberation to prove to others, as well as to ourselves, that our relationships are as legitimate as straight ones, that we are exactly like the most colorless of husbands and wives, that we do the same things, dream the same dreams, and pledge the same sort of undying true love while huddling around crackling fires sipping wine on chilly winter evenings. The saccharine excesses of many post-Stonewall ads can be viewed in part as a political affectation, the ideological grandstanding of a group of men determined to refute prevailing prejudices by furnishing incontrovertible evidence that, far from being a debauched band of sexual outlaws, gay men are in fact as normal, vapid, and unglamorously monogamous as ordinary men and women. Propaganda thus permeates the personal ads of the last 25 years, which function as an unlikely form of political protest, of sloganeering, a way of indoctrinating our readers with uplifting messages about our own suburban aspirations in the face of heterosexual revulsion.

The changes that have occurred during recent decades in the way in which homosexuals describe the men they are seeking, from "friend" in the 1960s to "lover" in the 1970s and "boyfriend" or "husband" in the 1980s and 1990s, provide an excellent barometer of the legitimization of gay relationships as we are assimilated into mainstream society, becoming more and more accepted and, regrettably, more conventional. The history of personal ads testifies to a crucial development in the gay sensibility: the gradual rejection of the equivocal terms with which we once soft-pedaled the erotic nature of our relationships, which we now perceive as identical to those of heterosexuals rather than fundamentally different from them, existing in some sort of desexed state of platonic bliss.

The heterosexualizing of gay love was also fueled by something happening within mainstream society itself, a development that can be summed up in the innocuous yet revolutionary word that, during the 1960s, essentially upstaged all other synonyms for sexual affairs: "relationship," the fashionable shibboleth of the human potential movement. Pop psychology, in conjunction with the rise of feminism and technological advances in contraception, radically changed the way Americans thought about their sex lives by replacing the institutional bond that once held two individuals together with a purely emotional bond between two independent free agents whose love for each other was sustained by their own personal initiative. By separating sex and procreation, the human potential movement secularized relationships, cutting them free of their traditional moorings in the family and fostering instead an autonomous, unencumbered type of attachment in which people met and made love, not to perpetuate established social structures, but for their own physical and psychological recreation.

Ironically, however, the human potential movement, which provided the ideological basis for gay liberation by sanctioning out-of-wedlock relationships, ended by making same-sex unions more orthodox than ever before. Pop psychologists may have contributed to the new hedonistic spirit with which people cohabited, but they did so while romanticizing intimacy and reviling casual sexual contact as a violation of their righteous insistence that sex occur only as an expression of love, as an interpersonal confirmation of a commit-

ted and meaningful "relationship." The movement was in fact profoundly sanctimonious, puritanical, and intolerant of promiscuity, of
the "free love" that belied its central tenet, that physical contact
should serve as an almost religious sacrament that deepened and
reaffirmed a couple's feelings for each other. While it helped create
the permissive background for the sexual revolution, enabling couples to live guiltlessly in sin, it was fundamentally Christian in its
outlook and, as such, represented an unprecedented phenomenon:
the emergence within American society of a new, highly moralistic
force that originated from the very heart of secular culture rather
than from its traditional source in religion.

Because pop psychology encouraged the climate of permissiveness
that led to the growing social tolerance of homosexuality, it is no
surprise that gay men should express their indebtedness to human
potential in their personal ads where they, too, began to express a
new puritanism, a contempt for anonymous sex, which they rejected
in favor of a priggish sort of cloistered monogamy. "I've outgrown
the novelty of sex without meaning, & desire 1-to-1 sharing of life,"
one human potentialist proclaimed in 1975, while another used his
ad as his own bully pulpit and stated indignantly that he "is not at
all interested in the sexual superbowl called city gay life," adding
disdainfully that he "dislikes guilt-ridden people who can't handle
where they're at with their own identity." These high-minded sen-
timents were echoed in another ad from the 1970s, which asked, in
the voice of a used car salesman in a TV commercial, "depressed
because so many contacts are driven by sex? Uptight when flippant
queens snigger at ideals? . . . Turned off by competitive promiscuity
of big city? Young men tired of all this, please write." "Tired of all
this" became the human potential rallying cry of many of the ads
placed throughout the late 1960s and 1970s, which often revolved
around a stereotyped "plot," that of a jaded young man, having sown
his wild oats in the wicked metropolis, repenting of the bar scene
and cheap tricks and turning to the personals in an act of contrition
in which he professes with evangelical fervor his readiness to settle
down to the homely amenities of a stable, if somewhat insipid, interpersonal relationship.

Since the early 1980s, the claustrophobia and uxoriousness of the new heterosexualized gay relationship have been intensified by an entirely unrelated phenomenon: disease. When coupled with our efforts to belie the prejudices of our opponents, AIDS has accelerated the reactionary direction of gay relationships, which have swerved precipitously to the right as homosexuals have begun to express an almost cultish sexual piety. The epidemic has not only had an extraordinarily regressive effect on intimacy between gay men, triggering a mass movement of born-again monogamists, but it has also become the turgid muse of a literary genre that is rapidly becoming one of the most representative art forms of this biological tragedy. Our efforts to institute radical changes in our sex lives have resulted in a strange form of overcompensation in which gay men trot out clichés of crackling fires and moonlit strolls as an antidote to our former whorishness, which we bury in an avalanche of purple prose, in "walks on the beach, romantic dinners out . . . brunches in undiscovered neighborhoods, [and] mystical reminiscing under full moons." The outpouring of emotion in these baroque flights of fancy reflects our self-conscious attempts to impose the ill-suited conventions of Harlequin romance on a subculture accustomed to the ready availability of recreational sex behind every bush and in every public toilet. The mythology of committed relationships has been absorbed like a sexual narcotic; it is the sentimental new catechism with which the gay community has brainwashed its members in order to curb their suicidally promiscuous behavior. Romanticism has become the psychological mechanism of repression, with matrimony serving as a form of hygiene, an extremely artificial way of purging ourselves of our profligate habits, which are so inveterate, so deeply ingrained, that we have been forced to combat them with a glut of amorous rhetoric.

AIDS also contributed to the heterosexualization of gay relationships by recreating the very conditions of atomization that originally gave rise to the need for the personals. The agonizing sense of isolation that was once caused by bigotry and social ostracism has now been revived by a microorganism, a retrovirus that has inspired more effusions about true love than all of the arrows in Cupid's quiver.

There is something distinctly stilted, far-fetched, and unspontaneous about the ads of the last ten years, which are permeated, not with love, but with fear, with a sense of beleaguerment, of being walled up in a besieged fortress, a feeling that expresses itself in a common leitmotif: the nest, the inner sanctum, the secure, womb-like space where the writer imagines himself clinging to his mate and burrowing under the flannel sheets and down comforter like hibernating animals. The image of the cave, of the den, where the advertiser lolls about in bed with his future boyfriend, oblivious to the perils of the outside world, recurs throughout contemporary ads, as when a man complains that he "can't find the right 'care bear' or 'care cub' to hibernate with or comb hair with" or when a man describes himself in unapologetically childish terms as "a teddy bear lover seeking a new friend or maybe a mate with whom to hibernate with in a fabulous cave." AIDS is the subtext of all modern gay relationship ads, which again and again return to the theme of hibernation, of sleeping in a glass incubator, where we curl up in fetal position and indulge in that most kittenish form of safe sex, the neonatal eroticism of "cuddling." The rhetorical expressions with which many sentimentalists extol intimacy are simply the pretty, picturesque fictions with which we have decorated our prison cells, protecting ourselves from the horrors of the plague.

AIDS is not the only factor that has shaped the modern gay relationship, however. Profound changes have also occurred in the whole economics of meeting and cruising other gay men. Well into the 1960s, sexual encounters between homosexuals often took place, not between two unattached equals, but between john and trade, sugar daddy and hustler, or even pederast and ephebe—relationships based on radical inequalities of income, age, and even sexual orientation. This imbalance was reflected in most gay newspapers, which, even in the years immediately following Stonewall, still did not divide their classified sections between relationship ads and ads for escorts, hustlers, masseurs, "houseboys," and "chauffeurs," but scrambled them all together in a crassly mercantile context tainted by the grim fiscal realities of sexploitation and prostitution. The failure to separate advertisements for genuine affairs of the heart from

those promoting the business ventures of boys for hire is highly significant in that it reveals that the modern gay relationship between
two financially independent homosexuals emerged out of the ineq-
uitable conditions that prevailed before the 1960s. During this time,
gay men were often forced into the demeaning position of either
purchasing sex or resigning themselves to unreciprocal encounters
with straight or bisexual trade whose coveted affections were won at
the price of contempt, if not outright brutality. It was only in the
mid-1970s that the prostitute was dislodged from the position of
preeminence he occupied in gay culture. As the personals began to
swallow up more and more columns of text, escort ads were finally
banished to their own disreputable section of the newspaper, a journalistic skid row of sleazy photographs of decapitated men squeezing
the bulges of their wet jockey shorts above headlines that read
"Throat Plug," "Eat at Pete's," and "Super Hung Fresh Grade 'A'
Stud."

The rise of the modern gay relationship has not, however, been
an unmixed blessing, for while the new heterosexualized romance
has leveled the disparities of income that once plagued gay men, it
has increased dramatically the materialism of the gay community.
The monogamous marriages for which we have advertised in our
newspapers for the last 20 years have often taken on the appearance
of corporate mergers between two gym-toned yuppies who open joint
bank accounts, set up housekeeping in gentrified "fix-its," entertain
lavishly, and embroider their hyphenated monograms on their "his
and his" towels. Before the 1960s, many gay men were forced to lead
a deeply closeted existence as double agents who emerged every
morning in three-piece suits to pursue high-powered, white-collar
careers that were kept entirely separate from the compromising realities of their private lives, which were sealed off in a vacuum of
secrecy and shame.

From the 1970s to the present, however, there has been an increasing integration of the homosexual's career and his love life,
which have become virtually synonymous features of an upscale,
quiche-and-brie "lifestyle" in which sexual fulfillment walks hand in
hand with economic prosperity. If gay relationships were once con-

ceived as the very opposite of one's career, as the skeleton in one's closet, the disclosure of which would shatter one's hopes and besmirch one's reputation, they have now become the very expression of one's career, its summit, the culmination of all of one's material aspirations—from the Jacuzzi and the Lamborghini to the Armani suit and the biannual jaunt to Maui. The separate provinces that were formerly impossible for the homosexual to reconcile have merged in disturbing new ways now that gay liberation has taught us that it is healthy and politically affirming to conflate our financial success with our romantic happiness, to hurl open the doors of the corporate closet and celebrate the joy of being gay through flamboyant displays of conspicuous consumption.

The result is what is known in the personal ads of the last 15 years as "the long-term relationship" or the "ltr," an expression that differs in one crucial respect from those used during the 1960s and 1970s when relationships were referred to as "permanent," "serious," "stable," and "long-standing." The phrase "long-term" emerged in the early 1980s when the American public, with the help of talk-show hosts, self-help gurus, and even New Age channelers, began to mix together interpersonal jargon with banking and business buzzwords. In its most literal sense, "long-term" refers to the length of time it takes for an investment to mature, an appropriate association for relationships based on the mutual affluence of two "professionals" who, swimming in disposable income, decide to pool their resources in a culture that has linked dating with spending, lovers with bank accounts. In the following two ads from the 1980s and 1990s, the type of intimacy sought is a direct outgrowth of the purchasing power of both the reader and the advertiser, who is not just looking for companionship but for someone capable of sharing, and even enhancing, his lifestyle as a go-getting corporate executive:

> I have been working very hard achieving a prominent position in one of San Francisco's Fortune 500 companies for the last three years and have not been able to find "the man of my dreams." . . . I long for someone to share my romantic dreams with—I love all the mushy stuff!

Wealthy man needed for building a life together. Brownie points for world class
cuddlers, blue eyes, a bit of a belly, bulging bank accounts, country homes,
and innocence that offsets worldliness.

For all of the modern homosexual's obsession with intimacy, the
new ltr is at heart deeply materialistic. It is imbued with the imagery
of the marketplace, with the conventions of advertising, pulp romance, and Hollywood movies, from romantic "weekend getaways"
and "long leisurely dinners" to day trips ambling around flea markets
in the wine country, afternoons simmering in hot tubs, and nights
of torrid passion that, according to the schematic fantasy of one humble soul, involve "holding or being held by a special man in a room
lit by a candle." We have left behind once and for all the era in
which gay relationships were profoundly one sided, full of dangerous
discrepancies of age and income, but in the process we have arrived
at a new and equally disturbing extreme of complete economic parity
in which, with the help of gay liberation, we have not just reconciled
our relationships with our careers but *equated* them.

By the 1980s and 1990s, the liberated gay marriage was so securely
established that the classical paradigm of the sugar daddy spoiling
his "kept" boy could be revamped and transformed into a titillating
form of sexual theater with which to spice up our love lives. In the
daddy/son craze of the last ten years, we have revisited an interesting
chapter in gay history and self-consciously evoked the old inequalities, the ancien régime of oppression and self-loathing, which has
reemerged in quotation marks as an innocuous fantasy involving a
consensual form of child molestation. Far from recreating the conditions of exploitation that prevailed in the first half of the century,
when old men were forced to pay for the sexual services of younger
men, the new daddy/son relationships cunningly lop off the "sugar"
from the "daddy" and thus enable older men to achieve a new sort
of sexual charisma by endowing them with the virility and erotic
appeal of paternalistic, pipe-smoking patriarchs. Similarly, even men
well past their prime can now cast themselves as "sons" looking for
"dads," who, in a system in which roles are dissolved and created
through verbal sleight of hand alone, are sometimes much younger

than the 40-year-old urchins they are supposed to have "fathered."
Roles that were once oppressive to gay men have now become extremely fluid and even liberating, freeing us from our biological ages
and allowing us to adopt imaginary ages simply by employing the
fountain-of-youth terms of "daddy" and "son," which function as
detachable labels designed for easy application and removal. Sex roles
are now chosen by preference, not by the dictates of age or sexual
orientation, so that men who would once have been forced to pay a
stiff fee for the unresponsive, heterosexual companionship of proletarian youths are now able to take advantage of the entire amusement
park of fictional roles that gay culture has created to accommodate
all of its members' needs.

The new control gay men exercise over their sex lives can also be
measured in the changes that have occurred during the last 30 years
in the language we use to describe our preferences in bed. Throughout the 1960s, men referred to themselves in their ads as either
"butch" or "fem," "dominant" or "docile." These expressions referred to more than just the roles they assumed during sex but to
their entire personalities outside of the bedroom as well, where they
hammed it up as screaming queens, making their desires known to
their potential partners through their effeminate gestures, mincing
gaits, and lisping falsettos.

In the 1970s, however, the expressions "Greek active" or "Greek
passive" and "French active" or "French passive" came into use,
expressions that pertain only to what goes on behind closed doors
and that are thus not as constrictive and defining as "fem" and "docile," which suggested that the gay man's sexual preferences were a
constituent part of his identity and even of his physical appearance.
The invention of the phrases "Gr/a" and "Gr/p" allowed gay men
to liberate themselves from the stigma of effeminacy by redefining
their passivity as a specific set of acts that occurred in a specific
location—namely, during sex—rather than as a general style of flaming behavior that they were forced to adopt in public.

In the late 1980s, we took this process one step further when we
abandoned "Gr/a" and "Gr/p" for the S/M expressions "top" and
"bottom," which define a man's sexual preferences even more nar-

rowly, not as an *act* that he likes to perform, but as the position he assumes in order to perform this act. Sex roles have thus become masks that we select from a whole wardrobe of sexual disguises, as demonstrated in a T-shirt manufactured by the gay company "Don't Panic" that reads "Bottom, top, top, bottom (Decisions, Decisions)"— a joke that suggests we can now easily straddle both sides of the fence, swapping roles that were once irreversible. Our preferences are no longer as asphixiatingly definitive as when men were martyrs to their sexual passivity, forced to use all of the blandishments at their disposal in order to captivate and seduce prospective sex partners.

The personal ads of the last 15 years also bear the marks of our new erotic "empowerment" in the specificity with which writers describe the sex they are seeking. While ads from 25 years ago could be very explicit, they were seldom as salacious as their contemporary counterparts, which electrify their readers with vivid reenactments of X-rated fantasies that draw on a vast repertoire of literary effects, from the anthropomorphism of "greedy holes" to the alliteration of "big bubble butt begs to be banged." In the 1980s, advertisers began to function as pornographers, as the creators of a highly concentrated and almost epigrammatic form of erotic literature in which they fleshed out their sexual desires in cinematic scenes that bring to life the taste and feel of sex.

Compare, for instance, the following ads, the first three from the 1970s, the last three from the 1980s and 1990s:

Male likes to take Gr. & Fr. initiatives but wants democratic partner who will reciprocate if asked.

Bearded bodybuilder with receptive rear, looking for well-endowed studs.

Looking for males who accept passive role in Greek.

● ● ●

Oil me up, bend me over and shove your meat up my butt while I wiggle and moan.

Horny top wants to yank down your pants, mount you in the rear & deposit his
hi-volume load up you.

Ride my wet tongue with your hot brown hole.

Although it would have been perfectly permissible in the 1970s for
an advertiser to publish an ad reading "into anal sex" or "into rimming," it is only in the 1980s that writers began to evoke the scene, to
create for the reader visualizations in which they conjured up the actual organs involved in the sex act, which were presented with precise,
if often apocryphal, measurements and invested with sensual characteristics like "wet," "hot," and "brown." In the 1980s, the ads were
suddenly flooded with the entire arsenal of pornographic rhetorical
conventions, with "yummy, greasy hairy shafts" and "quivering boy
pussies," phrases that came straight out of plain brown wrappers and
that lent the ad a dramatic quality absent from the matter-of-fact enu-
merations of preferences one finds in the 1970s. No longer content
simply to list our desires, we now narrate them, neatly packaging them
as stories. Throughout the 1980s, as homosexuality became more and
more assimilated into society at large, gay men developed increasing
competence in selling themselves, marketing their services as any
savvy businessman would plug the convenience and efficiency of his
product. Just as our emotional lives are increasingly structured by the
clichés of advertising, by gleaming white beaches, piña coladas, and
moonlit nights, so our sex lives exhibit a new vulnerability to the language of the marketplace, which is making deep inroads into the way
we think about sex. These novelized vignettes represent an advanced
stage in the commercialization of the subculture in that gay men now
perceive and represent sex through the lens of pornography, a highly
commercial genre that has become the screen or filter that blurs and
distorts our erotic experiences.

A central mystery surrounds the booming renaissance of personal
ads in the 1990s. The ready availability of new means for meeting
other homosexuals over the past three decades should certainly have
remedied many of the social problems we once faced, especially now
that we have fled from the desolate provinces and migrated to con-

gested urban ghettos where we clog the streets in our leather chaps and spandex shorts, swarming together in throngs from every hick town in the country. Unfortunately, however, the rise of an organized subculture has not provided us with a panacea, and we still find personal ads an effective means of overcoming the immense barriers that separate us. Divisions that were once geographic and social have now become psychological. We have recreated in our own minds the conditions that once stranded the lonely ballet buffs, embroidery aficionados, and whiskey-label mavens who advertised in *The Hobby Directory*. For the last 30 years, many men have attracted their mates, not by describing their own attributes, but by issuing a steady stream of self-righteous denigrations of other homosexuals, whom they dismiss in advertisements that amount to a public disavowal of gay life, a faithless defection from the subculture in which they brandish like "no trespassing" signs an interminable series of homophobic epithets including "no fats," "no fems," and "no fags." Gay personal ads are often organized around a parade of antitypes, a procession of effeminate monstrosities who are marched out and heckled by men who grovel before heterosexual society by referring to themselves as "straight-acting" and "straight-appearing," terms that reveal a degree of self-hatred unique among even the most conformist of ethnic groups, who would never stoop to such slavish behavior, fawning over the virility of their white masters. The picture of gay culture that emerges in many post-Stonewall advertisements is not that of the utopic consensus of a united group of committed freedom fighters but the furious enmity and self-loathing of a highly fractured society, torn apart by internal divisions.

Our acceptance by society depends not only on the improvement of our public image but on the evolution of our awareness of being part of a distinct group, of belonging to a closely knit tribe with common traditions and specific characteristics. The old-fashioned hobbyist who met potential partners through F.W. Ewing's thinly disguised dating service never wrote in the second person because he had no conception of what sort of man he was addressing. He spoke from a vacuum into a void, from his own isolation in South Dakota and Idaho into the vast empty expanse of windswept prairies in which homosexuals remained hidden in protective anonymity, trapped in the boondocks in one-horse towns and rustic villages where they lived without social support, unidentifiable to all but the most discerning observers.

The modern advertiser, by contrast, knows precisely what sort of man he is addressing when he tells his audience to "bend over and show dad what you've got" and can even visualize his reader's appearance, conjuring up a clear image of what he is wearing, where he works, and how he has decorated his apartment. The use of direct address in recent personal ads is representative of a larger development in gay culture: its nationalization. The gay sensibility now transcends regional borders, so the homosexual in Tennessee looks and sounds almost exactly like the homosexual in Arizona, sharing not only a common style of dress but a physical type, a linguistic accent, and a set of defining tastes in art, decoration, and music. In the space of only a century, we have gone from being a heterogeneous mass of frightened loners with few collective physical and behavioral characteristics, to a group so highly uniform, so consistent in appearance, that a clone visiting the Midwest from New York instantly recognizes another clone living in Dayton, and a bear visiting from Biloxi feels right at home in the same bar with his ursine brethren from San Francisco.

The globalization of the gay identity and the creation of the extraordinary homogeneity that now exists in our clothing and sensibility were brought about by changes in American society itself. Gay culture depends for its very existence on the technological developments that have revolutionized modern life during the last century. In order for us to achieve visual and psychological unity as a national group, whether we are living in Cheyenne or Amarillo, a high degree of centralization first had to take place in American culture, a wholesale elimination of geographical boundaries which have been erased by means of trains, airplanes, telephones, computer networks, and the mass media. Such forces have destroyed regionalism and unified a formerly sprawling empire of disparate communities, the loose federation of unconnected states that now have instant access to each other. A Balkanized America could not have produced a gay America. If the United States had remained an agrarian nation dependent on horse-drawn buggies and long-delayed mail deliveries, gay men would have remained in a state of atomization, deprived of the widely disseminated and by now international code of external signs with which we label ourselves for convenient identification. Had I myself not been exposed to film, to a medium developed by a culture that was fast achieving the cohesion, the "indivisibility," promised by the Pledge of Allegiance, I would not have acquired my own patrician accent, the fake British intonations I adopted as part of a common language of gestures and mannerisms used by many gay men, a lingua franca that enables us to reveal ourselves to other members of our tribe regardless of where we live.

Our fate as homosexuals, then, is intimately bound up with the fate of the entire nation, with its industrialization, with its emergence out of fractured provinciality into a world so cosmopolitan that we have become aware of ourselves as part of a group, of a nation within a nation, a minority that extends well beyond the towns in which we live. The centralization of American culture effected a major change in the homosexual's self-perception, allowing him to see himself as a member of an entire race of sexually transgressive iconoclasts rather than as a lonely and miserable aberration living in despised seclusion in an intolerant society.

We attained a collective consciousness as a minority by means of social forces that obliterate other minorities, that erode their awareness of being part of a specific group. Most ethnic differences are wiped out by centralization. Consider how television, which promotes a single, prescriptive style of speaking, is creating a homogeneous American voice and weakening all regional accents, from the linguistic mannerisms of New Yorkers to the lazy southern drawls of Mississippi rednecks, from the aristocratic precision of Boston Brahmins to the nasal twang of corn farmers from Kansas. The fragmentation of America once reinforced tribal solidarity, as in the case of the Amish, Quakers, Appalachians, Cajuns, and Indians who thrived on their geographic isolation from the dominant culture but are now threatened with extinction. The unique character of these formerly insular communities has been imperiled by the mass media, which conflates all subcultures into one undifferentiated group, a demographically identical mass market that listens to the same pop music and buys the same soft drinks. The centralization of a society almost invariably acts as a solvent of ethnic differences. But in the case of homosexuals, who have never lived in one place, looked alike, or shared the same language, but are dispersed and invisible, the process has been exactly reversed: the unification of America has proven to be instrumental in our achievement of a subcultural identity in that it has allowed a featureless group of individuals, strewn across every sector of society, to come together, establish esprit de corps, and communicate across the insurmountable barriers that once prevented us from seeking each other out. While the rest of the American public was being reduced to a monolithically uniform herd of consumers, homosexuals were discovering themselves as a unique kind of minority, one that flourished on the mass culture that levels the discrepancies between all other groups.

Ultimately, however, the consolidation of homosexuals through mass culture will result in the dissolution of our own sense of collective identity as well. Unification creates political empowerment, which in turn eliminates oppression and thus deprives the gay sensibility of its two main functions, that of providing both an oblique system of communication and a vehicle for rebellion against our philistine enemies, whom we belittle by means of our aestheticism. In addition, once we achieve national unity, we immediately attract the attention of manufacturers, who begin colonizing us as a market, thus hastening our assimilation into society at large. Only when we became a national bloc of consumers united by shared patterns of taste did we draw the attention of major manufacturers, who recognized the economic value of this peculiar niche of fiercely loyal men and women. Our unification as a minority thus created the conditions for our commercialization. Paradoxically, the very act of consolidation that made us politically powerful simultaneously made us economically vulnerable to the depredations of large companies.

If the change from "special friend" to "husband" encapsulates in the most laconic terms possible the story of our assimilation into mainstream society, so a comparison of gay glossy magazines from the 1970s and 1990s reveals that the discrepancies between gay and straight society have become so minimal that the publications serving these two presumably dissimilar constituencies are now distressingly alike. Gay journalists have become epigones of the saucy contributors to *Spy* and *Vanity Fair*. As the homosexual identity loses its definition, the thriving underground media that once provided an uncensored forum for the discussion of issues pertaining to the community deteriorate into wan, lifeless imitations of the featureless spawn of Condé Nast, the arch coffee-table magazines that corporations are now using as channels to achieve unrestricted access to the gay community.

The Invention of

the Teflon Magazine:

From *After Dark* to *Out*

THE FIRST GAY GLOSSY magazine came into existence, not in the 1990s, as the editors of such publications as *Genre*, *Out*, *10 Percent*, and *Men's Style* would have us believe, but in 1968, with the demise of a seemingly innocuous publication destined to undergo one of the strangest reincarnations in journalistic history. Catering to musically inclined blue-haired old ladies and golfers in Hush Puppies, *Ballroom Dance Magazine* was a recreational journal for the geriatric set. It was out of the ashes of a periodical devoted to such topics as waltzes, rumbas, and turkey trots that *After Dark*, an audacious mass-market experiment in gay eroticism, arose like a phoenix in all of its subversive splendor. Ostensibly covering Broadway, the arts, and showbiz in general, it was for its time an extremely racy publication, especially in its final years as it clung desperately to the market share it was gradually losing to skin magazines, whose images of bulging beefcakes with full erections were far more pornographic than anything its editors would ever dare to publish. Until its death in 1983, by which time it had already dwindled into a pitifully closeted anachronism, *After Dark* tantalized its readers with shockingly frank photographs of naked dance troupes displaying their voluptuous buttocks, prancing gymnasts thrusting their posing straps at the camera, and snarling athletes in tight baseball uniforms pawing their groins and slapping each other playfully on the butt.

After Dark's audience (more than 350,000 readers at the height of its success) was composed almost exclusively of gay men, who used its salacious photographs and color fashion essays on skimpy underwear that eliminated unsightly panty lines ("even under the snuggest pants") as masturbatory aids in the absence of other readily available forms of male pornography on the newsstands. And yet despite its huge gay following, it never officially declared its allegiances but played an endless game of hide-and-seek, cloaking its quite obvious sympathies for the burgeoning gay rights movement behind seemingly impartial coverage of homoerotic dance and theater. It also filled its pages with a dazzling array of openly gay advertisements for everything from Macho, an ingestible "personal hygiene spray for men" in three mouthwatering flavors, to Gay Bob, "the world's first gay doll" equipped with its own anatomically correct "private parts" with which he can play "without going blind."[1] The notorious Wall Street Sauna piqued the interest of potential patrons with an advertisement featuring a neglected housewife, sitting forlorn and abandoned in cheerless solitude, nursing a drink and staring out at the reader, whom she addressed accusingly with the words "it's five o'clock. Do you know where my husband is?" Taken as a whole, *After Dark* was a masterpiece of indirection, a magazine that was all insinuation, an elaborate dance around its unidentifiable subject, which emerged only in hints, winks, and nudges, in photographs of the muscular torsos of aspiring actors or of sultry Adonises sprawled invitingly on satin sheets.

If *After Dark* was the before image of the subculture, of a furtive underground with only one foot wedged indecisively in the closet door, the new gay glossies are the after image. The differences between the two reveal that, in the past 25 years, some of the most basic aspects of the gay sensibility have been altered almost beyond recognition. Whereas *After Dark* enshrouded homosexuality in eu-

---

[1] Gay Bob was later the subject of a lawsuit filed by Bob Yuill, an irate Canadian politician, who claimed to have experienced emotional damage from sharing the same name as "this disgusting toy," which had made him "and I expect other Bobs ... the butt of many homosexual jibes." *San Francisco Chronicle*, Aug. 12, 1978.

phemisms, recent gay magazines present a well-adjusted society of fun-loving bohemians who celebrate their newfound political enfranchisement in an endless variety of recreational activities, from skydiving out of airplanes in rainbow parachutes to boogeying shirt-less at jam-packed "White Parties" in South Beach. This mercilessly upbeat never-never land pulsates with wild, kinetic energy made all the more frenzied by advertisements featuring vivacious beauties do-ing cartwheels in prohibitively expensive grunge-wear or images of sweaty boys living it up at tropical resorts or socializing with phil-anthropic celebrities at swanky, black-tie benefits.

Full of lipstick lesbians and gym queens, *Out*, *Genre*, and the now defunct *10 Percent* convey a utopic vision of a post-gay-liberation subculture, a distinctly futuristic urban nirvana in which gay people are no longer persecuted and self-loathing. While professing to depict the contemporary realities of being gay in America, the new glossies are in fact a highly subtle form of escapist literature that operates on its readers much as Harlequin romances function for housewives, allowing them to indulge their fantasies about a nonexistent Shangri-la that embodies the homosexual's daydreams about a fully liberated gay future. Each issue is a guided exercise in wish fulfillment, in rewriting history, erasing the setbacks, whitewashing the defeats, and tacking onto the forever unfinished story of gay rights a happily-ever-after ending.

If *After Dark* can be faulted for the exasperating lack of candor with which it systematically refused to acknowledge its gay reader-ship, the new glossies are in many ways just as duplicitous in their cavalier dismissal of the grim conditions of contemporary gay life. Another world, quite different from the one they represent, lies just beneath the bright hues and the sunny smiles, the golden glow of cheerfulness that the editors use to gloss over the problems of a subculture ravaged by AIDS, splintered by ideological differences, and demoralized by political stagnation. Although the new maga-zines would have us believe they have nothing to hide and have proudly embraced gay life in all of its diversity, they too, like *After Dark*, are founded upon a calculated series of guilty omissions, of the inconvenient blemishes that they have airbrushed out of this contrived portrait. They feature, for instance, no braless diesel dykes flopping around in flannel shirts and spilling out of overalls, but only svelte lesbians who vamp around postmodern fashion spreads in haute couture, modeling slinky, latex cat suits by Versace and bitchy stiletto pumps by Manolo Blahnik. There are also disproportionately few photographs of people over the age of 40, with the exception of a few prematurely aged grey eminences who look oddly menopausal and out of place in this romper room of gorgeous ephebes constantly flying down ski slopes at gay "ski-a-thons" or kayaking over rapids at "Hotlanta"'s annual summer blowout.

But the most conspicuous omission of all is that of people in the advanced stages of AIDS whose wasted bodies have been censored from these lighthearted, dentist office magazines where they would have served as grisly reminders of the presence of death amid the revelry of this fool's paradise. In an interview with Derek Jarman in the final months of his life, *Genre* took the highly unconventional measure of suppressing photographs of the filmmaker altogether, tactfully describing him as "frail" and then illustrating the piece with inexplicably abstract graphics, which functioned as a bland and inoffensive substitute for images the editors undoubtedly considered too gruesome. Even *POZ*, the magazine specifically devoted to those living with HIV, attempts to circumvent the horrors of the epidemic by avoiding photographs of disease and printing instead rosy-cheeked images of HIV-positive athletes with spectacular physiques and silky white skin free of disfiguring lesions.

It is precisely because of their stunning omissions that the new glossies serve an important psychological function in contemporary gay culture. Far from being a celebration of our newfound freedom, they are in fact mood enhancers for a demoralized age, communal antidepressants that come in the form of visual pick-me-ups. Their celebratory air stems, not from a sense of triumph, from a conviction that we are marching toward the end of gay liberation's long and winding road, but from despair, from the extreme anxiety that feeds our urgent need for a readily available supply of fantasy literature whose empty reassurances provide, as *Genre*'s editor described it, "a breath of fresh air . . . amid the suffocating and overwhelming media deluge about the AIDS crisis."[2] The reader of the new gay glossies does not thumb through them looking for an accurate reflection of gay life but for a bowdlerized image, manufactured for easy, coffee-table consumption, of a make-believe gay world in every way safer and more glamorous than the risky and not always attractive one in which most of us live.

But aside from the fact that openly gay publications ironically have far more to hide than the closeted publications of the past, the new glossies differ from *After Dark* in another crucial respect. Since the 1970s, there has been a dramatic shift in the coverage of the arts in gay magazines, which no longer focus on traditional forms of high-brow culture, such as ballet, opera, theater, and classical music, but concentrate instead on popular entertainment, on Hollywood block-busters, prime-time TV, gangsta rap, and hip-hop. A distinct low-browing of the arts has occurred in gay journalism during the last two and a half decades that reflects a revolution within the gay sensibility itself, which was once inextricably linked to a kind of snobbish cultural elitism. This dilettantish superciliousness has all but disappeared from the shabby, pierced-and-tattooed "rave" culture of the so-called new clones who scoff at the piss elegance of ballet and opera and embrace instead the screeching, primal energies of Kurt Cobain and Nine Inch Nails.

The new involvement of the gay sensibility with popular enter-tainment is best understood within the context of the role that pre-tensions of artistic respectability formerly served in both *After Dark* and the first skin magazines, which began to appear in the mid- to late 1970s. Publications like *Mandate* and *Blueboy* were paradoxically obsessed with the most prestigious forms of institutionalized high culture and systematically juxtaposed naked pinups of leering body builders next to lengthy reviews of the performing arts, of ballets by Balanchine and productions of plays pivotal to the Western canon, from Marlowe's *Edward II* to Aeschylus' *Agamemnon*. The display of such genteel taste in such a raunchy forum was not accidental, for high aesthetics has a history of masking low lust. As far back as the

[2]*Genre*, June 1984, p. 10.

"physique" magazines of the 1940s and 1950s, which were full of solemn references to classical Greece, to amphoras representing Zeus dallying with Ganymede and statuary of Attic youths hurling javelins, high culture has served as the perfect disguise for erotica, a tasteful camouflage that permitted the magazine to get away with publishing arousing images by doctoring them with chaste artistic allusions. In this way, the editors threw a sop to both the prude and the censor, who could enjoy pornography only if it was packaged with earnest vindications, however implausible, of its cultural value. The editors of *After Dark* were particularly shameless about employing the fine arts as a fig leaf for their prurient material. Their arts coverage frequently served merely as a transparent pretext for displaying men in clingy leotards or the naked bodies of actors who spontaneously shucked their costumes and writhed around on the stage in the impromptu "happenings" of experimental theater troupes. In 1976, for instance, they somewhat disingenuously rhapsodized about the prepubescent body of a naked adolescent, gloating like pederasts over an image that "is not only a lovely picture of a nude youth, but also an evocation of a knowing innocence, a sensual, delicate piece of art" that was "chosen to appeal as much to the sensual as to the aesthetic appreciation of the reader."[3] Throughout its torrid history, *After Dark* undercut its readers' shame about ogling naked men by enabling them to scrutinize the male body through the lens of a lorgnette.

In the course of the 15 years in which the magazine was published, however, an interesting change took place. Nude photographs that were at first justified on artistic grounds became increasingly more gratuitous, until by the late 1970s the high-culture charade was dropped altogether, and erotic photographs, unaccompanied by guilty rationalizations, began to appear, not of dancers, but of distinctly plebeian hunks in undignified poses, cavorting on beaches in skimpy bikinis or tattered jockstraps. The trajectory of photographs in *After Dark*, from the arty image of the pirouetting ballet dancer leaping across the stage to the candid street shot of a grizzled trucker

---

[3]*After Dark*, Jan. 1976, p. 8.

stripped down to blue jean cutoffs scrubbing the cab of his tractor trailer, exactly maps the increasing abandonment of high culture as a clever apology for pornography. In the 25 years since Stonewall, as society became more tolerant of open displays of eroticism, gay culture ceased to use high-brow forms of art for the same purpose that they had well into the 1970s, that of defusing public outrage by wrapping homosexuality in the protective mantle of culture.

The shift from classical music to hip-hop, from ballet to slam dancing, from Antonioni to *The Flintstones*, also signals the gradual extinction of the high-art queen, the Oscar Wildean figure of the rapier-witted fop. As we have seen, throughout the twentieth century, the cultural expertise that gay men often demonstrated in self-conscious displays of their knowledge of the arts or their exotic preferences in interior decoration, in rooms cluttered with chinoiserie, gilt mirrors, gaudy antiques, and ornate pieces of sculpted crockery, has provided the homosexual with a way of setting himself apart from the vulgar masses. *Blueboy*'s selection of the erotic poems of Paul Verlaine, *Mandate*'s "think piece" on Andre Gide's *Corydon*, or *After Dark*'s adoring portrait of Nureyev were typical examples of the cultural elitism that was one of the homosexual's chief self-defenses against bigoted philistines. The contempt of his ignorant oppressors for his sexual preferences formed the psychological foundation for the implied reader of the early glossies: the dapper aesthete, the decadent epicurean, who waged a concerted campaign to retaliate against the emasculation he experienced at the hands of the American public by elevating himself above its egregious tastes in everything from household furnishings to clothing.

While *After Dark* provided generous helpings of the aristocratic culture with which the homosexual could nurse his injured sense of superiority to the prudish American public, the low-browing of the arts in the new gay glossies is a product of the gradual improvement in the social position of gay people, which has significantly alleviated the homosexual's need to cultivate a pedantic, hothouse aestheticism. Young gay men no longer feel compelled to exhibit their cultural refinement as a clever way of settling the score with the heterosexual mainstream but are quite content to skim the barbed prose of gossip columnists who dish the dirt about Cher's daughter Chastity Bono or such pop icons as Sandra Bernhard, Melissa Ethridge, and Courtney Love. The implied reader of the new glossies differs considerably from the implied reader of *After Dark*. Unlike the opera queens of the past, he is democratic; his tastes are rooted in popular culture, in the antics of Madonna and the vulgarities of Roseanne. The rapid assimilation of the gay community into American society is in this respect undermining a major aspect of the homosexual identity, its virulent streak of antiphilistinism.

The new gay glossies are also the product of a major demographic change occurring within the gay community: the rise of a separate gay youth culture. Ads featuring androgynous cherubs sporting nose rings and fashionably abstract tattoos swirling around their pierced nipples, or lesbian skinheads with diamond studs stuck in their cheeks, are the most conspicuous signs of a culture in the very act of splintering into two distinct camps: the members of the so-called generation X and the war-weary old clones who cling desperately to the fashions of the disco era and bemoan the loss of the good old days, their eyes permanently fixed on the ever-receding shadows of a bygone world. In the 1970s, there *was* no separate gay youth culture. The gay community was then far more unified, linked together by the shared exhilaration of being part of a new movement whose followers listened to the same Donna Summer songs, wore the same bomber jackets, danced the same dances, and exchanged copious quantities of the same bodily fluids in the orgy rooms of the same baths and action bars. The low-brow sensibility of the new glossies, with their breathless "fanzine" interviews with mega celebrities and their earnest admonitions about liposuction for the neck or "lymphatic drainage facial[s]," is a natural response to the increasing polarization of the gay community. Recent magazines have consolidated their economic base by catering exclusively to the needs of the emerging youth constituency and perpetrating pictorial genocide on men over the age of 40, who have been ethnically cleansed from their pages, leaving behind a racially pure group of young, prosperous beauties.

There are two major reasons for the formation in the late 1980s and early 1990s of the new gay youth culture. First, because gay men are coming out of the closet earlier than ever before, there are now more openly gay teenagers and people in their early twenties than there were in the 1970s. But just as importantly, the AIDS epidemic has created profound generational strife between the ancien régime and the X generation, between opera queens and grunge rockers, who are now driven apart by absurd, irrational, and potentially deadly equations of youth with health, maturity with disease. This association of age and HIV status is generating a whole new adolescent aesthetic, as seen in the fresh young teenyboppers with hairless chests and willowy bodies who, dressed in street gang paraphernalia, in chains dangling from their hips and pants sagging around their behinds, are plastered all over the new magazines. Today's glossies have profited from a kind of generational apartheid, exploiting the widening breach between these two sectors of the gay population and capitalizing on the mythologizing of youth as the embodiment of hygiene, of wholesomeness.

The editors of *Out*, *Genre*, and *10 Percent* would have us believe that their publications represent a new stage in the evolution of the gay "lifestyle," a proud assertion of an unprecedentedly self-confident homosexual identity capable of standing up to bigotry and parochialism. In fact, however, rather than representing a significant advance in the development of our self-awareness as gay people, the new magazines represent a profound erosion of gay identity, a wholesale collapse of the subculture into straight urban youth culture. The latter has become so androgynous and homosympathetic that it is virtually impossible to distinguish trendy young heterosexuals from the habitués of the flourishing club scene in gay meccas like New York and San Francisco. The merging of these two groups can be seen in the fact that the new glossies are uncanny impersonations of straight magazines. They attempt to pass themselves off as carbon copies of *GQ*, *Details*, *Vanity Fair*, and *Esquire*, from their advertisements and fashion spreads down to their grooming tips and relentlessly hip prose styles, from their columns for the lovelorn and their capsulized "picks and pans" to their notes on calf implants and advice on cosmetics for what one writer refers to as "nighttime glam."

As the boundaries between gay and straight culture have become blurred and permeable, subject to cross influences and mutual maraudings, groups that were once clearly differentiated, and even antagonistic, now overlap, sharing the same interests in film, music, and clothes. In fact, the collapse of formerly rigid demarcations has been so complete that many young gay men now have far more in common with young straight men than they do with older gay men.

Further evidence of the dissolution of gay culture can be found in the limited success that the new glossies have had in capturing a mass readership, in contrast with gay magazines of the past. A striking irony of the dated ambiguities with which *After Dark* jealously preserved its precarious sexual ambivalence is that the magazine attracted far more readers than all of its more forthright modern equivalents put together. Although the new magazines have ambitious plans to tap the immense audience that they claim will generate untold riches for pioneering advertisers, they have managed to secure a combined distribution of only 200,000 readers, or about 55 percent of the number who gleefully followed the often hilarious homoerotic pranks of *After Dark*. One would have expected the readership for gay magazines to increase dramatically as more and more homosexuals come out of the closet and gay culture becomes more open and more organized, but statistics show otherwise. The gay audience for glossy magazines, if not for the gay media in general, has paradoxically shrunk to a little over half of what it was at a time when buying a gay publication was fraught with the embarrassment of enduring the disapproving stares of news vendors and hiding compromising issues from the prying eyes of family and friends. Although magazine publishers today are convinced that the increasing visibility of gay culture and the growing social confidence of its members will swell the ranks of their subscription lists and line the pockets of their corporate sponsors, it is also very possible that assimilation will have the exact opposite effect and undermine the very need for such a publication. The largest gay magazine in history, after all, was launched, not in the 1990s, but at a relatively early stage in gay liberation, in the late 1960s, when it achieved a degree of success that even the shrewdest of Madison Avenue publicists have not been able to duplicate today.

The gay public's anemic response to the new lifestyle magazines is a symptom of the gradual fragmentation of the subculture as the very conditions that held it together—systematic discrimination, fag bashing, raids on bars, and sexual entrapment by vice squads—begin to improve, weakening our need to present a unified front to a hostile world whose prejudices shored up our strong sense of ethnic camaraderie. *After Dark*'s readership was far larger and more cohesive precisely because it was far more oppressed and therefore more unified as a secret brotherhood that shared the titillating complicity involved in recognizing all of the editors' in-jokes and responding to their wry captions and wicked doubles-entendres. No contemporary publication can inspire the same fervid loyalty with which *After Dark*'s readers eagerly devoured every issue because gay culture is slowly beginning to unravel at the very moment that many activists mistakenly feel that the gay sensibility is reaching its most "mature" and self-aware form.

The low-browing of the arts in recent gay glossies has gone hand in hand with a major change in the form and polemical tone of a standard feature of all coffee-table magazines, the celebrity profile and interview. In the past, gay writers rarely published anything other than uncritical homages to media superstars, doting accolades laid at the feet of such immortal heroines as a ravaged Bette Davis who, pottering around her kitchen in her stocking feet swirling her drink, swapped favorite recipes for Tuna Imperial and Quiche La Bette with *Mandate*'s star-struck interviewer. But whereas hagiographic portraits of matinee idols constitute one of the most frivolous forms of kiss-and-tell fluff in old magazines, the new gay glossies transform their coverage of celebrities into a means of securing a stamp of approval for gay rights. They anxiously solicit the blessings of such figures as jazz legend Jimmy Scott, who confers his benediction on the readers of *10 Percent* by telling them that he has many gay friends;[4] or of Belinda Carlisle of the 1980s girl group the Go-Go's, who appeases *Genre*'s interviewer by reaffirming her faith in

---

[4]*10 Percent*, Mar./Apr. 1995, p. 60.

the time-honored truism that "a person's sexual preference is no-body's business but their own."[5]

In the new glossies, plumbing the depths of a celebrity's personal life, as well as their attitudes toward homosexuality, transcends mere voyeurism to become a characterological inquest, a baptism by fire in which the star's credentials for humanitarianism are examined for potential heresies or stubborn refusals to toe the party line. In every issue, *Out*, *Genre*, and *10 Percent* convene a kind of kangaroo court that sits in judgment on a star's reputation, passing stiff sentences on their unpardonable waffling about their own homosexuality and, similarly, pinning medals of honor to the breasts of those who have exhibited unusual courage on the battlefield of gay rights. In the hands of the editors of the new glossies, this most prurient of genres breaks out of the yellow journalistic formula in which it has been trapped since it was first invented to become both a tendentious vehicle for propaganda and a way of recruiting cinematic gods and goddesses as our honorary *chargés d'affaires*, chosen to plead our case to the American public. When acid rocker Nina Hagen is featured in *10 Percent*, for instance, her interviewer is clearly delighted when the musician mouths the moral pieties to which celebrities must render lip service if they are to win the unqualified support of the gay community. Hagen transforms herself into a messianic caricature, a combination, as she calls herself, of "Mother Teresa and Nelson Mandela," who "would jump through fire for the sake of humanity" and who strives to be "such a perfect mother that all gay people can't help but search for refuge in me. It's like I'm a Divine Mother, and I shall lead them over the hills, over the Himalayas to the great lord Shiva."[6]

The monomaniacal fixation in recent gay magazines on what celebrities feel about homosexuality or whether they themselves are gay reflects a dangerous assumption, albeit one with a long history in the gay community, that is increasingly shaping the entire direction of gay rights—namely, that liberation lies, not with politicians, but with

---

[5]*Genre*, Nov. 1993, p. 113.
[6]*10 Percent*, Nov./Dec. 1994, p. 34.

pop stars, the unacknowledged legislators of mankind whom we have begun to fetishize as the primary moral force in our society, the high priests of American morality. This shift from electoral politics to celebrity politics, from ballot initiatives and voting booths to a charismatic new cult of personality, reflects the profound cynicism fueling the political vision of the new gay magazines, which have arisen in part as a response to a vacuum of leadership in the gay community, a void being filled by the likes of Elizabeth Taylor, Elton John, and Barbra Streisand. As state after state defeats antidiscrimination bills, pardons fag bashers, disqualifies lesbian mothers on the grounds that they are unfit parents, reinstates archaic antisodomy statutes, and champions the exclusion of homosexuals from the military, some activists are turning away from many inefficient types of post-Stonewall activism. Instead, they wage the struggle for liberation in the gossip columns, not in the legislatures, which have become so mired in gridlock and so openly hostile to the gay community that we are reexperimenting with silver screen politics, an activism by Hollywood proxy, a tactic based on a notion central to the new glossies: visibility. The concept of visibility, which underlies all recent celebrity profiles in gay magazines, assumes that the concrete legal changes that we have failed to realize through conventional methods can be enacted through a more media-centered approach, through a careful manipulation of public opinion either by "outing" high-profile figures or by extorting public endorsements from music and film stars.

To some extent, this new type of politics is simply an extension of gay men's inveterate habit of looking to Hollywood for the leadership they cannot find elsewhere, as we have done for generations. For what, after all, was the gay community's quasi-fascist cult of celebrity, which deified such screen sirens as Marlene Dietrich, Joan Crawford, and Barbara Stanwyck, but an expression of our political impotence? In the absence of more effective methods of lobbying for our rights throughout the early part of the twentieth century, we invented the greatest matriarchy in human history, an autocracy of divas who became the de facto political leaders of a vulnerable constituency that used popular culture as a means for achieving a collective identity. Gay activism arose from the sense of solidarity we created as fans, from our shared discipleship, and so, as we experience more and more legislative setbacks, it is perhaps not accidental that gay activism in the 1990s should, out of desperation, revert to one of the earliest and most primitive ways in which homosexuals originally established allegiances, through the slavish worship of personalities.

The resurgence of celebrity-centered politics is also part of a wider phenomenon occurring in recent gay magazines: the redefinition of gay activism to include all kinds of apolitical or even antipolitical things like shopping and careering. This redefinition can be seen in another regular feature of the new glossies: their profiles in courage, a genre that consists of biographical sketches of homosexual movers and shakers who are enlisted into what amounts to a mentoring program for young gay readers. Throughout these magazines, the editors are constantly singing the praises of enterprising people who have clambered up to the top of the corporate ladder and now lead prosperous lives as openly gay executives, TV producers, investment gurus, pulp novelists, soap opera stars, writers for sitcoms, fashion designers, and "vice-president[s] of . . . $100-million conglomerate[s]" who have "$700,000 Lear jet[s]," "seven-figure income[s]," "sun-splashed living room[s]" in Beverly Hills, and "gorgeous new home[s] perched high up on . . . bluff[s] at the northern end of Malibu."[7] These eulogies of members of the velvet mafia serve as an oddly religious form of inspirational literature consisting of an homiletic series of Horatio Alger stories about those who successfully parlay their mom-and-pop businesses into multi-million-dollar cartels, beginning as dowdy gay shop girls and ending as magnates and robber barons.

Not only do these rags-to-riches parables whet our appetite for success, they also cunningly transform the act of making money into a socially responsible form of activism, a way of seizing power and thus advancing the gay rights agenda by shattering the glass ceiling that has kept gays out of the boardrooms of corporate America. In other words, recent magazines provide an ideological justification for

---

[7]Jonathan Van Meter, "Sandy Gallin: Mogul Manager," *Out*, Nov. 1994, p. 68.

materialism and acquisitiveness which they glamorize as ways of entering the corridors of power, a world they evoke in their sumptuous photo spreads of the penthouse hideaways of wealthy lesbians or the rambling oceanside estates of Hollywood superagents and Fortune 500 CEOs. Social climbing is thus portrayed as an almost painful concession to Realpolitik, a way of blazing the trail to a more equitable and homosympathetic society.

The new glossy magazines are deeply rooted in the political philosophy of "economic clout," of "gay dollars," of putting our pocketbooks where our mouths are, and harnessing the natural resources of what the *Wall Street Journal* has called the "dream market," that of the so-called DINKs, "dual incomes no kids." Having failed to win social acceptance through the customary routes of political reform, we are experimenting with another technique of effecting change, one that involves strategic acts of shopping, of flexing our economic muscle, a Machiavellian scheme that attempts to mobilize the gay consumer in exactly the same way that more traditional forms of gay activism attempted to mobilize the gay voter. Consumerism is thus conflated in these magazines with politics and elevated into a concerted strategy that redefines both shopping and savvy career moves as a way of MasterCharging our way to liberation. The new glossies seem to suggest that the secret to ending oppression lies, not in the courtrooms and the legislatures, but in our wallets and stock portfolios, in the massive quantities of disposable income with which footloose-and-fancy-free gay men can buy their own manumission.

According to the theory of economic clout, the act of buying the products of the humane, tolerant, and courageous corporations that advertise in the new glossies, from Benetton to Benson & Hedges, from Absolut Vodka to Remy Martin, is a way of rewarding their far-sighted altruism, of requiting their kindness, as if they were the ones doing *us* the favor by appearing in our magazines rather than we who were doing *them* the favor by purchasing their products. The relentless materialism of these magazines, with their travel essays on Club Med package tours to lush tropical paradises encircled with jewel-like coral reefs and their lavish sections on "Boy Toys" (where one finds futuristic $200 pencil sharpeners and $100 designer chrome "in" and "out" boxes "guaranteed to suit any corporate image"), reveals the danger lurking at the very heart of this new economic strategy: in enlisting the help of Madison Avenue in the cause of gay rights, gay rights may in fact be enlisted in the cause of Madison Avenue. The corporations that the activist sets out to manipulate may, in the final analysis, end up manipulating him. The politicized consumer quickly degenerates into the consumerized politician, who serves the best interests, not of the gay community, but of the marketers courting this rich new slice of the population, which has such impeccable demographics, from our $55,000 average household incomes to our $500 billion annual spending power.

The fatal attraction of disposable income provides the most convincing solution to the otherwise inexplicable mystery surrounding the sudden proliferation of this new crop of glossy magazines, which are fighting fiercely for an ever-diminishing share of a lucrative market. The glut of mediocre journalism printed in these publications is not a response to a need from within the gay community for additional sources of information, but a response to a need from *outside* the gay community, from major U.S. corporations, which are scrambling to secure a foothold in this sexy and profitable new niche. Granted, as we have seen, *Out*, *Genre*, and *10 Percent* cater to a very real need among readers for an uplifting antidote to both AIDS and political stagnation. But the most compelling reason for the dizzying number of spinoffs from *Genre*, the leader of the pack, is that mainstream corporations have finally gotten around to making their first very tentative steps toward wooing the coveted gay market and have therefore conspired with gay entrepreneurs to invent an upscale advertising vehicle glitzy enough to showcase such products as Hennessy cognacs or the laptop PowerBooks of Apple. The new publications, in other words, are in large part market penetration devices. As such, they represent the point of entry for forces outside of the gay community to launch their incursions into virgin territory, a domain that, until recently, most businesses had been reluctant to cultivate for fear that the social stigma of these once anathematized consumers would sully the reputation of their products. *Genre* and similar publications are only secondarily magazines with significant editorial content but are first and foremost colorful advertising brochures, "channels," as *NEXT News* calls them, through which major companies funnel information about their merchandise. Because they are sustained by such blue chip companies as Saab, Apple, and American Express, they represent a revolution in the gay media, which, until the 1990s, were relatively immune to the forces of commercialism and therefore deeply entrenched in the community that supported them. The new glossies, by contrast, are merely immense "advertorials," the mouthpieces of corporations whose economic interests are quite extraneous to the needs of the gay community.

The fears of American companies of being tarred with the same brush as this attractive but potentially damaging consumer niche have led publishers to create an advertising environment morally hygienic enough to insulate the products featured in their magazines from the taint of erect centerfolds or sleazy personal ads seeking water sports enthusiasts or daddies' boys into diapers and woodshed discipline. The result has been the invention of what might be called the Teflon magazine, a publication so slick that nothing of the illicitness of gay culture, of its bawdiness and impermissibility, will stick to the advertisers. The most obvious way in which the designers of this shrewd marketing device have hastened to allay the apprehensions of their anxious corporate sponsors is to separate sex and culture, which, in a long-standing tradition in gay journalism, have always been inextricably linked. Throughout the 1970s and 1980s, discussions of the Met's new production of Wagner's *The Ring* or performances of the Bolshoi have resided comfortably with advertisements for butt plugs and tit clamps. Reviews of theater performances were published next to articles about the gutter etiquette of open-air cruising by writers who played the role of the Miss Manners of the meat rack, decrying the unspeakable rudeness of garrulous Chatty Cathys who talked too much in orgy rooms and cruise parks. The new magazines, however, have been completely desexualized, stripped of nude photos, risqué contact ads, and even advertisements for phone sex, as publishers strive to create a sanitized forum that will satisfy even the most conservative businesses. It is one of the cunning ironies of this decontamination process that publishers shift the responsibility for their expurgations off the shoulders of their financial backers and onto those of their readers, whom they are constantly characterizing as more "mature" and "well rounded" than gay readers of the past, whose reductively sexual image of gay life can presumably be seen in the blatant eroticism of *Honcho*, *Drummer*, and *Playguy*. The new magazines, in fact, are best viewed as self-righteous repudiations of the sort of sleazy bar rags published throughout the colorfully sordid history of gay journalism, high-minded mirror opposites of the soft-core porn that functions as the implicit subtext of the new glossies.

The invention of the Teflon magazine has also required editors to drive home to their advertisers the normality of gay people whose Middle American mediocrity is celebrated in article after article on such subjects as gays in the church, gays in the military, gays in sports, gays as parents, and gays as legally married spouses. These accounts of the assimilated gay lifestyle portray homosexuals as church-going Christians, patriotic soldiers, gung-ho athletes, rabid sports fans, perfect PTA moms and dads, and uxorious husbands and wives. The new glossies create infantilized, mythically pure homosexuals who are paradoxically described as infinitely wiser than the arch and urbane raunch queens of the past, the unblushing sophisticates who laughed at the naughty humor of *Mandate* and *After Dark*. What the new magazines characterize as a great leap forward in the gay sensibility—from the one-dimensionally sexual, curb-crawling slut of the disco era to the multidimensional, family-oriented careerists of the 1990s—in fact constitutes a wholesale regression of that sensibility, a reversion to an imaginary state of innocence that contrasts dramatically with the more promiscuous and nonconformist world of the 1970s. Indeed, the image of the gay man in both *After Dark* and the early skin magazines was not this insufferable house husband who dreams of dandling babies and living on cul-de-sacs in the suburbs but a countercultural rebel who rejected all of the trappings of normal heterosexual life and cultivated instead a more stylized persona, that of the sexual outcast, the insurgent whose behavior was an open affront to straight life, not a feeble imposture of it. Gay culture emerged from the counterculture of the 1960s, which provided the ideological impetus for gay liberation and allowed gay men to embrace their homosexuality as evidence of their anarchistic abnormality, of their self-flattering difference from the conventional families of four that the new wholesome gay man strives to imitate. Recent gay glossies represent the final severing of both gay culture and gay journalism from their roots in the radical politics of the sexual revolution which have now been finally laid to rest to make way for the new homosexual, the cautious conformist who fantasizes about bassinets and potluck suppers with members of his country-and-western square dancing club.

The methods of sterilization involved in creating an ad-friendly marketing vehicle capable of pacifying the fears of large corporations involves the annihilation of the gay identity, the eradication of every vestige of difference between ourselves and the heterosexual markets the advertiser is accustomed to addressing. The erosion of the gay identity discernible in the collapse of the subculture into straight urban youth culture has thus been accelerated by the needs of corporate America, which will court gay dollars only when we become unthreateningly similar to the most staid and monogamous of heterosexual consumers, turning our backs on the jaded hedonists of the past. The cultivation of the gay market necessitates its destruction, the erasure of the borders that once set it apart from mainstream America in whose image we are allowing ourselves to be recreated.

And yet at the same time Madison Avenue is gradually obliterating the cultural differences that presumably justify the very existence of the gay glossies, their editors loudly defend what they refer to time and again as the "gay lifestyle," which they insist merits coverage in a separate magazine. The crowning irony of these publications is that, as the gay identity begins to dissolve and homosexuals' interests become generic enough to be served by preexisting straight magazines, we become even more emphatic about the urgent need for a publication that "focuses on the people and stories that the general media has long overlooked," as *Genre*'s publicity statement puts it. The general media have not, however, been as remiss as *Genre* suggests. Indeed, in the final analysis, it is difficult to rationalize the need for magazines that advertise the same products as straight magazines, review the same albums, interview the same celebrities, profile the same vacation spots, feature the same fashion spreads, and recommend the same recipes for "sinfully luscious garlic-flavored mashed potatos" and succulent Atlantic salmon with tomato vinaigrette and salad Niçoise. The new magazines treat with reverence the gay lifestyle they have sold to the highest bidder, the ethnic identity that has become a casualty of the economics of mass production and mass consumption. The corporations that pull the strings of these journalistic puppets are colonialists of the most hypocritical sort, laying waste to the natural habitat of homosexuals and slashing and burning their way through the subculture, all the while professing their earnest commitment to preserving its most perishable features.

The economic exploitation of homosexuals has involved a painfully protracted courtship, a romance complicated by the fact that, in the early part of the century, another set of venture capitalists had already cornered the market—the Mafia, which, for its part, felt no qualms whatsoever about taking advantage of the business world's uneasiness with this potentially profitable group of untouchable outcasts. The shrewd bosses of organized crime were the first investors to recognize the economic viability of the gay market as a distinct social entity with its own special needs, an undomesticated cash cow that they milked dry by establishing an unregulated monopoly on gay bars and bathhouses, a stranglehold they relaxed only in the 1970s. Mobsters were the first pioneers in the century-long campaign to win "gay dollars," beating out by several decades the Calvin Kleins and the Kenneth Coles. The assimilation of the gay market into the overall economy began at the lowest level of the financial food chain, with its parasites and its bottom feeders, the opportunists who had no reputations to protect and, because they are accustomed to serving clients even more disreputable than homosexuals, aren't afraid of ruining their good names. The road from La Cosa Nostra to Saab, from the sleazy Gambino family to the pure, clean taste of Evian spring water, has proven to be a long and winding one. Paradoxically, however, the Mafia's exploitation of gay men was far less destructive to the subculture's unique character than its exploitation by respectable corporations, which are not content to leave the gay market as they found it but feel compelled to reinvent the homosexual, reshaping him in the image of the happily wedded heterosexual.

While gay men have long attempted to pressure companies into recognizing the error of their ways through boycotts of everything from orange juice and Coors Beer to catsup and ski lift tickets, it is only within the last few years that the politics of economic clout has become one of the central planks of the gay rights movement. The notion that liberation can be extorted by blackmail at the ATM and the cash register if not legislated at the voting booth has ironically simplified and streamlined the commercialization of the subculture, for gay activists have in effect turned themselves, with the best of intentions, into freelance rainmakers for corporate America. The conflation of politics and money has led many activists to work in tandem with Fortune 500 companies in order to bring them into a closer and more open association with the gay community in hopes that this marriage of convenience, of mutual self-interest, would at once whet corporate greed and hasten our integration into society. Progress in gay rights is often won at the expense of our indigenous, unacculturated idiosyncrasies as a minority which must be toned down or erased altogether in order for us to achieve complete social acceptance. Gay liberation and the gay sensibility are staunch antagonists. The stronger we become politically, the less of a distinct ethnic identity we are able to maintain in the face of assimilation, much as aboriginal tribes, untouched by Western culture, once forfeited their native customs and adopted foreign varieties of religion and dress.

As we have seen earlier, the very feature of the gay sensibility that was developed to fight against the prejudices of our society, our aestheticism, became the primary vehicle for our assimilation into it. Just as changes in personal ads and in glossy magazines show how easily gay men can be drafted into serving the interests of corporate America, so a comparison of our attitudes toward hygiene and grooming before and after Stonewall reveal how successfully companies have exploited our innate susceptibility to consumerism. They have made an effective bid to appropriate one of our most private possessions, our bodies, which we are slowly relinquishing to the ploys of modern advertising. Our efforts to counter the destructive effects of these economic forces and create an alternative body undefiled by the marketplace have, in turn, fueled our desire to suppress the gay sensibility and model ourselves on the physical image of the heterosexual male, a process that exactly mirrors our attempts to describe ourselves as "straight appearing" in our personal ads or to merge into mainstream youth culture.

A Psychohistory

of the Homosexual Body

I N 1899, PULP MAGAZINE MOGUL Bernarr Macfadden, the author of *The Superb Virility of Manhood: The Causes and Simple Home Methods of Curing the Weakness of Men*, published the first bodybuilding magazine to appear in America, *Physical Culture*, a publication that spawned literally hundreds of imitators in the decades to come, from *Muscles a Go-Go* to *Manorama*. For nearly 50 years, Macfadden advocated the revitalization of our country's masculinity, which he documented in photographs of naked athletes whose spectacular physiques he hoped would inspire the viewer to transform himself from an effete, potbellied slouch into a rippling, all-American he-man. As early as 1903, however, this eccentric entrepreneur, who later started his own cult, was alarmed to discover that an unwanted intruder had weaseled his way into the audience of *Physical Culture*, a type of reader who was not at all interested in trying out on his own body "the simple home methods of curing the weakness of men" but was perfectly content to feast his eyes on the effect of the cure on others. Disgusted by homosexuals' infiltration of his magazine, the mild-mannered founder of "Cosmotorianism," "the happiness religion," launched a lifelong vendetta against gay men and even went so far as to encourage fag bashing as a means of eradicating "the shoals of painted, perfumed,

kohl-eyed, lisping, mincing youths that at night swarm on Broadway . . . ogling every man that passes."[1]

Perhaps in response to the virulent homophobia of such ideologues as Macfadden, who turned *Physical Culture* into his own
bully pulpit to champion the cause of the American male in his
battle against effeminacy, gay men began to publish their own
physique magazines as early as the 1940s and 1950s. At first,
there was little to set these apart from their legitimate bodybuilding counterparts, but by the 1950s traces of camp began to
emerge in such audacious periodicals as *Grecian Guild Studio* and
Physique Pictorial. The editors made their proclivities particularly
clear in homoerotic art by such illustrators as "Art Bob" or
George Quaintance, whose sketches of half-naked telephone line-
men sweltering in the sun or frolicsome college athletes clad only
in jockstraps cavorting on dormitory beds "compare most favora-
bly," one author opined, "with the magnificent art treasures
handed down from antiquity."[2] *Physique Pictorial*'s "Four Alarm
Fire," for instance, depicted in explicitly sexual detail a room of
scarcely clothed firemen scrambling to pull on skin-tight uniforms
over their ample crotches and protruding rear ends, an image
that the magazine's editor claimed would remind readers "of the
tremendous debt of gratitude we owe these brave defenders of
our homes. Let us do all we can to lessen their burden. Follow
the fire safety rules."[3] Similarly, in "Mail Call," a cabin of bored
sailors on a ship receive their mail wearing scanty undergarments
even as they thumb through girlie magazines, an image that
dramatizes the "heartbreak of being forgotten" and the necessity

---

[1] *Gay New York*, p. 179. Defending the photographs in *Physical Culture* from those who
were more titillated than they were inspired, the publisher of such salacious trash as
the New York scandal sheet *Graphic* (nicknamed by its Manhattan readers "Porno-
Graphic") haughtily proclaimed that "there is nothing nasty, . . . vulgar, . . . [or] immodest in the nude" but that "the nastiness exists in the minds of those who view it, and
those who possess such vulgar minds are the enemies of everything clean, wholesome,
and elevating." *Gay New York*, p. 116.
[2] *Physique Pictorial*, Spring 1955, p. 27.
[3] *Physique Pictorial*, Summer 1955, p. 21.

of sending our boys overseas "good happy news of all the wonderful things happening all about you."[4]

Constantly harassed by the FBI and the U.S. Postal Service, the editors of gay physique magazines appeased government censors by striking exactly the right note of cloying virtuousness. Attempting to pass themselves off as members of a "persecuted cultural minority" victimized by a federal "crucifixion of the arts,"[5] gay editors indignantly filled their magazines with outraged self-justifications. They pretended to be sophisticated art lovers rather than lewd entrepreneurs who trafficked in dirty pictures of unsuspecting heterosexual teenagers, whom their photographers snatched off the football field and out of the boxing ring, often from right beneath the eyes of their adoring mothers. *Physique Pictorial*, in particular, always waxed poetic about its "mission" and self-righteously reassured its readers, as well as the government employees who steamed open its envelopes, that the admiration of "a fine healthy physique" is not a loathsome act of depravity but "a great compliment to our creator who planned for the utmost perfection in all of his universe."[6] "Just as infinite beauty surrounds us in flowers, music, [and] all of nature including ... the intricate galaxcies [sic] of the heavens, so in the perfect human body do we find limitless variations of harmonious rythms [sic] expressing a magnificent beauty which makes the soul sing."[7]

It was not until the early 1960s that the editors of gay physique magazines began to acknowledge publicly the prurient function of their photographs. They also became increasingly frank about the sexual orientation, not only of themselves and their readers, but of most of their models, the surly (and occasionally felonious) heterosexual auto mechanics, janitors, service station attendants, steel mill workers, paratroopers, plumbers, and farm boys who were often openly contemptuous of the gay photographers who took their pictures. "Dale left Los Angeles under most unusual circumstances,"

---

[4]*Physique Pictorial*, Summer 1955, p. 15.
[5]*Physique Pictorial*, Summer 1955, p. 1.
[6]*Physique Pictorial*, Winter 1954–55, p. 2.
[7]*Physique Pictorial*, Winter 1954–55, p. 2.

Physique Pictorial's editor reported of one model in 1960, "after a home in which he had been visiting was burglarized. This of course does not amount to an accusation."[8] By 1964, the editor had become considerably less coy and begun printing a lineup of the mug shots of "Delinquent Models!" who had robbed and beaten their tricks or, in the case of naughty Ronnie Akers, had tossed a man's beloved poodle into his outdoor swimming pool, thus "causing it to catch a cold which eventually resulted in its death."[9] Years later, *Physique Pictorial* even published an issue that featured the naked photographs of past models who had murdered, not just poodles, but actual gay men, such as adorable Danny who "is now serving a 25 years to life prison term for the brutal slaughter of a Bel-Air millionaire" or cherubic Kyle who "strangled [a trick] to death with [an] electric skillet cord, wrapped his frail body in a blanket and dumped it along the side of the upper end of the Hollywood freeway."[10]

From 1960 until its demise in 1983, *Physique Pictorial* regaled its readers with vivid descriptions of the misbehavior of its models, whose burglaries and homicidal escapades served as a perverse method of vouching for the boys' heterosexual authenticity as blue-collar rough trade. The editors never stopped reminding their readers of the vast differences of sensibility, class, and physical appearance that separated them from the men on display, who were both disparaged and romanticized as irresistibly masculine low life, at the same time that the reader was implicitly portrayed as law abiding and well behaved. Ultimately, however, these ironic captions celebrating the criminal activities of the magazine's straight trade were not entirely complimentary to the homosexual reader, for while he was praised for being a meek, defenseless gay man at the mercy of the underclasses, he was simultaneously denigrated as being unworthy of photographic representation. The vision of the gay body implicit in many physique magazines was that of a sexless sissy whose scrawny frame would have looked out of place amid the comely

---

[8]*Physique Pictorial*, Jan. 1960, p. 10.
[9]*Physique Pictorial*, July 1964, p. 29.
[10]*Physique Pictorial*, Nov. 1983, pp. 12–13.

parade of swaggering straight homophobes that early gay magazines held up as the very standard of the "superb virility of manhood."

As recently as the 1970s, the entire physique phenomenon both reflected and reinforced a culture of profound physical inadequacy in which gay men were indoctrinated to believe that it was the straight man whose body merited being seen and worshipped, while his own had minimal erotic appeal. Although gay physique magazines did publish photographs of homosexuals, usually of aspiring actors or dancers (whom *Physique Pictorial* scoffed at as "sylvan creatures . . . that flit about on tippy toe"[11]), by far the majority of the images that appeared were, by the open admission of their editors, of straight men. Until the last 25 years, gay soft porn was thus fundamentally unreceptive to images of its own readership, thus creating inevitable feelings of self-contempt, much as a black audience would have felt if all of the pornography sold to it before the 1970s had featured photographs of exclusively white people. From the very beginnings of gay culture, homosexuals' images of their bodies have been haunted by a sense of weakness, futility, and unattractiveness, of sexual subordination to the heterosexual Übermensch. As a result, the gay body is psychologically unstable and vulnerable to an infinite variety of cosmetic manipulations and surgical rearrangements as we attempt to overcome the sense of physical inadequacy expressed with such demeaning candor in physique magazines. Our pent-up reservoir of self-contempt has resulted in the extraordinary malleability of the gay body, which has been subjected to the grueling ordeal of everything from rhinoplasties and hair implants to weight-lifting regimens and electrolysis, from tattoos and UVA tanning to tummy tucks and pedicures.

With the emergence of the first skin magazines in the mid-1970s, the aesthetic of gay erotica changed dramatically. From the unkempt lower-class boys who strut through *Physique Pictorial*'s pages in combat boots and motorcycle helmets, we arrive at the suave centerfolds of *Blueboy* and *Mandate* where luscious yuppies, who are identifiably gay, lie around mountains of plush cushions photographed in an

---

[11]*Physique Pictorial*, May 1964, p. 3.

hypnotic soft focus. In the course of only a few years, the homosexual's desires seem to have leapt upscale from cement workers and street sweepers to collegiate jocks and budding bankers who, their eyes glazed [over] with lust, lounge around their bachelor pads after work in an enticing state of undress. For the first time in history, the manufacturers of commercial gay erotica seem to have responded to a desire on the part of gay men to see bodies that have the same highly groomed and fastidiously hygienic appearance as their own. Gone are the unwashed bodies of grease monkeys reeking of oily axle rods and leaking chassis, and in their place are the deodorized bodies of middle-class professionals who bathe regularly, douse themselves with expensive colognes, and style their hair with mousses and gels. The skin magazines of the disco era build an altar to what might be called the "bourgeois body" of the well-adjusted homosexual who, with the help of gay liberation, is slowly and painstakingly disengaging himself from the destructive spell of menacing straight boys and setting his sights on a more accessible group of his sexual peers.[12]

The bourgeois body of the modern homosexual was not, of course, the invention of gay liberation, but the political advances made during the 1960s and early 1970s did have a significant impact on gay men's appearance. Regardless of their social class, homosexuals have probably always tended to be overgroomed in comparison with the general population, to wear loud aftershaves, to fuss unnecessarily with their hair, to manicure their nails, or to experiment with the famous "beauty secrets" popular among gay men during the 1950s,

---

[12]I use the word "bourgeois" advisedly and in a special figurative sense. I certainly do not mean to suggest that there were no lower-class homosexuals before Stonewall but simply that many homosexuals, regardless of their class, were acutely conscious of the maintenance of their bodies and often cultivated an extravagant style of dress and grooming modeled on the deportment of upper-middle-class men. Even lower-class homosexuals would have been susceptible to this hyperfastidiousness, which would have set them apart from men at the same economic level. Blue-collar straight men would not have shared with their homosexual counterparts this typically gay self-consciousness about their hairstyles, skin care, methods of bathing, body odors (often concealed beneath loud colognes and aftershaves), and even their clothing, which was frequently expensive, even beyond their means.

such as placing wet teabags on the skin beneath their eyes to reduce the swelling or massaging Preparation H into their crow's-feet to eliminate their wrinkles. But if the proverbial vanity and physical self-consciousness of gay men has a long and venerable history, the political activism of the Stonewall era contributed a new element of urgency to the effeminate appearance of the homosexual's body. The rise of the gay rights movement created a climate of permissiveness that allowed homosexuals to exaggerate their already finicky style of self-presentation.

Until the 1960s, fears of social disapproval, as well as the una-vailability of skin-care products for men, held the bourgeois body carefully in check, thus driving many homosexuals into a kind of bootleg, beauty-supply underground where, out of desperation, they became self-medicating cosmeticians who filled rubber gloves with petroleum jelly in order to soften their hands and tied strips of cloth beneath their chins to prevent snoring, which causes wrinkles around the mouth. Gay liberation and the growth of the male beauty aid industry, however, freed the bourgeois body from its closet, from its makeshift elixirs and home brews, and stimulated a self-pampering narcissism that culminated in that encyclopedia of overgrooming, *Looking Good* (1977). Extremely popular among gay men during the late 1970s, this male fashion and beauty guide represents the very summit of the gay obsession with hygiene that fundamentally altered the look of our bodies in the years following Stonewall. The book offered extremely detailed recommendations about a wide variety of do's and don'ts: that we should douse our faces with a minimum of 30 handfuls of water before applying moisturizer; that we should cut our nails so they conform to the curve of the fingertips, since "ovals or points are *de trop*";[13] that we should blot—but never wipe!—our cheeks with a tissue when our bronzer begins to trickle down our faces from perspiration; and that, during a pedicure, we should sep-arate our toes with "cute little paper pompons."[14] Gay men had sud-denly found the courage they needed to cross a crucial psychological

---

[13]Charles Hix, *Looking Good*. Photos by Bruce Weber (Hawthorn Books, 1977), p. 182.
[14]*Looking Good*, p. 187.

threshold and coddle themselves with everything from cucumber facials and "Retexturing Whole Egg Masques" to mascaras that "come in colors for extra oomph" and eyeliners whose two basic shades, "champagne" and "mocha," "bring out the beauty of your eyes day into evening." Politics have thus played a pivotal role in the very appearance of the homosexual's body, permitting us to powder, spray, and scent it in ways that would have been impossible in the decades before Stonewall. The growing social acceptance of homosexuals' physical self-preoccupation gave us the license to act on long-suppressed desires to get into our mamas' makeup bags and smear our faces with bronzers, blushers, and foundation bases, cosmetics that only the most marginal members of the gay community had the courage to use before the 1960s. With gay liberation, the bodies of one major sector of the gay population were radically feminized.

Not all of the models in the first issues of the skin magazines published in the 1970s were perfectly coiffed specimens of the immaculate bourgeois body. Proletarians wearing construction hats, military fatigues, and police uniforms continued to appear, but they differed in one crucial respect from the lower-class boys represented in the physique magazines. The men in the early issues of *Blueboy* and *Playguy* were not real proles. They were *faux* proles, gay men dressed up to look like proles, dramatic impersonations of hayseeds in overalls chewing on straws, hillbillies with rifles and raccoon caps, and mechanics with neat streaks of axle grease daubed on their cheeks with aesthetic precision. In this complicated class masquerade, in which gay men assumed the tattered costumes, butch stances, and threatening demeanors of the blue-collar models in *Physique Pictorial*, we catch the homosexual in the very act of formulating an entirely new look for his body, one modeled on the image, not of the aristocratic dandy, who provided the paradigm for the pre-Stonewall gay body, but on that of the working-class male.

With the rise of gay liberation, the sexless homosexual eunuch acquired enough self-esteem that he attempted to overthrow his sense of physical inadequacy to straight men. Beginning in the 1970s and then gathering momentum in the early 1980s, as AIDS inspired a whole new type of anguished health consciousness, we started furiously lifting weights in order to claim our rightful place in front of the camera rather than perpetually behind it where we were previously forced to sit passively on the sidelines and reverently admire our dangerous heroes. As early as the 1950s, one segment of the homosexual population had begun to abandon the colorful cravats and brown suede shoes borrowed from the stereotype of the upper-class aesthete and actively adopted various badges and costumes associated with working-class men: the olive drab of the soldier, the chaps of the cowboy, the dark shades and motorcycle jackets of the biker, the facial hair of the Marlboro man, and the tattoos of the sailor (including such stereotypic designs as panthers that claw their way up biceps and kitschy Catholic images of bleeding hearts, weeping Virgins, and gaunt Jesuses pierced with crowns of thorns). The emergence of the *faux* prole, more widely known as the "clone," was a vivid indication of how completely, after decades of studying the bodies of heterosexual rough trade, we had absorbed their physical aesthetic, which led us to initiate a process of self-refashioning that has continued well into the 1990s.

Gay liberation thus produced two entirely contradictory images of the gay body, dividing it in two, creating our own subcultural Dr. Jekylls and Mr. Hydes. On the one hand, the license afforded by the growing climate of tolerance and permissiveness ushered many gay men into a whole new era of self-pampering, the slaphappy spirit of which can be summed up in *Blueboy*'s words of hygienic wisdom, "when you cleanse you moisturize. . . . *Never* one without the other!"[15] These radically feminized creatures guiltlessly transgressed sacred masculine taboos against narcissistic self-absorption by waxing tufts of hair off simian shoulder blades, twisting their facial features into grotesque expressions as part of a daily regimen of antiwrinkle, "faceometric" exercises, and even "matching the color of [their] eye shadow to [their] outfit or eye color," as *Genre*'s "Lipstick Shtick" column recently suggested.[16] On the other hand, gay liberation gave men the confidence they needed to wage war against precisely these

---

[15]"Grooming Beyond the Haircut," *Blueboy*, Dec. 1981, p. 58.
[16]*Genre*, Oct. 1994, p. 74.

effeminate stereotypes and to assert themselves in exaggeratedly masculine ways, cultivating an implausibly studied machismo. As a result, the feminized body of the dandy, brought to a peak of
perfumed, permed, and blow-dried perfection by the new male
beauty industry, collided head on with attempts to masculinize the
gay body. Rather than solving the self-image problems that had long
plagued homosexuals, gay liberation ironically created an entirely
new set of problems that divided a community that was once far
more uniform in its physical appearance into two warring factions
(each of which accused the other of being "unnatural," with the
bourgeois homosexual dismissing the clone as fake, "mainstream,"
and "conformist," and the clone, in turn, dismissing the bourgeois
homosexual as "synthetic," prissy, and affected).

The rugged, unkempt look of what might be called the "antibourgeois body" of the clone was resonant with disgust for the consumerized appearance of the beauty maven whose immaculate and
inviolable temple the new urban cowboys proceeded to desecrate in
highly symbolic ways, piercing their ears and nipples, tattooing their
biceps, growing hair on their faces, and even going unwashed for
days at a time to enhance their naturally fetid odors. Whereas homosexuals had traditionally modeled their bodies on the patrician
ideal of the clean-shaven, upper-middle-class aesthete, many men
now took an unprecedented step downscale and rejected this aristocratic appearance for an even more spurious blue-collar look loosely
based on quixotic images of old-fashioned frontiersmen and hearty
plebeians like marines and truckers.

As a device for improving the self-esteem of homosexuals, the
antibourgeois body was an extremely problematic invention, given
that the gay man's newly acquired blue-collar physique stood in
marked contrast to his bourgeois life and profession. The antibourgeois body was therefore conceived, like any modern, easy-to-clean
kitchen appliance, with the utmost consumer convenience in mind:
its piercings and tattoos could be easily concealed beneath the crisp
white shirts, expensive silk ties, and neatly tailored suit jackets of
traditional business attire. Because of this adaptability, the clone
could pursue the most conservative of professional careers without

betraying to the world the real man lurking beneath the mild-mannered facade of the bank teller and the office clerk who, as soon as the five-o'clock whistle blew, metamorphosed into a marine, a cop, or a cowboy in full working-class regalia. Even today, tattoo artists and piercers still openly acknowledge—and even praise—the duplicitousness of the antibourgeois body; they comment without a trace of irony on the "satisfaction of knowing that one is different underneath one's business suit" and marvel at their favorite customers who pull the wool over the eyes of their straight colleagues, such as the man who "has over 200 piercings and if you saw him on the street you'd just think he was somebody's grandfather. You'd never in a million years guess!"[17] White collar by day, blue collar by night, the antibourgeois body is a reversible body, a toy that can be taken out in the evening and put away again at the crack of dawn. While the homosexual is anxious to escape the effeminate stigma of his professional life, he is entirely unwilling to give up its material advantages and therefore attempts to straddle two separate classes, to have the best of both worlds, to attain the sexual charisma of the prole and retain the creature comforts—the glass coffee tables, Japanese prints, and porcelain figurines—of the bourgeois gay man. The clone thus leads a dual existence, living a fractured life with a fractured identity.

Ironically, both the bourgeois body of the queen and the antibourgeois body of the clone were vulnerable to a new form of insecurity. In opening himself up to the products of the cosmetics industry, the homosexual added another destabilizing factor to his physical self-image. As companies began to market to gay men "papaya peels," mint cold creams, and eye makeup that promised to "enhance the excitement of your come-hither gaze," they employed exactly the same techniques that they traditionally have used to coerce women into buying their products. Through advertisements that evoke in macabre detail the disfiguring effects of neglect, manufacturers have always threatened the female consumer with a form of facial blackmail in which they present graphic descriptions of the

---

[17]*Modern Primitives*, pp. 92, 154.

warts, wrinkles, and blotches that will permanently scar her skin if she is foolhardy enough *not* to buy their products. Behind every cosmetic advertisement in *Vogue, Mademoiselle,* and *Glamour* is the implied face of a ghastly pariah whose ravaged features, afflicted with a nightmarish array of dermatological disorders, form a cautionary portrait of the woman who failed to heed the cosmetic industry's apocalyptic warnings. Skin-care companies do not coax and seduce, they preach and terrorize. In order to force people to purchase their panaceas, they exaggerate the extreme delicacy of the face, its precariousness, fragility, and brittleness, its urgent need of "intensive care," "therapies," "formulas," and "face systems," the rhetoric of triage for the mutilated accident victim that only the "biological moisturizing agents" created in "the skin-care laboratories of L'Oréal" or Estée Lauder's "nonacnegenic" and "hydration"-promoting lotions can "salvage" or "rescue." When manufacturers discovered the gay market, they infected gay men with the same dread of the cratered visage of the rash and incautious shopper who flirted with disaster by using lotions that are "possibly dangerous to facial skin"[18] and scouring pads so abrasive that if "you scrub too hard . . . you'll bleed."[19] With the growth of the male beauty market throughout the 1960s and 1970s, this new source of anxiety begins to disrupt and complicate the homosexual's image of his body, which is now at the mercy, not only of the intimidatingly masculine physiques of homicidal rough trade, but the equally murderous cosmetic industry, which drives him to take ever more expensive precautions to stave off the encroachments of age.

In attempting to assuage our fears of disintegrating into the battered carcasses of worn-out old queens, we have succeeded in creating another problem altogether, the problem of what might be called homosexual artificiality. Many gay men are haunted by the conviction that, by anointing themselves with "hypoallergenic" lotions, "unique under-eye *crèmes,*" and the skin-care products of such openly gay companies as Dorian Grey Ltd. (which during the 1970s

---

[18]*Looking Good,* p. 73.
[19]*Looking Good,* p. 75.

sold Jeunesse), they have lost their naturalness and become ageless, artificial creatures with skin taut from too many face-lifts and pouting, bee-stung lips swollen with collagen injections. By succumbing to the extortion of the cosmetics industry and pickling ourselves in preservatives, we have become little more than virtuoso feats of self-taxidermy.

Straight men, by contrast, maintain their "naturalness" and masculine authenticity by allowing themselves to disintegrate and refusing even to lift a hand to arrest the process of aging. Examples of this uncultivated masculinity can be found in *Physique Pictorial*, where the editors harp, not only on the violence of the models, but on the alarming rapidity with which they age, as well as the indifference they manifest toward maintaining their beautiful bodies, whose transience becomes a measure of their virility. In order to reassure the viewers of the heterosexual "genuineness" of the men on the page, the editors compose extemporaneous carpe diem poems about the models even as they brandish in their readers' faces their police dossiers: "since this photo was taken, David has become considerably heavier and lost his 'boyish charm' ";[20] "Dust ... once had a far better build, but like many others, neglected it when life came too easy for him";[21] "Gerald Sullivan had gotten a bit mature at the time we did these studies";[22] "when we last saw Forrest he had more tracks on his arms than NY's Grand Central train station and he was worthless for modelling at that time."[23] In contrast to the gay body, the straight man's body has an extremely short period of perfection, coming to fruition for a few brief years in his teens and early twenties and then quickly sliding into a state of irreversible decline in which he gains weight, loses muscle tone, and then, within months, spreads and sags into premature old age. The speed with which the heterosexual's body goes to seed testifies to his lack of vanity and self-preoccupation, the girlish narcissism that leads the

---

[20]*Physique Pictorial*, Oct. 1964, p. 13.
[21]*Physique Pictorial*, May 1979, p. 3.
[22]*Physique Pictorial*, July 1972, p. 28.
[23]*Physique Pictorial*, Sept. 1982, p. 12.

homosexual to mummify himself in the quack cures of consumerism. In contrast to the careless blue-collar slob, gay men are timeless vampires, Dorian Grays who flaunt their perennial good looks even as their once youthful portraits, locked away in their attics, shrivel and turn to dust. Having become the slave of consumerism, which fed his fears of getting old, the gay man launches a restless, lifelong effort to rid himself of his guilty sense of fakeness, of artificiality, and to recover his "naturalness," which he restores through a series of elaborately costumed impersonations.

In the act of remaking themselves in the images of such mythical icons of American masculinity as gunslinging cowpokes and close-cropped leathernecks, homosexuals failed spectacularly to alleviate their nagging sense of inadequacy to straight men, whose unaffected sexual self-confidence continues to serve as the subcultural touchstone of manly authenticity. Rather than rejecting outright the notion that gay men are less "real" than straight men, the post-Stonewall subculture internalized this belief and embraced without reservation the standards of masculinity formulated by straight society, building around them the mystical ceremonies of a whole new folk religion. When we attempted to heal the pathology of the gay body by embarking on the costume dramas of the new machismo, we did not succeed in freeing ourselves from our belief in the heterosexual male's evolutionary superiority, nor did we accept on its own terms our overdemonstrative style of talking and gesturing. In fact, we did precisely the opposite, and became our own worst enemies, harsh, homophobic critics of the campy demeanor of the typical queen. In the process, we intensified the instability of the gay body, which was in some sense less psychologically disturbed when we were content simply to drool over the physique photographs of straight men rather than to reshape ourselves according to their physical paradigm. After Stonewall, many gay men did not engage in liberating acts of self-acceptance, as we are often led to believe, but in emotionally demeaning acts of self-cancellation.

However butch, tattooed, pumped up, and pierced many homosexuals have become since the 1970s, the acts of desecration we perform on the bourgeois body, scrubbed with astringents and reeking of Chanel No. 5, are never entirely successful. Even the most sub-versive efforts to masculinize the body are often suffused with the aesthetic sensibility of the designer queen, who fusses over his tattoos and worries over his nipple rings with the same distraught air of indecisiveness with which he might decorate his apartment, choosing the right color scheme and coordinating the pattern of the curtains with the carpets.

The process of selecting a tattoo, for instance, is often described in gay magazines, not as the drunken lark of sailors, who once chose naked ladies and grinning skulls from cheesy "flash" boards, but as a task as complex as that of an upholsterer who pores over fabric swatches:

> Pick where you want [it] to go on your body, and try to visualize it. . . . Your idea should be large enough that it can be perceived and understood from a few feet away. It should be placed in a way that complements your body, because when you move, so does the tattoo, and that is one of the subtle beauties of the art. . . . A little bitty rose is kind of lost on a big arm. . . . Think of your body as a moveable canvas with 18–20 square feet of surface area—approximately the same as one side of a normal door. [And remember that the sun] will fade out any delicate shading and promotes blurring. If you spend a lot of time in the sun, keep the color scheme simpler and darker, and even consider foregoing the tattoo work altogether, particularly if you prefer a nice tan.[24]

The writer describes an act of self-vandalism, so popular among the lower classes, in distinctly upper-class terms, as if the gay man were trying on a designer suit or vacillating over a radical haircut at a beauty parlor, rather than trying to impress schoolgirls, as proletarian boys did during the 1950s when they frequently tattooed their left biceps so they could display them outside of their car windows as they cruised past the drive-in diners and drugstore soda shops. In an article entitled "Tattooed Tit Enhancement" in the gay S/M maga-zine *Drummer*, the author advises his readers that, before they engage

---

[24]*Drummer*, no. 141, Aug. 1990, p. 19.

in the common practice of enlarging and darkening the aureole around the nipple through tattooing, they collaborate with their lovers in sessions of "colorization foreplay" in which they decorate their breasts with felt-tip pens and experiment with the "design, color, and size of the aureole"; such sessions make "great Tit Scenes in themselves," we are told, "as the Tit Coach works out with the Tit Jock savory visions of how big the aureole and how dark the ink of the burgeoning nipples."[25]

As these examples reveal, the gay man's body has become a living, breathing battlefield in which the queen and the clone grapple for supremacy. No matter how macho the gay man tries to be, his strut inevitably becomes a mince, his deep voice a husky Marlene Dietrich contralto. His tattoos and piercings are refracted through a deeply embedded and ineradicably bourgeois sensibility, which cannot be suppressed but pops up inappropriately right in the midst of the most manly rites of passage in which the real person emerges like a flower arranger or a window dresser who flounces around making tough aesthetic decisions, his brow furrowed, his pinkie stabbing the air.

Over the past two decades, the very rituals of body defacement that once served the subversive function of defiling the aesthete's prissiness have gradually been transformed into methods of body beautification, as can be seen in the complete change in the nature and purpose of tattooing and piercing in contemporary gay culture. Whereas the tattoo was once inspired by the male-bonding rituals of sailors, criminals, and gang members, who bequeathed it to their gay tricks as a symbol of their masculinity, it has now assumed a central role in the new unisex look of androgynous chic and as such has been completely voided of its previous manly associations with the blood brotherhood of felons and merchant marines. Moreover, whereas the cheap "flash" art of anchors, eagles, and "In Memory of Mother" 's originated among the lower classes, the custom-designed tattoos of the fin de siècle "auteur" school originate in the highly individual sensibility of the cultural elite who plan their tattoos in consultation with professional illustrators as if they were one-of-a-

---

[25]*Drummer*, no. 143, Oct. 1990, p. 20.

kind art objects. Similarly, the clone's piercings, which once served a narrowly erotic function (specifically of heightening sensations in the nipple), have now become distinctly ornamental, appearing in nostrils, septums, eyebrows, navels, cheeks, and even tongues, which are punctured with a glittering array of studs, hoops, amulets, and brooches. Likewise, the bristling walrus mustaches, mutton-chop sideburns, and straggly beards popular during the 1970s and early 1980s have been converted in the 1990s into dapper goatees, which, far from indicating chest-thumping burliness, are meant to be neat and tidy, suggesting the natty style of a fastidious and carefully tweezered aesthete. Even homosexuals' strenuous bodybuilding workouts, which we first used to butch ourselves up, have ultimately become a sign of the queen's obsessive interest in grooming and self-maintenance. By the early 1980s, when the new extremes of AIDS-inspired health consciousness drove homosexuals to immerse themselves in what has been called "gym culture," muscularity had become so synonymous in the minds of most people with gay narcissism that a well-toned physique was an almost certain giveaway of one's sexual orientation. In the course of only a few years, the masquerade of proletarian machismo that homosexuals adopted during the 1960s and 1970s has begun to collapse, and the sensibility of the aristocratic dandy has begun to reassert itself through all of the testosterone-induced fantasies in which it was buried for over a decade. The bourgeois gay body has gradually eaten through the husk of cartoonish virility in which it was imprisoned and begun to aestheticize even the most recalcitrantly macho things, which have been turned into dainty body illuminations, intricate embellishments, and exotic arabesques.

One part of the homosexual's anatomy in particular has become the subject of an almost allegorical struggle between the bourgeois and the antibourgeois body: the foreskin, a sacrosanct part of the penis that the *faux* prole has fetishized as a distinctive physical feature of lower-class American men, who are in fact circumcised less often than their middle-class counterparts. The impassioned manifestos against circumcision that homosexuals are constantly nailing to delivery-room doors are filled with intense indignation, especially those disseminated by USA, the Uncircumcised Society of America, a sort of Save-the-Whales group for the prepuce whose members have actually written anthems in celebration of the foreskin. The following, for instance, is intended to be sung to the tune of "America the Beautiful":

O hood divine, O skin sublime
O foreskin dark or fair . . .
O wrinkled tip, O pouting lip,
Your beauty is all there.[26]

The subject of hymns, poems, monthly magazines, and even a whole line of specialty pornography, the pouting lip is now an endangered species championed by hordes of gay supporters ready to take up arms in defense of the "natural beauty" of the "unadulterated cock." Magazines like *Uncut* comb medical literature for examples of atrocities perpetrated against foreskins, which over the centuries have fallen victim to such groups as Muslim warriors who, during the Middle Ages, "scalped" their European opponents on the battlefield, carrying away their foreskins in trophy bags or impaled on their spears. Similarly, anticircumcision propagandists commemorate World War II as the armageddon of the foreskin, the final showdown when savage physicians in the U.S. Army engaged in foreskin witch-hunts, flushing out innocent victims whose "wingflaps" one particularly insidious doctor in the South Pacific gleefully threatened to add "to my collection of pickled foreskins."[27] In anecdote after anecdote, the anticircumcision brigade invents for itself a history of oppression and harassment, a colorful martyrology that abounds in horror stories of uncircumcised schoolboys tormented in the locker room by their sadistic "clipped" peers, or hairbreadth escapes by enlisted men who narrowly manage to evade the scalpel of the army surgeon, who mows down recruits in a vast holocaust of foreskins, decimating the American population.

---

[26]*Blueboy*, Sept. 1984, p. 78.
[27]Bud Berkeley, "A History of the Foreskin," *Drummer*, 6 (54), 1982, p. 27.

For the homosexual who is striving to suppress the finicky bourgeois gay body, which abhors the smell of smegma as much as it
adores the scents of the cosmetic counter, the wrinkled tip becomes,
not only a symbol of proletarian "naturalness," but a badge of resistance against the puritanical forces of hygiene and regimentation that
are attempting to reduce the gay man's body to something as odorless
and antiseptic as a test tube. The proud owners of antibourgeois
bodies nurse their own persecution complexes, savoring delusional
fantasies that they are the victims of the sexually backward machi-
nations of the medical establishment, as well as of mainstream gay
men, who stalk them wherever they go, snipping the air with gleaming surgical scissors. Many who have had the misfortune of being
circumcised have gone so far as to act on these nostalgic longings for
the pristine masculine body. They try out complex restoration techniques that involve stretching the skin of the penis with bizarre
scopelike contraptions or using do-it-yourself kits that require tying
the head together with loops of thread and then stuffing the pocket
with items like cotton balls, marbles, and BB pellets.

In the heated debates that gay men wage over the foreskin, the
ironies and contradictions of the antibourgeois body emerge with
painful clarity, for while homosexuals often hold up naturalness as
an antidote to the artificiality of the cosmeticized body, they are
willing to undergo the most *un*natural cosmetic techniques to combat
this artificiality. Moreover, they are blind to the contradiction of decrying circumcision as a criminal violation of the male body in its
natural state while at the same time violating their own bodies by
skewering their nipples, nostrils, navels, penises, and testicles with
disfiguring piercings as invasive as any botched circumcision. The
antibourgeois body is allegorized in profoundly inconsistent ways,
which demonstrate how artificial the whole enterprise of recovering
one's lost, pristine masculinity really is.

The emergence of what the gay community calls "bear culture"
provides yet another example of the civil war being waged in the
physical aesthetic of our bodies between the young, hairless studs
featured in porn films and the self-styled mountain men and redneck

brutes who are trying to subvert the subculture's oppressively un-realistic standards of beauty. The bear phenomenon, which origi-nated in the mid- to late 1980s, represents one of the most violent assaults that gay men have made to date against the overgroomed bodies of urban homosexuals whom the editors at *Bear* magazine despise as perversions of masculine authenticity. Reviling "buffed baby boys,"[28] "hairless little flips," "18 year old bar bunnies," and "pretty cityboys with pretty preppy dreams dancing in their heads,"[29] bears hold up as the paradigm of real, "honest-to-God" men miners, loggers, lumberjacks, and Hell's Angels who rev up their "hawgs," guzzle moonshine, develop enormous beer guts, and wear grizzled Whitmanesque beards like Old Testament prophets.

A pornographic bear short story entitled "Mountain Grizzly" (by "Furr") revolves around the conflict between men who like the dep-ilated buttholes and squeaky-clean bodies of blond surfers and those who prefer the ripe pits and mats of wooly chest hair of "rough, tough, big-bearded dudes carousing around a campfire, playing har-monica, fiddle . . . guitar, [and] passing the jugs of 'Pie.' "[30] After a ranger rescues a city slicker whose tent was washed out in a moun-tain storm, he apologizes to his guest for his raunchy smell, having lived alone in the wilds of the Rockies for such a long time. This confession inspires his guest to launch into a vitriolic lay sermon against gay overgrooming, during which he tells his host, "I think the perfumes and garbage most 'city folk' wear are a lot more ob-jectionable than the way a person smells naturally."[31] To prove his point, he promptly jams his nose into the man's armpit and then dives for his crotch, rubbing his "stache" in the ranger's natural juices. These coy gestures of flirtation have their desired effect and his host, variously referred to in his guest's ecstatic exclamations as

---

[28]*Drummer*, no. 140, June 1990, p. 26.

[29]*Drummer*, no. 119, July 1988, p. 19.

[30]Jack Fritscher, "How to Hunt Buckskin Leather Mountain Men and Live Among the Bears," *Drummer*, no. 119, July 1988, p. 22.

[31]*Drummer*, no. 119, July 1988, p. 29.

"Daddy Bear," "Grizzly Bear," and "Daddy Grizzly," proceeds to sodomize "baby bear" up his "cubby-hole."[32]

Such attempts to aestheticize hairy, out-of-shape bodies are in part motivated by fatigue with the amount of energy required for the onerous maintenance of the bourgeois body, which can be kept at its deodorized peak of svelte perfection only through back-breaking regimens of diet and exercise. But the cult of burliness is also fueled by an unprecedented new spirit of acceptance of a physical phenomenon once dreaded in the gay community, the unspeakable taboo of aging. While the old queen was once the pathetic laughingstock of gay culture, a much-derided spinster who collected antiques and knitted tea cozies, in the age of the bear she has been taken out of her mothballs and recast as "Grizzly Daddy," a figure whose physical disintegration has been invested with the authority and virility of an aging patriarch. As the incarnation of older gay men's impatience with the tyranny of the youthful body, which is always sleek and hairless, the bear might be defined as a Dorian Gray who has destroyed his own portrait. The bear is a man who allows himself to age in public, refusing to reverse the ravages of time by burying them beneath Max Factor foundation bases, face-lifts, Grecian Formula rinses, and hair replacement systems.

If the bear movement is inspired by perfectly reasonable frustrations over the prevalence in the gay community of a single prescriptive body type, its hirsute ideal of rugged masculinity is ultimately as contrived as the aesthetic of the designer queen. While bears pretend to oppose the "unnatural" look of urban gay men, nothing could be more unnatural, urban, and middle class than the pastoral fantasy of the smelly mountaineer in long johns, a costume drama that many homosexuals are now acting out as self-consciously as Marie Antoinette and her entourage dressed up as shepherds and shepherdesses. The bourgeois urban sensibility emerges all too clearly through the agrarian facade of these "shit-kicking . . . bearded guys in full leather buckskins, wearing fur animals on their heads . . . spending their . . .

---

[32]*Drummer*, no. 119, July 1988, p. 30.

winters out trapping skins and fur [until], come the spring thaw, YEE-HAW!—these American bear-trappers come down from the high country."[33] The contradiction implicit in the bear aesthetic between the ghettoized mind-set of the urban homosexual and his bucolic fantasies, which hark back to the bygone era of the Hatfields and McCoys, becomes especially evident in the closing scene of "Mountain Grizzly." Here, Daddy Bear proposes to his "cub" that the next time he comes up to the mountains they erect a fist-fucking sling in a clearing, a strange urban non sequitur imported straight out of the famous sex club, the Mineshaft, and set up incongruously in the placid, Arcadian setting of the forest primeval. Just as the designer queen inevitably peeps out from beneath his blanket of blue-collar tattoos, so inside of every bear there lurks . . . a Goldilocks.

The entire bear phenomenon is unnatural in another respect as well. Although bears profess to venerate the paternal authority of older men, it is difficult to imagine a more infantile preoccupation. Regression is ironically one of the major aims of the new religion of maturity. The movement is tainted with the kitsch of "The Care Bears," as can be seen in the personal ads in *Bear* magazine, which are full of "furry little critter[s]," "papa bear[s]," "baby bear[s]," "teddy bear[s]," "honeybear[s]," "cuddly grizzlies," "older fur balls of quality," "cute little daddy's boy[s]," and "warm fuzz[ies] in [their] 30s" who want "to hibernate in [a] den" or engage in "den play," "denning," or even "den shopping." Images of pedophilia are central to bear sex scenes, which often revolve around the hairy bogeyman's invasion of the nursery, as well as the violation and misuse of soft, squeezable stuffed animals, of plush koalas and silky pandas who are seeking "brawny, uncut papa bear[s]" to "expand an already sick-minded cub's limits" or to engage in "fuzz therapy" with "gosh-darned really good [bears]" ("no morbidly obese bears, please").

While the bear movement projects hostility toward the perennially youthful bourgeois body, it, too, is based on a central fantasy of boyishness and vulnerability, on the infantilism of the decrepit. If

---

[33]Fritscher, "How to Hunt," p. 22.

you skin the bear, you find, not a toothless hillbilly with a shotgun
and a still, but the typical age-obsessed queen with a subscription to
House Beautiful and a Japanese tea garden. Just as the tattoo has
become a brooch, so the bear's fur is really a mink stole. It is ultimately impossible to imprison the bourgeois body, to deprive it of
its lotions, starve it of its eaux de colognes and depilatories, and stuff
it in the hair shirt of apelike masculinity. Its effeminate refinement
infuses everything it comes in contact with, reappearing in the course
of time like an image that has been painted over, a pentimento that
shines through the fading tattoos and the thinning hair, the Mardi
Gras masks and Groucho Marx noses in which we have disguised
it, hidden it away out of shame.

The commercialization of the gay man's body was one of the
inadvertent consequences of gay liberation, which, after rescuing us
from our closets, placed us at the mercy of our vanity cases and our
medicine cabinets, where we stockpiled the rejuvenating ointments
and the vanishing wrinkle creams that had previously been used only
by women. While the aestheticism of maladjustment is the source of
the subculture's major attraction to manufacturers, the gay community serves other economic functions as well. Most importantly, it
can be used as a pilot market, an experimental laboratory in which
corporations introduce controversial commodities that they ultimately
hope to sell to the more mainstream and conservative heterosexual
shopper, who is far less adventurous in his habits of consumption
than gay men. Because of our complex psychological involvement
with shopping, we have always been on the cutting edge of trends
in consumerism, functioning as a marketing avant garde in everything from men's purses to platform shoes, from tanning salons to
track lighting, from Lycra gym trunks to Soloflex exercise machines.
We offer companies a test group of eager guinea pigs willing to wear,
display, drink, inhale, and ingest risky products that the rest of the
American public would be too timid to buy unless homosexuals had
not first made them fashionable, laying the groundwork for their
acceptance by society at large. Our value as a bridge market becomes
particularly clear in the case of the men's health and beauty industry.

Manufacturers have taken advantage of the homosexual's more liberal attitudes toward grooming in order to set an important psychological precedent in the minds of the average macho American who
will buy lip glosses, hair spritzers, and "glycolic peels" that offer "a
special blend of nature's own alpha hydroxy acids" only when the
companies that produce them have succeeded in overcoming their
emasculating association with feminine vanity and self-indulgence.
Gay men have helped such firms as Estée Lauder, Clinique, and
Calvin Klein break into the burgeoning men's market by destig-
matizing patterns of consumption once characterized as exclusively
female, thus opening doors to business opportunities otherwise barricaded by centuries of male prejudices. In a later chapter on the
origins of the underwear revolution, we see how the gay community
has provided a similar sort of bridge market for the selling of another
ideologically problematic commodity, men's underwear, an untouch-
ably sacrosanct article that is only now, in the 1990s, catching up
with women's lingerie after decades of being sealed off in a state of
museumlike inviolability.

Long before homosexuals were accepted by mainstream society,
we had become so financially useful to the business world that our
integration as respectable Americans was inevitable, for how could
any ethnic group that contributed as heavily as we did to the nation's
economy be ostracized forever? Gay men achieved economic viability
years before they achieved political viability. Indeed, the question
arises whether gay liberation would even have occurred had society
not first recognized our potential as a source of revenue and therefore
realized that, because we were less profitable as second-class citizens,
it had a vested interest in our assimilation. Liberation happened, not
only because drag queens hurled Molotov cocktails, set trash cans
ablaze, and uprooted parking meters at Stonewall, but also because
we had become too valuable to corporate America to be ignored,
relegated to the exclusive fiefdoms that the Mafia had established in
every major city. If companies were to take advantage of the financial
power of this troublesome natural resource, which seemed to offer
so much promise and yet bring with it so much peril, social inequalities that degraded and marginalized homosexuals needed to be

eliminated so that we could be welcomed into the fold of ordinary shoppers rather than excluded as a class of pariahs from which businesses were anxious to separate themselves. The recognition of our economic potential, in other words, was a prerequisite for our moral redemption and our political empowerment.

We are inclined to look at gay liberation as the sole factor leading to our acceptance into society, as if we had achieved the progress we have made in gay rights exclusively by locking horns with our enemies and putting up stiff resistance in the face of police brutality, when in fact the preconditions for the strides we have made are far more complex. It is not an accident that we were accepted by mainstream America first as consumers and only second as morally respectable individuals. The one did not simply precede the other, it made it possible.

In this sense, the integration of homosexuals into society is precisely the opposite of that of African Americans. Blacks achieved political equality first through government sanctions but have never succeeded in achieving their economic equality, a fact that explains why they remain marginalized and oppressed while homosexuals, who were acknowledged from the beginning as an elite group of shoppers and tastemakers, have been more readily endorsed as responsible members of the white-collar work force. The enormous discrepancy between the relatively successful gay rights movement and the floundering struggle against racism shows how a minority's moral status is directly related to its commercial value to society.

Before homosexuals began buying "rejuvenating" mint-avocado facial peels and Pacific-sea-kelp-and-algae astringents, they bought copious quantities of another type of commodity, pornography. Our libidos were one of the earliest aspects of our lives to experience the full impact of commercialism, which exercised an extremely destructive influence on our already troubled images of our bodies.

The Evolution
of Gay
Pornography: Film

LONG BEFORE HARD-CORE PORN films became available to the general public in the 1970s, small audiences of venturesome gay men defied their local vice squads and gathered together in stifling rooms to watch what were called "smokers," the silent, 16 mm shorts produced by a handful of underground pioneers during the 1950s and 1960s. In these unventilated theaters, guilt-ridden homosexuals watched such unspeakably obscene things as naked teenagers skinny dipping in mountain lakes, bare-assed cowboys in G-strings and Stetsons tackling unsuspecting Indian braves, and pensive artists sketching nude athletes in the tasteful poses of classical discus throwers. In *The Captive*, a Roman centurion taunts a disobedient slave in a tiny cache-sexe who, like a damsel in distress, pleads for mercy as he unconvincingly yanks on the chains that bind him to two teetering plaster pillars. In *Marble Illusion*, a melancholy Pygmalion chisels away at a Herculean figure, who miraculously comes to life, strutting about the studio in a scanty "posing strap" and gazing benevolently at the sculptor, who swoons girlishly over his flexed biceps.

No matter how arousing gay men may have found the euphemisms of vintage erotica, which the modern audience laughs at as little more than puerile kitsch, the films of such studios as the Athletic Model Guild (AMG), Zenith Pictures, and Apollo Films fell far short of actual pornography. They contained no penetration, no erections, and, most importantly, no frontal nudity, at least until the mid-1960s when they began to offer a parade of jiggling penises after the Supreme Court ruled that nudity in itself was not obscene. Even something as innocent as touching was portrayed in an extremely stylized manner and was sanctioned only if it was presented in one of three ways: (1) as a maniacal tendency on the part of the actors to engage in unmotivated bouts of wrestling, the adolescent rough-housing that, in the absence of more intimate contact, serves as a form of surrogate sex; (2) as "appreciation" by an admiring artist who circles around a static, muscle-bound figure on a pedestal, squeezing his arms and tentatively prodding his taut stomach; and (3) as a homoerotic form of rescue, as in the many instances of drowning in these films or in scenes involving heat exhaustion on African safaris where a parched beauty collapses limply on the shoulders of his heroic companion. Embracing is rarely permitted as an expression of affection, let alone of desire, but is allowed only in the form of mindless aggression or if one of the actors is defenseless, immobile, unable to reciprocate, paralyzed as a living statue or as a semiconscious accident victim languishing helplessly after a close brush with death.

When gay directors finally made the leap from erotica to pornography in the very early 1970s and abandoned such sophomoric sex substitutes as wrestling and posing for actual penetration, plot—and not just the nervous agitation of what AMG called "kinetics"—suddenly became much more central to the entire stag-film industry. The ironic result is that, as erotica became more raunchy and less euphemistic, it also became more artful, more literary, more narrative. The growing emergence of plot was simply a practical response to the pitfalls of filming explicit sex acts, which were liable to incur the wrath of vigilant censors unless directors carefully padded their films with a perfunctory quotient of socially and artistically "redeeming" material. In addition, plot quickly became essential to the misguided psychology of arousal basic to these films, which were premised on the naive assumption that the audience would become more excited if the sex scenes were staggered throughout the movie, separated from each other by long sequences of inaction that served as a form of striptease, of narrative foreplay, a way of deferring gratification until the viewer was worked up into a feverish pitch of impatience.

Throughout the 1970s and well into the 1980s, directors produced baroque monuments of inertia and aimlessness, *Last Year at Marienbad*s of dreamy, somnolent filmmaking. The 1972 film *Left-Handed*, for instance, consists largely of arid stretches in which the characters stroll through the streets of New York or take leisurely Sunday drives through the countryside followed by trancelike moments of presumably transcendent lovemaking blurred by the effects of pot and mescaline. Similarly, in that big-budget extravaganza *The Centurions of Rome*, the sex scenes are set off from each other by murky episodes of an entangled plot involving a kidnapping in the first century A.D. The movie reaches its climax when Caligula, surrounded by Praetorian guards with towering papier-mâché helmets that shake precariously on their heads as they sodomize each other beside the Hellenic bric-a-brac of Doric columns and plaster busts, chooses a slave to satisfy "my naughty, naughty lusts," ordering his prey to "take me with your large, strong, classical, sensitive hands!" The directors of such films set out, in some sense quite deliberately, to bore their audiences, for boredom was crucial to their tactics of delay. Plot served, not to engage the attention of the viewer, but precisely the opposite, to make him restless, to make him champ at the bit, to sit on the edge of his seat until his lusts could be slaked in the highly desultory moments of explicit sex that followed lengthy sections of sluggish narrative prick teasing.

Heavily plotted pornography became increasingly rare in the mid-1980s and 1990s (with the notable exception of such films as *Romeo and Julian*, an unintentionally ridiculous X-rated musical in which two troubled lovebirds burst into lip-synched duets before they make love, serenading each other with such lyrics as "does he want me? I just can't tell" and "it feels so good to fall in love"). But despite the existence of a number of examples of overplotting, the entire role of storytelling changed dramatically during the 1980s. Protracted narrative foreplay no longer satisfied an increasingly educated and demanding consumer who wanted his sex on the spot, with no foot dragging, no drumroll, just the act itself within seconds of popping the cassette into his VCR. As a result, plot has either been eliminated altogether and the curtain rises *in medias res* on a situationless act of copulation taking place in a barn, a locker room, or even on a trampoline, as in that acrobatic tour de force *Slam Bam (Thank You Man)*, or it is telescoped into brief expository scenes where it is prevented from getting in the way of the sex. Instead, it is marginalized into a humorous frame, a decorative border rather than a constituent part of the pornographic experience itself.

In contrast to the often humorless films of the 1970s, plot has become much more playful and ironic but at the same time much less intrusive, as in Catalina's *Secret Sex* trilogy, a clever remake of Arnold Schwarzenegger's *Terminator* series in which the characters conspire, not against machines, but against the "Sex Police," the diabolical henchman of twenty-first-century ultraconservatives. The latter have criminalized sex altogether, driving underground a group of erotic terrorists who call themselves the "Sex Radicals" and live in a labyrinth of dark, smoky tunnels crawling with police moles and would-be defectors from above who are inevitably converted as soon as they taste the forbidden fruits of sin. Sex has been so thoroughly suppressed that one rookie cop from the Sex Police is forced to ask his more seasoned sidekick, "I mean, do they really, you know, put their things in their mouths? . . . And do they, you know, take it up the, well, you know?"—whereupon his obliging instructor, breaking the law for strictly pedagogic purposes, teaches him, through hands-on training, that they do indeed put their "things" in their mouths and take it up "the, well, you know."

Even the most popular form of plot in pornographic films, the picaresque tale of an itinerant character who has a series of disconnected sexual encounters while traveling on the open road, is gradually becoming obsolete. As skeletal as this basic story line is, its episodic structure is unable to withstand the new commercial pressures to decentralize plots and break the stranglehold on the entire casting process of a single star protagonist who, because he appears in all of the scenes, is liable to bore those who insist on seeing a whole smorgasbord of beautiful bodies. The new mandate for variety is incompatible with plot, for narrative presupposes a stable set of recurring characters, whereas most contemporary porn films have large casts of actors who participate in one scene and then, with neither explanation nor apology, simply vanish. Modern pornography is thus antiheroic rather than picaresque. It precludes from the outset a story that centers on one charismatic personality whose role has now been fragmented into dozens of bit parts and brief walk-ons. Contemporary cinematic erotica is heroless, devoid of leading men, consisting entirely of chorus lines, the supernumeraries who have divvied up between them the role of the presiding diva who once gave pornography more structure than it has today.

The most corrosive influence on plot, however, is neither literary nor commercial but technological: the fast-forward button, the ultimate solvent of narrative. Before the mid-1980s, the audience, which was forced to consume pornography in movie theaters, was at the mercy of the pacing of the director, who could draw out his precoital narratives for as long as he chose in the sadly mistaken belief that he was adding fuel to the fire and heightening curiosity. Now, the roles are reversed and the director is at the mercy of the VCR-owning consumer who, with a simple flick of his wrist, exacts revenge for past boredom. With his remote control always closely at hand, he shapes the entire narrative experience of pornography in such a way that he can peek ahead, much as a reader might peek ahead to see how a novel ends, thus bypassing all of the tedious preliminaries, the storytelling striptease, and throwing himself into the thick of the action. Pornographers now create their films with the fast-forward button firmly in mind, drastically foreshortening the story's expository sections. Because watching porn is no longer the sequential, chronological experience necessary for the very existence of plot, it has become a nonconsecutive, nonlinear event in which the audience leaps from moment to moment in a fitful, discontinuous type of viewing that dissolves narrative into a series of discrete orgasms ideally suited for the MTV audience. Once again, we are returning to AMG's "kinetics" after a decade of watching monotonously drawn-out films in which the sex was buried in a thickly padded plot like a prize in a Cracker Jack box.

The use of plot as an instrument of delay is not the only factor that makes early gay films difficult to watch today. The obstructive presence of narrative was heightened by the bad lighting of early pornography, which frequently envelops the actor's entire body in impenetrable shadows, obliterating his genitalia, which, at the most crucial moments, disappear altogether from the screen for seconds at a time, fading into pitch blackness. For many years during the 1970s, most films were so dark that certain parts of the male anatomy remained unexplored erotic territory, an unfathomable wilderness that defied the budget constraints and limited technological resources of companies working with bulky equipment and low-watt bulbs. Despite the fact that they filled the screen with obsessive closeups, directors had great difficulty throughout the 1970s and even into the 1980s in overcoming the darkness of the regions surrounding the groin, which were made even more mysterious by the long hair of the actors, which draped over blow jobs like curtains, hiding erections from the audience. Until the early 1980s, inadequate lighting also rendered the anus largely unfilmable, hidden away under a bristly fleece of coarse hair that prevented all but the briefest and most unsatisfactory cameo appearances of a barely discernible puckered opening surrounded by a thicket of frizzy curls.

In part, the funereal gloom of the films made during this period was simply the result of the nature of the medium of film (as opposed to that of video) and of technical incompetence. Yet this darkness was not entirely inadvertent, for bad lighting also served a specific ideological function. It contributed to the decadent atmosphere with which directors linked gay sex in an effort to incorporate the forbidden nature of homosexuality into the very mechanism by which they aroused their audiences. When sex occurs in many of the films produced during the 1970s, we enter what might be called a dreamscape, an hypnotic and decidedly ill-lit world, suffused with a highly moralistic sense of sin, in which the characters exist in a timeless state of drugged arousal, floating disembodied through indeterminate landscapes that have no clear physical reality. In one of the darkest and most brooding films of the 1970s, *Destroying Angel*, a priest experiencing religious doubts is chased around Manhattan by a de-

monic twin who appears at his bedside when he is making love,
stepping out of mirrors and cackling with sinister glee over his
brother's ungodly abominations as Hitchcockian scores of dark cellos
and screeching violins reach deafening crescendos.

The sex of early gay pornography often occurs in a setting that is
explicitly demonic and otherworldly, an infernal realm in which perverted acts, engulfed in the misty vapors of fog machines, are filmed
in slow motion or in diabolical shades of red. But although the allusions to purgatory can be quite direct, such moody, Dantesque
twilight zones crop up even in the most realistic films where the
characters no sooner pull down their pants than they leave the bedroom behind and enter a trancelike state of sexual rapture whose
intensity temporarily suspends the normal operations of space and
time. As the characters make love, the viewer is transported out of
the everyday world into a vague and kaleidoscopic no-man's-land
divorced from reality, a delirious mirage where the ravenous fingers
of faceless phantoms snatch at wayward undergarments slipping
down rock-hard thighs. The final scene of an otherwise quite naturalistic film, the 1976 production *Kansas City Trucking Company*, for
instance, takes place in a bunk house for truckers so dark and so
permeated with a sense of shame that it is impossible to tell if the
whole episode is not in fact a figment of the characters' feverish
imaginations, a fantasy in which headless truckers, tormented by
unnatural lusts, lunge at the protagonist's defenseless body with an
air of starving desperation.

In the years immediately following Stonewall, the neogothic strain
that taints many gay films appealed to homosexuals' internalized
guilt, their belief in their own moral turpitude, a stereotype that
pornographers exploited by arousing their viewers with subliminal
images of decadence and degeneracy. Haunting dreamscapes in
which darkness served as a physical analogue of the depravity of gay
sex struck a deep chord with a subculture that had always been
marginalized as a promiscuous underground, a hellish world of furtive cruisers, condemned to anonymous sex, who flitted in and out
of parks and public rest rooms in pursuit of unmentionable passions.
Over the subsequent two decades, however, the eroticizing of gay

oppression lost its control over our sexual fantasies as homosexuals acquired greater confidence about the healthiness of their preferences and thus responded less and less to the dated conventions of these nightmarish tableaux. In fact, the entire history of gay self-acceptance since Stonewall can be discerned in the changes that have occurred in the lighting of gay films, from the spectral settings of the 1970s to the brilliant, clinical lighting of present-day films, which take place in spaces free of guilt, of the erotics of sin. Contemporary pornography is anchored in the here and now, in real bedrooms and real cars, rather than in indeterminate fantasy realms whose flickering light and dramatic chiaroscuro provide an almost allegorical representation of the stealthy conditions under which homosexuals were once forced to meet and cruise.

Many of the films produced during the 1970s were also undermined by the heavy editing of the sex scenes, which were sliced up into shots as brief as one or two seconds and then scrambled into a sort of cubist collage. Well into the 1980s, the viewer was presented, not with intact bodies that we are allowed to examine in their entirety, but with a mosaic of details. A shot of one lover's arm was juxtaposed next to a shot of the other's thigh, a nipple next to a foot, an eagerly lapping tongue next to a curling toe, or a mouth drooling in anticipation next to clawing fingers raking down a frenziedly thrusting back. In the course of 60 seconds of a particularly chaotic sexual encounter in *Destroying Angel*, for instance, the director makes a total of 37 cuts, or one cut every second and a half. The result is a garbled patchwork of incoherent blowups stitched together in such a way that the viewer cannot even determine which cock belongs to which character. Contemporary pornography, by contrast, tends to present an average of only four to five shots every minute, a number that produces far less fractured images than those found in the mangled episodes of older films, which seem to have been invented from scratch by splicing together random loops of film on the editorial chopping block.

The medleys of body parts in early gay pornography were not simply a result of the director's ineptitude but were the consequence of his conviction that an endless succession of rapid jump cuts and tumultuous sequences of blurry, dismembered shapes contributed something irresistibly erotic to the sex scenes. Pornographers believed they were filming two people, not in the act of fucking, but of merging, of coalescing, a process that involved the dissolution of their separate physical identities as they melted together, losing their definition as individuals. Sex was supposed to effect a mystical union of two lovers whose spiritual integration in the heat of passion was represented aesthetically by actively confusing their bodies, carving them up into small pieces, and then grafting them back together in intricate visual puzzles. Much as obsessive closeups were based on an extremely literal notion that the proximity of the lens to the body brought the viewer closer to the scene, so these erotic collages, which often spoil the films of the 1970s, were based on the literal notion that erasing clear visual demarcations between two bodies allowed the audience to relive the sweaty exhilaration of actors melding into one.

The fragmentation that occurs in films made in the 1970s was also the product of the context in which they were watched, a setting that changed dramatically in the wake of the home video revolution of the mid-1980s, which liberated viewers from decrepit burlesque palaces with sticky floors and dilapidated seats plastered with wads of gum. Until the last decade, the viewing of pornography was a communal event, taking place in darkened cinemas where restless audiences migrated from seat to seat in a game of musical chairs, knocking knees, playing footsie, and gathering together for sex in abandoned balconies or the cramped stalls of bathrooms. Because the vast majority of people viewed pornography in a public setting, early gay films really served more as an enhancement for cruising, a form of visual Muzak for sex, than they did as an end in themselves, as engrossing full-length features that monopolized the viewer's attention to the exclusion of all else, holding him spellbound as they meandered at their own exasperating pace through rambling and convoluted plots. In its early years, gay pornography was more glimpsed than it was watched. Its splintered images were designed for the most careless and intermittent attention. They allowed the viewer's eyes to dart back and forth between the screen and the audience, the fidgety and restive spectators who function as the unstable subtext of early pornography.

With the commercial success of home videos, the entire appearance of gay pornography was transformed as the nature of the audience's involvement with sexual imagery changed from the glance to the stare, the absorbed concentration of the man on his sofa who used pornography, not as an excuse for staging impromptu orgies on ruinous mezzanines, but as a masturbatory aid. Over the next decade, the pornographer attempted to accommodate the spectator's new level of alertness by dramatically reducing the amount of editing and the number of confining closeups for viewers who were increasingly devoting their undivided attention to the television screen. When pornography retired from a communal to a private setting, from the theater to the living room, its blurry and inchoate images snapped into sharp focus, the pieces of the shattered bodies were reassembled, and, with the flick of a switch, the stage settings in which sex was filmed were flooded with light as unsparingly brilliant as the incandescent lamps of a surgical theater. Moreover, in an effort to coordinate the action on the screen with the viewer's own masturbatory rhythms, the director created a strict new chronology of sex acts. He unscrambled the unpredictable sequencing of early porn films, where various kinds of sex were conflated together, presented simultaneously, with a few seconds of fellatio collapsed into the same footage with a few seconds of penetration or of French kissing, as if they were all happening at once. Contemporary films, by contrast, set the acts off from each other in clearly marked and rigidly hierarchical segments. As the audience becomes more aroused, the intensity of sharply differentiated positions and types of intercourse builds incrementally in excitement, escalating from the relatively prosaic yet obligatory blowjob to a more suspenseful interlude of rimming, which in turn culminate in the grand finale, both the actors' and the viewer's: the orgasmic climax of anal intercourse.

Well into the mid-1980s, the audience's estrangement from the surrealism of the dreamscape was heightened by the absence of sound[1] and the practice of dubbing sex scenes with voice-overs of disembodied groans and echoing tirades of expletives. The action was also set to music, to inappropriately lighthearted supermarket jingles that skipped merrily along, totally at odds with the thrusting pelvises pummeling each other on the screen. When the ghostlike inhabitants of misty purgatories began to speak and groan in their own voices and to do so in instantly recognizable settings presented without the perceptual distortions that make older films so hallucinatory, the viewer suddenly achieved the feeling of what might be called "presence," of being in close proximity to the sex. We have moved from the ecstatic love ballets of early films, in which sex transcended the realm of the physical, to the work of the last ten years, which, far from being dreamy and trancelike, strives to create something infinitely more down to earth: "hot" sex, sex rooted in the physicality of actors who remain firmly planted in the locations in which they make love rather than lofting up into an otherworldly state of euphoria where they convulse and shudder through acts of sodomy and fellatio so heavily romanticized that they resemble New Age out-of-body experiences. We have thus gone from rapturous pornography to crude and exclusively carnal acts of unapologetically obscene fucking and sucking, from transcendent sex, which was primarily an emotional and spiritual experience, to sex that takes place in the mundane realm of beds with creaking box springs.

And yet the decline of disembodied sex and the arrival of "hot" sex created as many problems as it solved for the modern pornographer: as soon as pornography came down from the clouds, it was difficult to conceal the stars' egregious acting, not to mention their intense anxiety and obvious lack of excitement. When the viewer is finally permitted into the room where the sex is taking place and is forced to listen to dopey blond surfers and burly numbskulls dressed as plumbers delivering their lines in a dishearteningly hammy and unconvincing way, he comes face to face with the alienating theatricality of pornography in a way that he had never experienced be-

---

[1]Before pornographers changed from film to video, synchronized sound was prohibitively expensive. The change to video also brought about brighter lighting.

fore. He immediately realizes that pornography seldom evokes fireworks but more often resembles a stroll through a wax museum in which talentless automatons flog each other with limp pricks, all the while howling, grimacing, and gnashing their teeth. Ironically, it is the untempered realism of modern pornography that is its downfall. The more lifelike the films become, the more phony they seem, haunted by the inauthenticity of actors chanting monotonous refrains of "oh baby" and "take it" even as they stand before us trembling and impotent, professing with such fervor the burning passions they clearly do not feel.

It is not only the sex that has become clearer since the video revolution but the locations in which the action is staged as well. Up until the mid-1980s, the backgrounds in gay films were usually irrelevant, consisting simply of someone's cluttered living room strewn with dirty socks and old newspapers or their grungy garage slick with pools of coagulating oil. These settings were chosen solely because of their availability and not because some well-paid scout had scoured the neighborhoods in search of the perfect location. It is precisely because of their irrelevance that the glaringly superfluous details of these backgrounds are so conspicuous today, so obtrusive, luring our eyes to the peripheries of the scene, to the hideous nonessentials that deflect attention from the sex itself: the appalling knickknacks on the coffee table, the half-eaten jelly donut on the chipped plate at the foot of the plaid sofa, the orange shag throw rug lying on the pea green wall-to-wall carpet, or the filthy high-top sneaker abandoned on top of the red vinyl ottoman.

By the 1980s, however, pornography became less and less a seller's market in which any amateur who dabbled in film could hawk his dingy and defective products to buyers willing to settle for whatever they could find in the stores. As a result, directors have become as sensitive to the aesthetics of their films, to uncoordinated patterns of upholstery or walls with peeling paint, as the cinematographers of commercial Hollywood releases. Unlike the cheesiness and vulgarity of the "found" locations of older films, the tasteful decors of contemporary pornography are actually *meant* to be seen and appreciated, to be processed along with the sex, which they complement, creating a seductive ambience of well-heeled elegance that exerts as strong an influence on the audience as the sexiness and stamina of the actors. Surrounded by original works of art and tasteful antiques, characters now make love in sleek, minimal environments, beside the marble hearths of crackling fireplaces or in living rooms that look almost unoccupied, like designer showrooms free of the unwashed coffee cups and dirty ashtrays that littered the sets of older films. Footloose bon vivants, fresh from Waikiki, now dally in luxurious swimming pools and then screw their way through every room of the entire mansion, taking the viewer on a kind of guided tour, from the ultra-modern kitchen, where they copulate among islands of gleaming appliances, to the master bathroom where they make love in the jacuzzis and walk-in showers.

Even settings that are *meant* to be dirty are now presented in such a way that they look squeaky clean. The yuppification of gay pornography, which now functions as a sort of open house in which the director squires us around the stately homes of the landed gentry, is neatly illustrated in a comparison of two public bathroom scenes, the first from the 1973 film *The Back Row*, the second from a film made over 20 years later, the 1994 release *Trip to Hopeful*. The former was clearly filmed on location in the filthy toilet of a dirty movie theater where the actors grovel in the stalls and wallow on the cold tile floor, the authenticity of which is verified by the camera, which gives us a clear shot of the soles of their feet, blackened with grime. In *Trip to Hopeful*, however, the bathroom was manufactured for the occasion with fresh wood, sparkling fixtures, and spurious graffiti. Even the glory hole is a designer model cut and sanded by an efficient stagehand who carefully beveled away the rough edges to protect the actors from splinters, while the dirt on the floor is trompe l'oeil filth created from paint splattered around the room like a Jackson Pollock to give the impression of squalor. We have grown so accustomed to seeing sex in affluent settings, which rival those found in *House Beautiful* or *Architectural Digest*, that even the minimal doses of raunch that we can tolerate have been sanitized for the disease-conscious consumer. (Like the decors, intercourse has also become obsessively clean and odorless. Directors now conscientiously suppress the sex prep, the application of the lubricant and the condom, which magically appears on the active partner's erection, unlike in older films in which the viewer was allowed to see the greasy application of gobs of pure white Crisco which get matted in clots in the furry pelts of actors' unshaven rear ends. Our insistence on maintaining hospital-like hygienic standards is so strong that the contemporary viewer recoils during a pastoral scene in the 1973 film *Just Blonds* when a leaf flutters down from a tree and gets stuck in the crack of one actor's ass, which is soon after visited by a blue-bottle fly, buzzing around inquisitively.)

The revolution in the decor of recent pornography is a symptom of a much larger phenomenon: the emergence of a new gay archetype. X-rated films were, like their audiences, once in perpetual flight from the subculture and consequently celebrated such nongay proletarians as truckers, construction workers, farmers, cowboys, policemen, mechanics, soldiers, sailors, athletes, fraternity brothers, and even criminals—blue-collar studs whose "authentic" masculinity tantalized their effete admirers. With the rise of the *House Beautiful* aristocrat whose sexual adventures function both as pornography and as a fanciful tour of a prime piece of expensive real estate, we are witnessing the rise of a new sexual hero, one that originates from within the subculture rather than from without it, from the ranks of homosexuals themselves rather than the elusive proles whose uniforms and mannerisms gay men once slavishly imitated. While porn films still celebrate the lumpen proletariat who screws in the cabs of tractor trailers, over wooden trestles at construction sites, or on bales of hay in the lofts of barns, these comely plebeians are gradually being crowded out and the viewer is left watching sex between idealized versions of himself, carbon copies who are as sexually charismatic as the primitive laborers of older pornography.

On the one hand, as we have seen previously, the search for sexual models from within the subculture represents an advance in the education of the homosexual libido. Many gay men are no longer at war with themselves, turned on exclusively by the act of self-cancellation that lies at the very basis of early films, where homosexuals have sex with the proverbial Other, with grease monkeys and horse wranglers, and assiduously avoid their emasculated subcultural counterparts. On the other hand, the fact that porn films increasingly focus on posh and gentrified images of gay men marks an insidious shift in the psychology of pornography, which used to glorify masculine icons with whom the homosexual viewer shared nothing in common and who were thus sealed off from him in such a way that their influence was carefully minimized. In recent films, by contrast, the viewer and the actor are compatriots, accomplices, brothers-in-arms, and the man on the screen is not simply an object of lust but of imitation, a model rather than a sex object, a figure who represents the bland summit of gay materialism. The porn star is increasingly the embodiment, not only of the gay man's sexual desires, but of his social and economic desires as well, his aspirations to lead the carefree life of a lounge lizard swimming in disposable income and basking in the sun around his crystalline pool where beautiful boys in bikinis silently skim the leaves from the waters and then succumb wholeheartedly to his sensual whimsies. As a result, pornography now eroticizes an entire lifestyle which has become as sexy as the sex itself, as in the 1989 film *Two Handfuls II* in which each change of scene is set apart, for no apparent reason, by lingering shots of such high-priced appurtenances as Louis Vuitton wallets, portable compact disc players, high-tech electronic gadgets, and bottles of vintage burgundy.

Contemporary pornography eroticizes all kinds of extraneous, nonsexual things, chandeliers and Persian carpets, Porsches and convertible coupes, jade figurines and silver candelabra, all of the status symbols that crop up on the inanimate fringes of the picture, where they are invested with erotic significance as searingly intense as the sexual images in the foreground. Thus, while it may represent a small step toward self-acceptance that we are turning away from the cult of the macho Other, the phobia of the subculture implicit in archaic erotica served its purpose, for when we begin to choose our archetypes from within our own ranks, pornography begins to exert a degree of control over us that it has never had before, shaping our social and professional aspirations as well as our sexual ones.

In addition to providing an economic model for the gay com-

munity, which reflects the ever-increasing pace of our commercialization, the rich new playboys of recent pornography present an
intimidatingly unrealistic physical model. As we have seen, throughout the 1970s and well into the 1980s, the bodies of the actors were
so fractured or examined at such close range that the viewer often
didn't have a clear sense of which leg belonged to which man, let
alone what each character looked like or how well endowed he was.
The erotics of coalescing produced a style of pornography that was
profoundly indifferent, not only to the luxuriousness of the settings,
but to the identity of the star, who was usually not a magnificent
specimen, a champion thoroughbred rippling with muscles, but simply an average man off the street, a slender but not necessarily gym-
toned individual with bad teeth, bony knees, and a boyish paunch.
Because the actor's personal appearance was all but irrelevant, collage
sex was the porn of anonymity, a style of filmmaking in which the
central character was simply *a* man, any man, unlike the ambrosial
youth, the autocracy of ectomorphs, promoted by such studios as
Falcon or Colt, which groom entire stables of actors, paying their
gym memberships and issuing decrees about the length of their hair
and the darkness of their tan lines.

The rise of such examples of the new gay archetype as cult stars
Jeff Stryker, Ryan Idol, and the late Joey Stephano contributed to
the obsession with fitness that continues to jeopardize gay men's sense
of physical and sexual well-being. With the spread of pornography,
we have been inundated with so many irresistible images of hand-
some jocks and prime slabs of beef that we have stampeded to the
gyms where, out of intense inadequacy, we attempt to sculpt our
flaccid bodies into shapes they were never intended to assume. The
proliferation in the mid-1970s of such glossy beefcake magazines as
Honcho, *Mandate*, and *Blueboy* saturated gay culture with an unprecedentedly coercive body of masculine iconography, the electrol-
icized images of the buffed, bionic males who now strip in our clubs,
strut down the runways of our fund-raisers, sprawl spread-eagled in
our calendars, and leer suggestively, in all of their hairless splendor,
from virtually every page of our newspapers. Throughout the 1970s,

gay men began to ingest massive quantities of prescriptive images manufactured by a highly commercialized industry that helped invent an illusory ideal of an unreal and unattainable individual, forever outside of our reach, inaccessible to all but the most conventionally beautiful people. The repressed, censorious, and moralistic culture that preceded the sexual revolution had at least one distinct advantage over its modern, hedonistic counterpart: its squeamishness prevented the free dissemination of the sexual images that now victimize gay men by providing the punitive standard against which we measure the mediocrity of our sex lives, as well as the inferiority of our bandy-legged, stooped-shouldered bodies. Gay liberation and the climate of permissiveness fostered by the counterculture inadvertently liberated us into a new state of heightened sexual self-consciousness, placing an aspect of our lives that had been relatively immune to the forces of commercialism at the mercy of the marketplace, which quickly began to bombard us with photographs and films depicting an all-powerful sexual elite.

To compare the actors of old pornography, whose bodies were scrawny, hairy, sallow, untanned, pimply, scarred, wrinkled, and buttless, with the groomed, buffed, tanned, shaven, oiled, tattooed, and pierced Adonises of contemporary films, is to see the entire history of the last 25 years of the commercialization of gay culture summed up in the most tangible way possible. Before the 1970s, homosexuals and heterosexuals were physically identical. There may have been gay clothing, gay gestures, gay walks, and gay voices, but there was no gay body, no equivalent of Semitic noses, Negroid lips, or Asian eyes. Pornography, however, contributed to the creation of the gay body. It left the traces of the commercialized gay subculture burned into the anatomy itself, which it resculpted, recolored, and reshaped, polishing it to a satiny finish with electrolysis, turning it a healthy and unseasonable shade of brown in the tanning salon, fattening it with steroids and protein powders, and pumping it up with free weights and Nautilus machines. The body was the final frontier that mainstream gay culture invaded, coopted, and commercialized, and one has only to take a nostalgic glance back at the unprocessed bodies of early pornography, with their scruffy beards, dirty feet, and cadaverous complexions, to see how profoundly our bodies have changed since Stonewall.

The new gay archetype is not only wealthy and muscular but also untouchable, a cold-blooded creature whose primary purpose, like the immaculate suites of palatial bedrooms and lavish solariums over which he presides, is largely ornamental. If the directors of older pornography created out of two separate individuals a single montage that was intended to suggest spiritual fusion caused by the surreal intensity of lust, recent films strive just as conscientiously to keep the bodies of the actors apart, to prevent them from coalescing. Directors now limit their characters' interaction in order to showcase the stunning physiques of a parade of raging prima donnas who are not having sex so much as they are striking flattering poses, mugging for the camera, and flaunting the laborious achievements of the hours they spent torturing themselves at the gym. We have come full circle to the AMG films where living statues, tastefully slumped against Doric columns, were meant to be admired from a distance, like works of art that could be seen but not touched. Just as wrestling once served as a surrogate for sex, so sex now serves as a surrogate for posing. Whereas the men in pornography from the 1970s freely wrapped their arms and legs around each other, contemporary directors rarely permit full-body embracing for more than a few seconds. Horizontal sex, in which one character drapes himself over the prone body of the other so that they become virtually indistinguishable, is strictly forbidden on the grounds that such extensive contact would impair the audience's vision of the showpieces on display. The cameraman manipulates intercourse to create a schematized, televisual sex that is in no sense whatsoever like the sex we have in real life, something he achieves by prying the actors apart, thus preventing them from concealing each other, from *converging* rather than simply *penetrating*. Unlike older pornography, in which anatomically incoherent and ill-lit ensembles of entangled limbs writhe to the dulcet strains of Muzak, sustained body contact in the films of the last ten years is so minimal that the actors are joined, like Siamese twins, at the single point of entry where one character's penis actually penetrates his partner. As a result, for purposes of clarity, the characters in contemporary pornography do not make love with their entire bodies but are confined to touching each other with their genitals alone.

This desire to maximize the exposure of the protagonists' bodies in order to allow the audience the best possible view results in a number of strange mannerisms: the actors appear to be pulling away from each other, shrinking back rather than rushing forward, as if their partners in some way repelled them, as can be seen in the absurdly diffident way in which porn stars often kiss. While people in real life press their faces together so that their tongues can explore deeply within each other's mouths, the tongues of porn stars frequently do not enter the orifice but simply touch at the very tip, flickering in the air like those of serpents so that this most apocryphal of cinematic kisses can be captured by the camera. The director expressly choreographs sex to create the best visuals, the optimal conditions for viewing. During anal intercourse, he instructs the active partner to place one hand behind his back in an inappropriately stilted, Napoleonic pose that simultaneously shows off his washboard stomach and prevents his erection from being hidden by his forearms as he clasps his partner by the hips. The actors also reduce sex to an occasion for exhibiting their massive quads and bulging lats by performing more literal forms of posing, including folding their arms voluptuously behind their heads, flexing their biceps, and doing pushups while drilling the mouths of their lovers who lie helpless beneath them, serving as human fulcrums for these gratuitous acrobatics. Even the harmless slaps the actors often give each other, pounding their partner's pecs with their fists or playfully swatting their rear ends, are not masterful S/M slaps meant to inflict a pleasant sting, but are a means of demonstrating to the audience the tautness and tone of their bodies, which the characters take turns displaying to the viewer as if they were car dealers showing off the special features of their merchandise, kicking their tires and adjusting the luxurious bucket seats.

But perhaps the moment that reveals most clearly that the real subject of modern pornography is not sex but a prurient examination of the sculptural perfection of spectacular physiques is the eccentric way in which orgasm is represented. Astonishingly, what industry insiders call the "money shot" seldom occurs during intercourse, from friction with another body, but is relegated to separate scenes in which the actors suddenly stop having sex altogether so that one man can bring *himself* to orgasm through masturbation as the other simply sits back and watches, offering feeble words of halfhearted support and encouragement, like a midwife presiding over a difficult birth. Instead of having simultaneous orgasms, which are relatively rare in gay pornography, the actors politely take turns, spelling off in such a way that only one man assumes center stage at a time, allowing the viewer to savor the thrill of each cum shot individually. Thus, paradoxically, at the very moment when the two lovers should be conjoined, merging in mutual satisfaction, they are most alone, withdrawn, and independent. The cum shot provides a metaphor for the pathology of modern pornography, which is highly solipsistic and resistant to the whole idea of merging. Contemporary pornography is at war with its very subject, sex, an act that involves a type of communion anathema to films more preoccupied with the appearance of lovely specimens than with the quality of their interaction with each other.

Older pornography looks as chaotic as it does because directors were trying to show sex from the point of view of the actors, whose excitement they mimicked in a reeling, vertiginous series of jump cuts, which were meant to provide the objective equivalent of a highly subjective state of arousal. The operative assumption was that the audience would get excited if the pornographer could devise a sufficiently compelling image of what was taking place inside his actors' heads, of the intensity of the tactile impressions being experienced in the porn star's consciousness. In the course of the last 20 years, however, directors have abandoned the notion that pornography works by empathy, by the transference of pleasure from the consciousness of the actor experiencing it to that of the audience watching him. While older films focused on what the actors were *feeling* when they had sex, more recent films focus on how they *look* when they engaged in it. Pornography has gone from being intensely, inscrutably subjective to alienatingly objective. Old pornography was about pleasure, about how pleasure feels. New pornography is about aesthetics, about how pleasure looks. In other words, the entire point of view of pornography has changed from the actor's point of view to the audience's, from the first person to the third, from their perspective as participants to ours as passive spectators loitering on the sidelines experiencing the scene from the outside where we watch an activity that is primarily a visual event rather than a sensual one.

If pornography once served merely as a mood enhancement for sex and cruising, the AIDS epidemic has made it an outright replacement for sex, both for those of us who have chosen celibacy and those of us who, having drastically reduced our number of partners, have made an uneasy truce with our libidos by settling for the tepid pleasures of mutual masturbation. AIDS has radically transformed the function that pornography plays in gay culture, elevating it from its former role as an aphrodisiac, a titillating way of whetting our appetites before we ourselves engaged in the act, to its present role as a wholesale substitute for sex, a safe alternative to the perils of the meat rack. We are rapidly becoming a culture of voyeurs, a society that delegates its sexual experiences to a special class of proxies, of stand-ins and understudies, who, like stuntmen in action films diving into circles of flame and leaping from careening automobiles, hurl themselves into a deadly battlefield of viruses where they take on all of the sexual risks that we ourselves are unwilling to assume. AIDS has turned us into cowardly bystanders who increasingly know sex secondhand, safely ensconced on our sofas where we indulge in the vicarious thrills of an absorbing spectator sport that we participate in only with our eyes. As intercourse becomes an exclusively visual, nontactile event, which we experience in a compromised, incomplete, and unsensual way, our pornography begins to cater solely to Peeping Toms who watch sex more than they participate in it, looking but never touching.

The Mafia introduced the gay community to the first product ever sold directly to it, alcohol, whose destructive effect on our livers bears silent witness to the earliest stages of our development as a growing market. The second commodity sold to the gay consumer was far safer, causing less wear and tear on our bodies and, what's more, an altogether different sort of intoxication: pornography, a product whose manufacturers, like the crime bosses who owned the first gay bars, were utterly indifferent to the possibility that their own reputations as businessmen would suffer from the unsavory reputation of their clients. But although the saturation of gay culture with pornography was easier on us physically than its earlier inundation with alcohol, the commercialization of our sex lives through the absorption of erotic images has caused its own peculiar type of psychological malaise.

Until the late twentieth century, sex was only rarely a spectator sport. The vast majority of people could experience it only by participating in it rather than by spying on others, gluing their eyes to keyholes or, like villains in old-fashioned mystery movies, peering through slits gouged out of the eyes of portraits. As a result, for thousands of years, we had a relatively imprecise notion of what sex actually looked like, having seen it either in fleeting glimpses of couples caught in flagrante delicto or in albums of rare erotic prints that presented—to the connoisseur who could afford to collect them—an at best schematic image of the appearance of our bodies when we penetrated each other. With the rise of readily accessible, commercial pornography, however, our perspective on sex was revolutionized, turned inside out from a subjective point of view to an objective one. People whose knowledge of intercourse was confined to firsthand experiences and direct tactile sensations acquired a whole new line of vision now that they could see people making love through the lens of a camera, well above the fray of passion. Pornography has acted like a tape recorder that has enabled us to hear our voices for the first time, to record an act that was formerly so private, so carefully hidden from view, so closely protected from unwanted interruptions, that we remained largely ignorant of its appearance. We perceived it only in a fragmentary way, through the tunnel vision of our own limitations as aroused participants handicapped by a kind of blindness that forced us to concentrate on sensations over aesthetics.

The startling innovation of this new commercial genre has caused radical changes, not only in the way we think about sex and judge our partners' bodies, but in the pornography itself, which is increasingly "told" from the point of view of the audience and the cameraman, not the actor. As our culture is permeated with erotic images, the perspective of pornography slowly migrates from that of the participant to that of the witness. In a world without pornography, we would be far more tolerant of the physical imperfections of our lovers, whom we now constantly appraise by means of the punitive and highly unrealistic criteria for attractiveness purveyed by an insinuatingly commercial medium that has turned intercourse into a beauty pageant, a wild dash down a runway at a fashion show. Pornography shows us how sex *should* look, not how it really looks. Its effect is essentially prescriptive and judgmental. It vitiates our sense of touch and exaggerates our sense of sight, promoting dissatisfaction with our real-world lovers and distancing us from the actual sensations of an experience that many now perceive exclusively through the stylized representations of it available on the store shelves. Because advertising often works by infecting the consumer with fear and insecurity, as we have seen in the case of the cosmetics industry, the commercialization of the gay community almost invariably means that homosexuals will become more fearful and insecure. The achievement of our economic viability as a market entails an enormous loss of self-confidence. We exchange guilt about our sexuality for apprehension, growing out of remorse and maturing into anxiety.

The Evolution of
Gay Pornography:
Literature

L ONG BEFORE EXPLICIT LITERARY pornography became legal in the United States in the 1960s, a thriving
underground cottage industry provided readers with sexually titillating mimeographed manuscripts that could be purchased for as
little as—even the price was pornographic—69¢. This contraband
was sold by neighborhood porn brokers who, during the 1940s and
1950s, smuggled their stock in from Tijuana where it was cranked
out on ditto machines by such clandestine operations as Esoterica
Press or 7 Zephyrs Press. Focusing on the racy, picaresque adventures
of hitchhikers, farm boys, and sailors on leave, these 20- to 30-page
booklets were dashed off by barely literate writers and were riddled
with typos, misspellings, grammatical errors, and an endless series of
such quaint euphemisms as "love muscle," "ding-donger," "my de-
lightful pogo stick," "that little thing-a-jig," and "my itching chasm."

Unlike the highly literary pornography of the eighteenth and
nineteenth centuries, which was written for an educated upper-
and middle-class reader, the populist gay pornography of the 1940s
and 1950s was probably some of the first explicit material produced for the working class. The coarse, unpolished stories of the
Mexican samizdat occupy a unique place in the transitional period
between the belletristic erotica published before the twentieth century for the jaded bibliophile and the hard-core material churned
out for the uneducated masses after the 1960s when the grassroots

hacks of the Tijuana cartel were squeezed out of the market by the well-paid entrepreneurs of the new sex industry. Although most of the authors of this interim period wrote in a concise, elementary, and even patently illiterate style ("he touch the cheek of the boys ass," "he jassed me hisself,"[1] "the hottness of his lips tongueing my bruised hole sent thrills shoting [sic] all through my body"[2]), others harbored frustrated literary ambitions and frequently lapsed into chaotic purple prose. In a story from the early 1950s, "Boy Meets Boy," the author waxes poetic about the postcoital bliss of a man whose now flaccid penis, "lovingly besmerched [sic] . . . with fine unsalted tea butter," "rested limber and slack like a dew-worm in the dilated, wetted and slimy aperture," finally slipping out of "the small convulsively jerking [opening] which, concealed between the fleshy masses, was blooming in obscurity."[3] The bootleg literature of the 1940s and 1950s is a genuinely vernacular pornography in which the grand periphrastic style of such erotica as *Teleny* and *Memoirs of a Woman of Pleasure* clashes dramatically with the low-brow solecisms of unprofessional writers whose gutter slang frequently degenerates into an incomprehensibly obscene pidgin English.

Given the repressed era in which this pornography was published, it is somewhat surprising how guiltlessly it describes gay sex. A kind of exuberant polymorphousness reigns in stories in which gay and straight sex exist side by side and in which totally indiscriminate bisexual heros shoot "great blasts of hot sticky lust liquid"[4] into whatever orifice happens to be at hand, all the while exhibiting an enlightened sexual tolerance that seems well in advance of its time. Moreover, unlike the pornography of the present, which is fixated on hot studs with magnificent bodies whose every vein and hair follicle are examined in punctilious detail, there is very little description of the physical appearance of the characters, with the exception

---

[1] Donald Love, "The County Jail" (7 Zephyrs Press, 1955), no page numbers.
[2] Donald Love, "I Love Men" (7 Zephyrs Press, 1955), no page numbers.
[3] "Boy Meets Boy" (Esoterica Press, no date), no page numbers.
[4] Eldon Barnard, "Navy Daze" (Esoterica Press, 1945).

of their erections, which are, of course, immense, so large in fact that "my bottom started to twitch"[5] and "my eyes nearly popped out of there [sic] sockets."[6] The gay pornographic hero of the 1940s and 1950s was not "sexy" in the modern sense of the word. Rather, his appeal was measured by something altogether less tangible, his lack of physical inhibitions. The star of early gay erotica was not an Adonis; he was a swinger, a playboy, a libertine, or, as the narrator of the 1945 story "Navy Daze" describes himself, "a real sexbox, as bisexual as a honeybee." These erotic renegades didn't need to be beautiful, simply ready and willing. Horniness and enthusiasm mattered far more than prettiness and muscularity. The allure of these Don Juan figures emanated from their liberal attitudes toward sex, their promiscuity, and the audacity with which they outmaneuvered the sex police and ignored the moral injunctions of a society that did everything in its power to outlaw gay sex. In the repressive world of the 1940s and 1950s, the speed with which these characters met and made love must have seemed miraculously instantaneous, like sex at first sight, effortless conquests that bypassed all the tedious preliminaries, the roadblocks of moral righteousness. In early gay erotica, readers were far less interested in the aesthetics of sex than they were in its sociology, in the cleverness with which characters were able to sidestep psychological barriers and inhibitions, the taboos that this pornography efficiently dismantled, conjuring up an illusion of sexual plenty in a culture characterized by enforced abstinence and restraint.

Instead of dwelling on how the swinger hero looked when he made love, as is the case in contemporary pornography, stories from the 1940s and 1950s, much like early pornographic films, focused on how he felt, on the pleasure he was experiencing, with the result that he seemed to be in a constant state of apoplectic delirium, as can be seen in such pronouncements as "I felt as if an electric eel had been forced into my sweet tender part"[7] and "[I experienced] a terrfic

---

[5]"Runaway Sex" (7 Zephyrs Press, Oct. 1953). By "a new author from Sand [sic] Diego."
[6]Donald Love, "I Love Men" (7 Zephyrs Press, 1955).
[7]"The Arizona Nights" (7 Zephyrs Press, no date).

[sic] spasm of the most soul-shattering glorious ecstasy."[8] Orgasms were not only religious experiences, they were natural disasters:

> He thembled [sic] and shook, In the most devastating spasm imaginable; Like some giant tree of a forest that has Been seared by a great bolt of lightning. Never in my life have I seen anyone So overcome by a transport of passion. It was as though a rocky avalanche had Come crashing down upon his body, To leave him limp—but not wxhausted [sic]![9]

These stories revolved so exclusively around the subjective state of the swinger hero that his body disappeared into a haze of euphoria, a mystical state of bliss that engulfed the entire scene.

Starting in the 1950s and lasting until 1966, when the U.S. Supreme Court adopted a more permissive definition of obscenity that effectively legalized the representation of explicit sex, a second, entirely unrelated type of gay pornography began to appear. This cautious and, by contemporary standards, extremely tame variety of inexpensive pulp fiction was tolerated by the authorities only if its authors confined themselves to frantic scenes of genital-less frottage, steering away from blatant descriptions of anal sex and fellatio. Unlike the illegal vernacular pornography of the 1940s and 1950s, in which randy bisexuals shamelessly scattered their wild oats, the legal soft porn written before the 1966 decision was full of guilt, of heavy-handed evocations of a world of stealthy perverts who, daubed with makeup and reeking of perfume, were "willing to endure anything ... to quell the beast called desire."[10] If the hero of older pornography was a swinger or a "sexbox," the hero of this more recent material was a remorseful, conscience-smitten closet case who, wrestling with uncontrollable urges, struggled unsuccessfully to stifle his longings for men and assert his beleaguered heterosexuality. The cover of the 1962 novel *All the Sad Young Men* was adorned with a garish painting apocalyptically entitled "The End of the World," an

---

[8]Eldon Barnard, "Navy Daze" (Esoterica Press, 1945).
[9]"Golden Minarets" (7 Zephyrs Press, 1950s), no page numbers. No author.
[10]Anonymous, *Male Bride* (Kozy Books, 1963).

apt image for this harrowing cautionary tale about a happily married man, the father of two lovely children, who is sucked into the Sodom and Gomorrah of "this tragic twilight world," "the world of the homosexual, the world of all the sad young men who are neither men nor women, only lost souls."[11] "Read the FACTS most books on the subject DARE NOT REVEAL," the cover of the 1963 novel *Male Bride* announced: "in this scorching novel are HOMOSEXUALS who walk along dark and twisted paths in search of love and satisfaction. These are people whose desperate yearnings make them players in the wildest game of passion."[12] In the opening scene of the novel, we are ushered into the hellish landscape of a "filth-lined pit,"[13] Club Indifference, a gay bar where the jukebox blares out the sinister refrain of a decadent song ("yah gotta, yah gotta, yah gotta do the twist") and tormented queens, braying with shrill, mocking laughter, lurk in the shadows, their smirking faces illuminated by the flickering lights of smoky candles.

While such homophobic books as *Dynasty of Decadence*, *Cursed*, *Faggots to Burn*, *Sin Travellers*, and *The Half-World of the American Homosexual* hammered home their basic themes of iniquity and corruption, their stern moralism was almost certainly not a reflection of their authors' real disapproval of homosexuality. Rather, this scathing didacticism was a pose, a way of evading censors, of camouflaging prurience as a socially responsible investigation into a nightmare realm, "revealing the real inside of HOMOSEXUALITY" where painted inverts seduce "innocent boy virgins."[14] In order to keep the FBI at bay, the pornographer masqueraded either as a crusading journalist or a sneeringly clinical sex researcher who aroused his readers with mildly erotic descriptions of gay encounters even as he fulminated against the unspeakable vices of the very audience he was secretly titillating.

Throughout the 1960s, pornography as a genre underwent a sort

---

[11]Anonymous (Wisdom House), from cover blurb, 1962.
[12]*Male Bride*, from jacket copy.
[13]*Male Bride*, p. 8.
[14]Carlson Wade, *Queer Path* (L.S. Publications, 1967), back blurb.

of literary identity crisis. It assumed one of three very unlikely disguises, that of a muckraking exposé, that of a dry yet derisive sexed textbook, or that of a damning psychological treatise on the complex origins of perversion. This implausibly tendentious material was full of contradictions: it professed to disgust the reader when in fact it aroused him; it made a great pretense that it was intended to satisfy the salacious curiosity of the uninformed outsider when in fact it was really written for the informed *in*sider. It is one of the major ironies of gay pornography that it did not progress historically from a period of repression and shame to a period of unapologetic homoeroticism, as one would have expected, but moved in quite the opposite direction, from the exuberant, guiltless world of the illegal porn of the 1940s and 1950s to the furtive, guilt-stricken world of *Male Bride* and *All the Sad Young Men* whose authors' prudish sermonizing must be understood as a pragmatic, if highly disingenuous, disguise.

The hypocritical need for the authors of soft pornography to express shock and disapproval, even as they obviously relished their characters' desperate gropings, had a direct impact on the way in which they represented sex. Because pleasure was so consistently masked as disgust, erotic encounters were often depicted as acts of rape, of coercion. In the 1965 novel *Mr. Muscle Boy*, a young weightlifter, whose "body would have fetched sacks of gold in the days of slave traders when muscular blond boys were priceless," is raped in the shower room of his gym where, "riddled with guilt and shame," he is forced to participate in "a form of love that has been condemned since the days of Greece's decline."[15] Likewise, in *The Gay Jungle*, a homeless 16-year-old waif, loitering around bus stations, his teeth chattering from the bitter cold, is driven into hustling on the windswept pavements of Time Square. Here, he loses his innocence to lurid johns "who cared not if the world knew of their perverse ways" and who "use [him] in a brutal manner," beating him black and blue and forcing him to "slither . . . into [a] wispy nylon posing strap" as

---

[15]Donald Evans, *Mr. Muscle Boy* (Selbee Publications, 1965), pp. 40, 13.

he "flinched, twitched, and shivered in so many spasms under [one john's] explorations and disportions."[16]

The rhetorical mandate of sanitizing gay sex with heavy doses of moralism had the paradoxical effect of intensifying the violence that accompanied each pornographic scene, which, in order to seem sufficiently sinful, often featured nonconsensual acts in which one of the participants resisted the debauched desires of his assailant. Whereas in the illegal pornography of Esoterica Press and 7 Zephyrs Press fun-loving sensualists freely espoused such liberal doctrines as "sex was fine as long as no one was hurt and they both received a climax,"[17] the duplicitous nature of the soft pornography of the early 1960s turned sex into a ferocious battle of wills that became ever more sadistic as writers strove to shore up their legitimacy in the eyes of vigilant members of the courts. Every act of penetration was allegorized as part of an epic struggle against evil, a declaration of war in which caresses became blows, moans cries for help, and the bedroom was turned into a potentially deadly arena in which men engaged, not in lovemaking, but in hand-to-hand combat. While this compulsion to sermonize was clearly a ruse, gay men nonetheless consumed pornography tainted by guilt and coercion, ingesting images of gay sex that undoubtedly complicated their already problematic relation to their homosexuality and that, in the worst instances, even made violence an integral part of the very mechanism by which they became aroused. The change from the zipless fuck of the 1940s to the morality play of the 1960s had profound consequences for the very nature of many gay men's sexual fantasies, which, out of pure legal expedience, were refracted through the filter of revulsion.

Until 1966, the authors of this legally published pseudo-porn often represented sex through an anticlimactic use of ellipsis. The novelist brought the reader to the very brink of intercourse and then, just as his characters began to fumble with their flies to release "tumescent manhood[s]" and "miasma[s] of maleness," suddenly cut away to the

---

[16]*Mr. Muscle Boy*, p. 40.
[17]Donald Loew, "I Love Men" (7 Zephyrs, 1955), no page numbers.

postcoital cigarette or the embarrassed adjustment of rumpled clothing. A second, somewhat bolder technique of concealing explicit sex was the use of what might be called bodice-ripping rhetoric, a dense tissue of cryptic euphemisms ("his upthrust rigidity," "his twitching membrane," "his heavenly tumescence") that dropped a discreet curtain of incoherence over the sex scenes, which immediately dissolved into an unintelligible mist of abstractions. In the following passage from the 1965 novel *Queer Daddy*, Lena, the transvestite nanny who cares for the children of a married man, the pillar of his community, throws himself upon his employer, who responds with equal fervor, crushing between his "hot petulant lips" "another luscious grape from the vineyard of passion":

> [Lena] wanted to scream, wanted to seize, wanted to cast himself into the flame of satiation. . . . Like a kitten kiss, he touched the warm, soft round of flesh and the world exploded. Lena clutched his mouth to keep from screaming. The convulsions rolled and hammered and squeezed his body and he could not voluntarily move. He knew what he was doing, what was cascading over the pink warm body, and the shock of ecstasy made movement impossible. In his excruciating expenditure, he straightened and arched and it no longer mattered that he had raised away from the suddenly moving body on the bed.[18]

It is ultimately impossible to tell what is actually happening in this passage. What type of sex is it evoking? Where are the hands and where are the legs? The more passionate it becomes, the more garbled the image. The flame of satiation blinds the reader with its brightness. The bodice is ripped but beneath it one finds . . . another bodice. Filled with a strong sense of the unmentionable, the turgid periphrasis of this amorphous rhetoric served an extremely practical function, that of self-censorship, of blocking out the picture on the screen through the artful imprecision of a style deliberately designed to obfuscate rather than to describe. The characters' bodies lose all definition, experiencing a sort of semantic meltdown that provides

---

[18]Helene Morgan, *Queer Daddy* (Satan Press, 1965), p. 81.

the linguistic equivalent of the black dot placed like a fig leaf over the sex organs in pornographic photographs, a black dot composed of words, of a mass of inchoate generalities.

Like vintage gay pornography from the 1940s and 1950s and the films of the 1970s, the bodice-ripping pornography of the 1960s emphasized the emotional states of the lovers over their physical appearance, which was eclipsed by frenzied rhapsodies of uncontrollable passion, by "the brain-bursting spasms that shook his entire body."[19] These soulful outbursts transformed this pornography into a strangely mystical sort of religious literature, full of grotesque epiphanies. Before the legalization of explicit descriptions of intercourse, the assumption that sex operated like an hallucinogen to induce trancelike experiences served the same function that periphrasis and abstraction served in the passage from *Queer Daddy*: self-censorship. As soon as the scene gets impermissibly steamy, a sort of rhetorical blackout occurs in which the characters' loss of emotional control elicits a similar loss of control in visual clarity, so that the lights are suddenly flicked off and all we are allowed to see are veiled and murky forms thrashing about in the dark.

Even after the 1966 Supreme Court decision, pornographers still described sex as if it were a fundamentally irrational experience, an exclusively subjective event in which the physical component is secondary to the transcendent intensity of pure, disembodied sensation. In the 1966 novel *The Song of the Loon*, an outlandish cowboy-and-Indian horse opera widely credited with being the first explicit example of gay pornography, the author continues to rely heavily on the conventions of the genre even though the legal incentive to do so has vanished. In the following scene, the white man Ephraim is given "labial, lingual joy" by an Indian who "set[s his] swollen nerves ablaze [with] a supine sweetness, [a] warmly rising burst," by jabbing his finger into the "mystic hidden vortex underneath":[20]

---

[19]Russ Trainer, *His Brother Love* (Satan Press, 1968), p. 132.
[20]Richard Amory, *The Song of the Loon: A Gay Pastoral in Five Books and an Interlude* (Greenleaf Classics, 1966), p. 172.

In a single flash of warm, sharp sensation, Ephraim felt the mouth on his cock, warm and pressing, the beard prickling against his thighs—and the finger thrust, long and powerful. He arched, strained, clutched, lived wholly in the warm sweetness gathering force, pivoting wildly on an axis at the center of his being, strangely, oddly off center, reaching up to his vitals as the finger whirled up his anus, then the sweetness snapped, and it was the big man's mouth, tongue, teeth, the sweetness surging into the center of the earth, down, down, into black oblivion—[21]

Unlike the scene from *Queer Daddy*, which was published only one year before *The Song of the Loon* and in which the sex is obliterated by the author's nebulous rhetoric, it is actually possible for the reader to visualize what is going on in this passage. And yet despite this new degree of clarity, the underlying assumption shaping the author's description of sex remains the same: intercourse causes a form of temporary madness, an ecstatic swoon that triggers an automatic shutdown in the amount of information the reader is receiving.

The passage also reveals another fundamental assumption of bodice-ripping pornography: in order to create a sense of heightened emotional turmoil, the narrator must become as excited and uncontrolled as his characters, mimicking the state of ecstasy in his syntax which, as orgasm approaches, disintegrates into fragments, unraveling into unstructured run-on sentences. Although these pyrotechnic stylistic displays continued well into the early 1970s, bodice-ripping rhetoric became increasingly anachronistic in the years following Stonewall when a new kind of rational pornography appeared, one that dispensed with the self-censoring ploys of such language as "exquisite agonies," "spasms of consummation," and "showers of shooting stars." Instead of wails of indescribable pleasure and "scalding, volcanic passions" that explode into "boiling geysers of lust," we are offered a much more controlled, almost photographic style of narration by authors who no longer feel obliged to participate in the action, to get as worked up as the blurry shapes on the page, to

---

[21]*The Song of the Loon*, p. 70.

gnash their teeth in unison with their characters and pant breathlessly along with them. In the early 1970s, we move from this delirious and highly artificial poesy to a prosaic series of shorter, tighter, and more tactile sentences in which the authors remain both calmly detached and painstakingly descriptive right up to the point of orgasm. In the following passage from the 1974 novel *Tall Timber*, a gay man is sodomized in the outhouse of an Oregon logging camp by a burly lumberjack with "lemon-sized balls" and an erection so large that, during a jaw-breaking act of oral sex that occurs later in the novel, he actually chokes and asphyxiates one of his comrades whose throat becomes "a sarcophagus" for the logger's cock:

> Quince held the cheeks of Ebon's ass wide apart and took aim, touching the fist-size head of his cock to that small pink circle. Because of the difference in their heights, Quince had to bend his knees a bit and gave a quick upward scoop with the haunches, and the horsecock broke into the first barrier. Ebon almost went head first into the commode. . . . He felt a tearing as the massive pole of flesh moved up into him and broadened with every new inch . . . [Quince] grabbed the boy around the hips with both hands and forced him back hard against himself, so that the remainder of the rocklike shaft broke into him and Ebon let out a muffled Ummmmmmmnnnnn.[22]

Had this novel been written even five or six years earlier, it is unlikely the author would have provided such a clear, unobstructed view of anal intercourse but would have forced us to look through the distorting lens of an emotional kaleidoscope that would have fractured the bodies into lyrical, if utterly unintelligible, pieces.

As gay liberation gathered momentum, the focus suddenly shifted from the subjective state of the characters to their physical appearance, which is captured in highly concrete, pictorial images purged of the emotional mannerisms of bodice-ripping rhetoric, as can be seen in the preceding passage in which the reader is given access to the characters' internal feelings only in the unembellished phrase "he felt a tearing" and in the subdued expression "Ummmmmmmnnnnn."

---

[22]Wolfe Bronson, *Tall Timber* (Hamilton House, 1974), p. 70.

This new pictorial rationalism is not only the result of the decline of the legal need for splintered collages, but of the new sense of gay pride after Stonewall which fundamentally altered our attitudes toward sex in ways that had a direct impact on pornography. As we have seen in the case of X-rated films, gay liberation ultimately relocated intercourse from the murky, surreptitious darkness of the proverbial "twilight world" featured in pornography from the 1960s to brightly lit spaces in which there was no need to swaddle sex in thick veils of euphemisms, to shield the reader's eyes like a watchful mother at the crucial moment. After a decade dominated by a Dionysian, sexual mysticism, our political empowerment ushered in a naturalistic school of pornography characterized by a new mandate to peel back the bowdlerizing black dots of rhapsodic emotion and describe sex in unflinchingly specific visual detail, from the size of the balls to the bulge of the basket.

The new naturalists actively deflated the high-flown style of old pornography, which they rejected in favor of a harsh, antipoetic language that was as crass, tasteless, and obscene as bodice-ripping pornography was fussy and grandiloquent. A radical transformation occurred in the diction used to describe erections, for instance, which were no longer "temple[s] of Priapus," "love emblem[s]," "hunk[s] of animated ivory," "marble scepter[s]," or "untouched virgin sapling[s]," but instead "big, wet hillbilly cock[s]," "hard cock[s]," "massive cock[s]," "horse cock[s]," "damned prick[s]," "ripe dick[s]," and "hard pecker[s]." Whereas the penis was once Latinate, it suddenly became Saxon. Whereas writers once strove obsessively to vary the vocabulary used to describe erections (so that they became the object of a distractingly tedious exercise in rhetorical virtuosity), post-Stonewall pornographers created an austere and strictly functional style that relied on a dissonant, monosyllabic slang consisting of words like "prick," "cock," "dick," "dong," "tool," and "meat." For centuries, pornographers as different as John Cleland, Oscar Wilde, and Aubrey Beardsley inflated the language they used to describe sex, using lavish displays of ornate rhetoric to soften the impact of obscenity (with the unintentional result that a strong undercurrent of the mock heroic runs through erotic literature, which frequently seems far more formal and florid than its subject merits). After Stonewall, however, pornographers reacted against this saccharine preciosity and sought to cheapen their language with raunchy idioms in order to create a suitably base and graceless style adapted to the new confrontational mood of outspoken crudeness.

The obscene effects of the new antiliterary style were heightened by the microscopic specificity with which writers described sex, which they began to represent with such uncanny precision that the anatomical minutia of dilating orifices and throbbing erections ultimately displaced narrative, crowding out plot and characterization which gave way to uninterrupted orgies. Sex not only becomes clearer as we move out of the 1960s and into the 1970s, it becomes hyper-real, laden with infinitesimal details, as in the following description of fellatio, which is as meticulous as an anatomy lesson:

> Jerry's tongue slipped around the ridge under the head of Billy's dick. He slithered his tongue under the foreskin and pulled it up to close it over his tongue. Billy liked the way that felt, the way that Jerry's tongue ran around and around the thick head of his cock as he gripped it tightly in his hand. . . . Jerry then moved his tongue up to the top of the head of Billy's dick and slid it over the piss slit, pulling the edges of Billy's cockhead to force the little hole open. He slid his tongue into the groove and Billy sighed with pleasure at the feeling that Jerry was causing in his peter.[23]

The passage provides us with a stroke-by-stroke account of every lap of the protagonist's tongue as it grazes over an area of skin that comprises at most two or three square inches, an expanse of flesh the author magnifies into a full-fledged landscape. This myopic view of sex brings the reader closer to the physical act of intercourse than he has ever been before, as if he were Gulliver examining the moles, warts, and blemishes on the breasts of the Brobdingnagians. And yet post-Stonewall pornographers are rarely content simply to examine the pores and freckles on the outside of the body; they often try to increase the level of explicitness and obscenity by actually entering

---

[23]*Come Hungry Sinners* (Finland Books, 1980), p. 32. No author.

various orifices and providing the reader with a sort of x-ray of sex, as in the 1980 novel *Beach Bum* in which the "clinging ring of sphincter muscle" in one man's drum-tight asshole "held onto [his lover's] prick like a baby holds its bottle . . . sucking the come out."[24] Some writers go even further and slip past the prostate like a probe into the lower intestine or down the urethra, inching through the vas deferens to the testicles, where they investigate how the semen travels, like liquids for unclogging clogged drains in television commercials, through complicated whorls of crystal tubing.

Even the way in which characters touch each other undergoes radical changes from the late 1960s, when men stroke, pet, and nuzzle their partners, to the pornography of the post-Stonewall era, in which they don't so much caress as collide, slamming into other naked bodies like inert objects. The language with which writers describe sex in the 1970s and 1980s suggests an entirely different sort of physical interaction than the passionate embraces with which the characters in *The Song of the Loon* enfold themselves in each other's arms, merging into one, struggling to get ever closer, to fuse into a single, writhing entity. Compare, for instance, a random selection of the concussive, high-impact verbs from the 1980 novel *The Cocky Cowboy* with a random selection of the far gentler, almost touchy-feely verbs from *The Song of the Loon*:

> *The Cocky Cowboy* (1980): shove, yank, smash, hammer, saw, stuff, ream, ram, pile drive, attack, crack his rocks, pound, slap, plug, piston, grind

> *The Song of the Loon* (1966): explore, touch, thrust, pull, press, writhe, rub, take in the mouth, stroke, seize, shudder, lower gently, possess, play, caress, grind, slide, pound in, stroke, twine, grope, roll, brush, probe, clasp, cradle, nip lightly, fondle

While the bodies in *The Song of the Loon* seem to liquify at the merest flick of the tongue, melting together under the heat of passion, in *The Cocky Cowboy* they rigidify when they touch, turning

---

[24]*Beach Bum* (Finland Books, 1980), p. 27. No author.

into blocks of ice and caroming off each other's hard surfaces, which sturdily deflect the blows raining down upon them. Moreover, if during the 1960s the prevailing metaphors for the texture of skin were "silk" and "satin," their counterparts in the 1970s and 1980s were "stone" and "steel."

Just as the visual, nonsubjective nature of pornography in the 1970s can be attributed to the climate of guiltlessness following gay liberation, so the rise of this unsensual, high-impact sex can be ascribed to gay men's post-Stonewall self-confidence which led to highly paradoxical changes in their attitudes toward both their bodies and their masculinity. One would have expected that the representation of sex after gay liberation would have become more sensual, more loving, more intimate, more interested in the voluptuousness of gay sex. As homosexuals felt less and less shame about expressing their sexual impulses, it stands to reason they would have demanded pornography that extolled the glories of homoeroticism and revelled in the physical pleasures of male-to-male contact. In fact, however, the exact opposite occurred, and the representation of sex became *less* loving, *less* sensual and, in many ways, even *anti*sensual.

As we have seen in the case of the antibourgeois body described in an earlier chapter, in the act of denying the stereotypic image of the effeminate pansy in the course of the 1970s, gay men asserted their masculinity in overcompensating ways that gave rise to a distinctly militaristic appearance. This style of behavior also carried over into the bedroom where homosexuals played out fantasies of bestial couplings free of feminizing affection and tenderness. Intercourse that emphasized sensual pleasure and intimacy over aggressive contact between two dehumanized, hypermasculine sex machines would have compromised the new machismo, which fostered a type of pornography that stripped sex of its sensuality, as well as of the ludicrous emotionalism that now seemed both hilariously dated and despicably effeminate. Thus, ironically, if the pretense of guilt in the soft porn of the early 1960s increased the level of coercion, so, in a sense, did gay liberation, which inspired a rough-and-tumble, no-holds-barred type of hard-core sex. (Even the violated and deflowered rectum became macho after Stonewall. In the late 1960s, it was typically described as a delicate, quivering flower, a passive, plundered aperture that timidly accepted the assaults of the active partner, as in the 1970 novel *Fag Chaser* where the lead character's anus is constantly invoked in a precious series of girlish metaphors including "the open blossom of his virginal ass flower"[25] and "the butterfly of his cave entrance."[26] The new militarized, gay liberation asshole, by contrast, doesn't just simply lie down and take it but actually fucks back, sloughing off the fancy floral similes invented by the rectal poets of the 1960s to become an active agent, a "hungry, greedy" meat eater that devours its prey, as in *The Cocky Cowboy* where one man's carnivorous asshole "seemed to swallow up [a man's penis] . . . as if it was going to eat all of his cock up."[27])

While the rational, pictorial sex found in post-Stonewall pornography may be easier to visualize than that found in pornography from the 1960s, it is by no means more realistic. In fact, it is just as highly stylized, although stylized in an entirely different manner. If the characters in older pornography seem as ethereal as disembodied souls, the characters in more recent pornography are enormous hulks with bionic bodies, rippling pecs, quads the size of tree trunks, and erections the thickness of fire hydrants and baseball bats. After gay liberation, the standards of verisimilitude in pornography were drastically inflated until the characters took on the distinctly surrealistic appearance of steroid monsters who engage in what might be called superhero sex. The pictorial equivalent of this exaggerated type of protagonist are the drawings of Tom of Finland, who created sexual utopias in which burly cops, with nipples as protuberant as pacifiers and bubble butts as round as beach balls, take on entire motorcycle gangs, whacking their bare bottoms on the seats of their souped-up Harleys or raping them over bar stools and tree stumps. Such novels as *Hard Hat, Ride a Hot Marine, Mountain Stud, Hard Truckin' Sucker, Cop Licker,* and *Brutal Seaman* take place in a caricatured world of lumbering giants who fiddle with their pickup trucks, chop

---

[25]Warren Brown, *Fag Chaser* (Pec French Line, 1970), p. 33.
[26]*Fag Chaser*, p. 147.
[27]C. K. Angus, *The Cocky Cowboy* (Rough Trade, 1980), p. 59.

wood, "wrastle" with their buddies, sweat like hogs on oil rigs, and operate ten-story cranes and hydraulic forklifts while living in female-free paradises populated with the entire pantheon of iconic subcultural heroes—truckers, cowboys, frat jocks, policemen, linebackers, farmers, construction workers, sailors, swat teams, and firemen. Unlike the pornography of the 1960s, which featured large numbers of screaming queens, as well as heterosexual women, the superhero pornography of the 1970s has been purged of all traces of femininity in order to create an atmosphere of fascist masculinity.

The plots of superhero pornography often involve the conversion of heterosexuals. A typical scenario is the discovery by a presumably straight man that he actually enjoys gay sex, which he experiences during a chance homoerotic encounter, a passing grope in the sauna of an empty gym or an impromptu blow job through the glory hole of a truck stop toilet. Bodice-ripping pornography also revolved around tragic retellings of this basic conversion narrative. Novels from the 1960s frequently featured a tormented bisexual, "a slave to unlooked for passions,"[28] who struggled to restrain his perverted impulses, to turn away from the "twilight world" of Club Indifference. The 1968 novel *His Brother Love*, for instance, dramatizes the turmoil of an accountant at a fashion firm teetering on the brink of a sexual abyss. After sleeping with the entire staff of gay designers, he finally embraces heterosexuality and marries Pam, a homophobic prig who discovers that homosexuals across the globe are engaged in a diabolical conspiracy to turn all women into dowdy frumps by designing ill-fitting dresses as unflattering as burlap bags.

By the 1970s, the conversion narrative had lost such dark and sinister undertones, but it still remained one of the most popular storylines. It constitutes the central erotic plank of the progay propaganda that forms the heart of superhero pornography, which is founded on a misguided tenet of gay folk wisdom: that deep down inside every man is gay or, as a character in *Tall Timber* puts it, "there's [no] such thing as a *straight* guy. A man will take a piece of

---

[28]*Male Bride*, from back cover blurb.

ass any time, any place, hetero or not."[29] In the 1979 novel *The Cockfighters*, two South Bronx street gangs, the Wild Ones and the Sharks, feud over the same turf, abducting and humiliating their rivals, only to discover, as they grapple naked in wrestling matches staged in order to resolve heated disputes, how much more they prefer the sensations of gay sex to those they experience with their girlfriends. In the most tendentious, gay-positive novels, the pornographer even transforms the conversion narrative into a vehicle for revenge, for defilement, a way of taking the most macho and homophobic groups of our society—marines, hard hats, football players—and, through a malicious act of inversion, turning them into the most avid of sexual recruits who enthusiastically ravage every man they encounter.

If the superhero pornography of the 1970s and 1980s is outspokenly homosympathetic and self-affirming in its underlying message, it remains profoundly self-denying in fact. The propagandistic use of the conversion narrative to incriminate the entire gender, to blacken with homosexual aspersions every quarterback and auto mechanic, may at first sight seem like a clever form of liberating sexual sabotage, but on closer scrutiny, it proves to be fundamentally self-loathing. The dominant mythic figure of post-Stonewall pornography is the nongay homosexual, a member of the *lumpenproletariat* who, while engaging in gay sex, manages to retain the masculine identity of a straight man untouched by the look and sensibility of the subculture. The nongay homosexual is gay only in the bedroom, while in public he easily passes as a dyed-in-the-wool heterosexual, no matter how many cowpokes he services in the bunk house, how many tomahawk-wielding Indian braves he seduces in their wigwams, or how many members of the varsity wrestling team he lures into the bleachers. Despite his formidable stamina and sex drive, he is a solitary sensualist who has no stake or interest in a collective homosexual identity but has eliminated all telltale signs of urban gay life from his behavior, which strictly conforms to the style of the most virile of tobacco-chewing, beer-guzzling, stogie-smoking good old boys.

---

[29]*Tall Timber*, p. 133.

Although there are many openly gay characters in superhero pornography, one of the most disturbing ironies of the genre is that all too often the hero is not, in fact, recognizably gay but rather is a composite creature from a sexually imprecise limbo, an ambiguous erotic half-breed who has the libido of a gay man but the body and mannerisms of a truck driver. Despite the progay propaganda that post-Stonewall pornographers disseminate, their work remains rooted in the assumption that men who have erased the stigma of homosexuality from their behavior—whether found in loud colognes, elaborately coiffed hairdos, or the high-pitched laughs of braying queens—are intrinsically more sexy than the jaded denizens of urban gay ghettos. Just as gay men were once forced to consume pornography poisoned by guilt, so after gay liberation they must read a type of fiction that reflects serious reservations about their very sex appeal. The cumulative effect of this literature is to undermine the reader's erotic self-confidence, instilling him with a sense of his own inadequacy to these nongay chimeras, even as the post-Stonewall pornographer somewhat hypocritically celebrates homosexuality in countless declarations of the goodness and normality of gay sex.

Superhero pornography is a refugee genre, in constant flight from the sexually compromised world in which its readers reside, the ghettoized subculture that the pornographer finds such an uncongenial setting for his stories. Each novel testifies to the decline of the gay sensibility, involving a ritualistic act of purification in which the contaminating evidence of the conventional gay lifestyle is carefully suppressed and the characters are transplanted out of the depleted atmosphere of piano bars and bathhouses to fresh foreign soil, to ranches and police academies, Indian reservations and battleships, locker rooms and army barracks. In this most macho of never-never lands, anti-subcultural characters in an exotic array of uniforms engage in an unending costume party, a game of dress-up, a masquerade ball in which the customary dramatis personae of the gay fantasy life participate in a bizarre and stately minuet, with the cowboy pairing off with the Iroquois tribal chieftain, the corporal with the captain, the deputy sheriff with the felon from the county jail.

Tall Timber provides a perfect example of the allegorical act of flight and self-cancellation that forms the basis of superhero pornography, the great escape from the claustrophobic barrios of the Castro and West Hollywood into the infantilized world of dress-up. After two gay men become dissatisfied with the paucity of butch tops in the Bay Area, they respond to an ad placed in a gay newspaper by the madame of a brothel at a logging camp in Oregon, a woman so disgusted with the filthy habits of her slatternly whores that she fires her entire staff. She replaces them with spic-and-span gay men, whom she employs, not only to cook meals, scour pots and pans, and swab out the camp's overflowing outhouses, but to service the gruff, undiscriminating heterosexual loggers who live in this paradise of authentic masculinity. With remarkably little hesitation, the lumber-jacks accept the eager ministrations of these unlikely courtesans who have shunned the effeminate and devitalized subculture, beating a hasty retreat from urban sexual blight into the unspoiled northern frontiers of the Wild West, a pastoral wilderness where, as one character puts it, "men are Men."[30] Much as recent personal ads reflect an active effort to undermine the gay sensibility and much as pot-bellied bears attempt to transform themselves into rustic heterosexuals, so our erotic literature reflects our eagerness to assimilate into mainstream society, offering a utopic vision of an imaginary world in which the subculture has been eradicated.

In contrast to *Tall Timber* and countless other examples of super-hero pornography, pre-Stonewall novels were much more closely rooted in the pedestrian realities of the gay community and drew upon—if admittedly only to a limited degree—the daily lives of their homosexual readers, the quotidian details of which they reworked into imaginative, and yet plausible, narratives. Rather than avoiding urban gay life, pornographers from the 1960s set their novels in such decadent haunts as action bars and cruise parks and recorded, with a pretense of scandalized distaste, the full variety of sordid metro-politan lowlife, from hustlers to drag queens. While such would-be exposés as *All the Sad Young Men* and *Male Bride* sought to maintain

---

[30]*Tall Timber*, p. 13.

an accurate, even journalistic relationship to gay life, superhero sex seals itself off in a literary vacuum, a rhetorical construct, a world that exists only on the page. Because of its essentially dismissive attitude toward the subculture that sustains it, it has become an arid abstraction, a highly conceptual narrative that, in its refusal to represent the conventional gay lives it finds so abhorrent, has become bloodless and cerebral, free of the unwanted and unarousing presence of the men who constitute its market.

Although superhero pornography no longer needs the brooding atmospherics and stern moralizing that once provided a socially responsible disguise for prurient material, it still requires guilt, an emotion that remains essential to the process of arousal long after feelings of shame have been largely eliminated from the psychology of gay sex. Because so few homosexuals experience the same degree of guilt they suffered before Stonewall, it must be artificially created in scenes in which characters feign shock, panic, and even horror at being propositioned in shower stalls, fondled in the lofts of barns, and smooched against their wills by lecherous mashers who entice them into the cramped cabs of their tractor trailers. While the characters of modern pornography are anything *but* defenseless in appearance, they are constantly whimpering and begging, their voices cracking and quavering as they make such beseeching entreaties as "stay away from me ... please!",[31] "n-nobody ever did this to m-me before,"[32] "I ne ... never did no ... nothing like this,"[33] and "you ... r-raped me,"[34] all the while praying—fruitlessly—that their merciless assailant will be "too much of a gentleman to take advantage of [the] situation."[35] Superhero pornography is plagued by the ploys of the big-bad-wolf syndrome. As unmitigatedly macho as these strapping, Tom of Finland giants are, they exhibit an inappropriate kind of false maidenliness, the frightened diffidence of bashful virgins who

---

[31]*Tall Timber*, p. 119.
[32]*Stable Boy* (Rough Trade, 1980), p. 151. No author.
[33]Bert Shrader, *Gay Stud's Trip* (Pec French Line, 1968), p. 9.
[34]*Stable Boy*, p. 135.
[35]*Fag Chaser*, p. 15.

balk at the prospect of being ravished. As soon as some big bad brute has the audacity to leer suggestively at them or make indelicate remarks about their imperiled virtue, they behave like damsels in distress roped to the railroad tracks. In *Stable Boy*, for instance, a blushing adolescent wearing a prep school uniform—a blue blazer, a string necktie, and skimpy shorts—wrings his hands helplessly, sobbing "never, never!" and "y-you w-wouldn't!" just before he is raped by the novel's dastardly villain, a wealthy ranch owner who ignores his frightened pleas and violates "the most precious gift that [the boy's] pure, virgin body can offer."[36] The lady doth protest too much but she ultimately gives in and the "please no!" 's inevitably turn into "yes, more!" 's as she is mauled by the feverish fingers of her relentless admirer.

The rise of the big-bad-wolf syndrome is symptomatic of a crisis occurring in contemporary gay pornography. The need for shame, resistance, and coercion still persists, despite the new climate of permissiveness that is destroying the taboos necessary for the creation of effective pornography. The modern writer's angst-ridden methods of arousal are at odds with an era that has normalized gay sex, reduced guilt, and alleviated the reprehensible social conditions in which homosexuals formerly met and cruised. The scarcity in real life of pornography's secret ingredient, shame, is leading writers to take more and more outlandish measures to create an increasingly improbable simulacrum of this old-fashioned and ever elusive emotion, which must be produced through the hammy manipulation of maladroit literary devices. In *Come Hungry Sinner*, for instance, the author is so desperate to invent an adequate guilt substitute that will give his sex scenes the high voltage they require that he focuses his story entirely on the antics of a charismatic, born-again preacher who sodomizes his innocent disciples while forcing them to sing "Jesus loves me, this I know, 'cause the Bible tells me so": " 'Yes!' Plunge! 'Jesus!' Plunge! 'Loves me!' Plunge! 'Yes, Jesus loves me, the Bible tells me so!' "[37]

---

[36] *Stable Boy*, p. 111.
[37] *Come Hungry Sinner* (Finland Books, 1980), p. 25. No author.

The openness about sex fostered by the sexual revolution in the 1960s has placed a particular burden on gay pornography, which feeds off of the residual traces of the surreptitiousness and paranoia that once dominated our lives and that we are unwilling to relinquish as the stage setting for our fantasies. As society becomes more liberal about sex, pornography becomes more conservative, more anxious about maintaining the homosexual's dwindling conviction of sin, regressing to outmoded narratives about cowboys and Indians, boy virgins and nefarious rapists, false maidens and the heartless marauders who have their way with them, defiling their "precious gifts" for the sake of their own selfish pleasures. Gay pornography is haunted by *nostalgie de la boue*, by perverse cravings for the puritanical state of mind that prevailed during the presexual revolutionary age. In this era of pristine guilt, there were no Oprahs and Donahues to broach the topic of cross-dressers and married bisexuals on every broadcast, no talk-radio sexologists to offer insipid admonitions about the virtues of self-acceptance, and no syndicated advice columnists to spell out the etiquette for gay weddings and explain the complicated protocol for coming out to unsuspecting parents.

Since the 1960s, gay pornography has attempted to repeal the conditions of candor and tolerance that are threatening the sustaining force of pornography, to roll back the political advances we are making in gay rights in order to create a make-believe world of antiquated taboos where sex is more shameful than in real life and therefore more exciting. Although the success of gay pornography has gone hand in hand with the development of gay politics, it is in fact politically retrograde. Gay liberation is its enemy, not its friend. The sexual fantasies to which it panders have a stagnating effect on our emotional and political progress as a minority, making us yearn for the shadows in which we once lurked, skulking around johns and bus stations, where we hoped to meet men who were, as some would have us believe, "Men." First Amendment apologists for free speech often insist that the exuberant eroticism of pornography is intrinsically militant, even subversive of the status quo, and it is difficult to disagree with them when one considers the unsavory positions with which one allies oneself in entertaining the alternative:

the dour moralism of the New Right or the pious hysterics of such prophets of doom as Andrea Dworkin and Catherine McKinnon, who presume an absurdly literal relation between fantasy and reality, between fictional violence and the epidemic of spousal abuse or actual street crime against women. And yet how healthy in the long run *are* the fantasies that modern gay pornography devises for homosexuals, the self-denying images of nostalgic false maidens and gigantic dolls with priapic endowments who cast such wistful glances back to the Dark Ages of gay culture when gay sex was a crime that destroyed careers and ruined lives?

It is interesting to note that the vernacular gay pornography produced in the genuinely repressive years of the 1940s and 1950s, well before the sexual revolution, is so free of the guilt that distinguishes the pornography written during and after the 1960s. A basic axiom of twentieth-century erotic literature is that there is an inverse relation between the moral tenor of the pornography of any given era and the society it serves. In a sexually inhibited society, gay pornography revolved around people guiltlessly fucking, playing a light-hearted game of musical chairs, pairing off with multiple partners who good-naturedly offered their services to any man they encountered. In a sexually open society, by contrast, gay pornography revolves around people furtively and shamefacedly fucking, feigning dismay and resistance, putting up a brave fight before surrendering their virtue. The sexual fantasy of a repressed society is a pornutopia, a world in which people can get as much sex as they need when they need it, gorging on an inexhaustible banquet of appetizing dishes. The sexual fantasy of a liberal culture, however, is a dystopia, a world in which sex is dirty and embarrassing, in which the food is spoiled, and in which starving debauchées devour with famished frenzy a delicious repast of forbidden fruits.

The commercialization of sex through pornography has profoundly damaged the homosexual's erotic responses. The more images he consumes, the more his own subjective point of view as a participant is modeled on this stylized genre's unsparingly external perspective, which teaches him to focus on appearances over sensations and to rely on artistic conventions to understand an experience that authors and directors inevitably parody and distort. As we absorb the new prescriptive aesthetic criteria of this crassly commercial commodity, we begin to appraise other men's bodies by highly inflated standards, thus experiencing a perpetual sense of inferiority to the picture-perfect vision of sex purveyed by a product that bears virtually no relation to reality. We have ingested so much pornography that the sex we have in real life is now accompanied by an erotic subtext, a peep show projected in the private viewing booths of our minds where we watch a film that runs parallel to, and comments on, our own inept lovemaking, the desperate, unconvincing imitations we make of the beautiful images flickering on our internal screens.

The before and after comparisons of the subculture I have been making throughout this book have shown how the commercialization of homosexuals often involves the active suppression of the gay sensibility, a process in which manufacturers divest us of our subcultural identity. Just as literary pornography is often based on acts of disavowal, as in the case of the nongay homosexual, a figure who embodies the disappearance of gay culture, so the eradication of our ethnicity can be seen in the changes that have occurred in gay men's attitudes toward an article of clothing that encapsulates the entire history of the gay sensibility's rise and fall: men's underwear, a garment that frequently mimics straight men's underwear (which, in turn, in a never-ending game of cross-influences, plagiarizes the audacious fashion experiments of homosexuals). Like alcohol and pornography, underwear was one of the earliest products to be openly sold to homosexuals and therefore merits special attention as a commodity on the cutting edge of gay consumerism. It is no surprise that the first advertisement ever to appear in a gay magazine was an underwear ad, a full-page spread in the October 1954 issue of *One*. It featured a photograph of a man in a diaphanous satin nightshirt and see-through nylon harem pants next to a drawing of a pair of rhinestone-studded underwear that came in two colors, plain white or "black magic." Dismissing readers' complaints that the ad "besmirch[ed] your format" and was "disgusting," the editors responded that "for the first time in two years of our existence a genuine, commercial, bill-paying advertiser has appeared voluntarily."[38] This statement could be engraved like an epitaph on the tombstone of the subculture, which has finally collapsed before the onslaught of "bill-paying advertiser[s]" who have come forth in such extraordinary numbers ever since "WIN-MOR of California" first offered their "originals for your discriminating approval," thereby inaugurating several decades of the ruinous cultivation of the gay market.

---

[38]*One*, Nov. 1954, p. 25.

The Origin of

the Underwear

Revolution in

the Gay Subculture

IN DECEMBER 1992, AN arresting image of the rap singer Marky Mark, the brawny yet petite *Playgirl* pinup featured in Calvin Klein underwear ads, appeared on bus stops across the country. Wearing only a pair of Lycra boxer shorts that hugged his muscular thighs and bulged provocatively at the crotch, he stood laughing directly out at us, tangled up in his baggy pants which had collapsed around his ankles as if someone had just yanked them down from the preposterously low-slung position in which he customarily wears them.

Although images of men in underwear had appeared in bus stop advertisements before (albeit in a somewhat neutered state, the faint imprint of their genitalia having been carefully airbrushed away to create a sexless, antiseptic look), the photograph of Marky Mark was in some sense unprecedented. Its impact stemmed, not from its partial nudity, but from the way in which it emphatically represented an act of undressing, an exposure, a staged incident of de-pantsing in which the viewer was forced to confront underwear in a context that dramatized its forbidden intimacy. Advertisements for Jockey and Hanes feature cool, collected, unembarrassed models who exhibit no consciousness whatsoever of being undressed and whose nakedness is therefore subtly understated, rendered innocuous by a tasteful pretense of nonchalance that gives them the appearance of being fully clothed people. Marky Mark, by contrast, is inescapably disrobed, stripped bare, kicked out into the streets in his shorts, openly giggling about appearing in the midst of people at bus stops, who are both captivated and appalled by his gleefully unabashed expression of amusement.

Given the way in which Mark's self-satisfied exhibitionism undercuts the convention of obliviousness that underwear advertisements had traditionally used to sanitize their images, purging them of erotic content, the Calvin Klein campaign represents a pivotal moment in the history of fashion. An article of clothing that we had either emasculated or kept out of sight entirely has now broken out of its sartorial prison and emerged into public view as the object of nothing less than a mass cult, a collective act of fetishization that testifies to the influence of the gay sensibility on mainstream culture. In the course of the last three decades, this national obsession has become so widespread that it is blurring the most fundamental distinction in fashion: the irreconcilable difference between outerwear and underwear. Since the late 1980s, we have become extraordinarily immodest about a garment that was formerly hidden away in furtive isolation but that currently serves as an acceptable form of dress for semipublic encounters among homosexuals who frequently wear elaborate creations by Calvin Klein and Joe Boxer as brazen surrogates for gym trunks or even summer shorts.

While in most instances large corporations have commercialized the gay subculture by exploiting it for their own financial gain, men's lingerie provides a peculiar example of reverse commercialization because it is the subculture that has actually helped commercialize an aspect of the dominant culture. Up until the 1960s, when fashion inspired by the sexual revolution, as well as by the widening influence of the gay sensibility, introduced into the market brightly colored men's bikinis by Poco and Fruit of the Loom, underwear had been a relatively unchanging commodity, a bland staple in one monochromatic style, insulated from the vicissitudes of seasonal innovations. Underwear was not considered a component of "fashion" but was regarded as just an unglamorous necessity immune to fluctuations of taste because it was sealed off in a state of timelessness created by the prudish constraints placed on its representation in advertising. The moment this carefully preserved artifact was hoisted like a flag as the sexual banner of pre-Stonewall gay America, however, it acquired an entirely new status as a commodity and was elevated from being simply a glorified pants liner to an object of intrinsic aesthetic interest subject to innovation and change. The gay man's upgrading of underwear from a necessity to a luxury, from a hygienic requirement to a stylish accessory, resulted in an extravagant period of research and development by its manufacturers. They have taken this recalcitrantly uninteresting and monotonous staple and made it a playground of market forces, a wild experiment in the ingenuity of the free enterprise system, which has at last conquered the final frontier of fashion, the plain white brief. This immaculate uniform has been transformed into a dazzlingly gratuitous array of fabrics, colors, and styles, all of which now change with the same volatility and urgency with which other fashions have fluctuated for centuries.

Underwear fetishism has played such an important role in gay culture, not only because homosexuals naturally take erotic pleasure in men's lingerie, but also because male underwear catalogs, which made their first appearance as early as the 1950s, functioned as a form of pornography manqué in the absence of other readily available images of naked men. The historic scarcity of gay erotica before the 1970s placed the underwear catalog at the very center of the homosexual's masturbatory fantasies. The underwear revolution of the 1960s thus drew much of its inspiration from the frustrated libidos of gay men who were so starved for representations of the male body that they rifled through whatever material existed on the market. The most deprived and secretive of individuals were even driven to such unlikely sources of soft-core pornography as illustrations of the briefs and long johns featured in the Sears, Roebuck and Montgomery Ward catalogs with their sexless models bereft of genitalia.

The promotional brochures of specialty underwear manufacturers of the 1960s, including Regency Square of Hollywood, Ah Men, The Town Squire, and Parr of Arizona, catered explicitly to the needs of their predominantly gay markets by selling exotic lines of "torso tingling" briefs and "Persia Pasha pajama loungers." These mail-order companies also carried such openly gay paraphernalia as dildos called "Stimulant Massagers," which were "shaped to work on hard to reach areas"; decks of cards decorated with naked men; books with titles like *Entrapment* "about defiant perversions in conflict with the forces of law"; and elaborate contraptions that functioned as prosthetic buttocks, consisting of polyethylene pads sewn into underwear, a device ostensibly designed to "give . . . positive rear guard protection" to those who participate in contact sports. These catalogs provided their readers one of the earliest visual representations of a distinctly homosexual subculture, offering photo albums of "the male nude," "inhaler pendants" for carrying amyl nitrite, and aphrodisiacs like the "Vice Spice," a sort of Spanish Fly whose "stimulating potential can create a greater awareness of the sensual parts of your lover." Here, outlandish drawings of vampish figures in one-piece jumpsuits with plunging necklines did more than just sell underwear. They provided a desperate set of closeted consumers, who had little or no contact with other gay men, with a glimpse of a hidden sexual underground whose members cavorted in "lounge sets" made of sheer chiffon, gold lamé "Turkish Turn-on" harem pants, and underwear named the Bait Box, which the manufacturer warned you to "wear at your own risk! People have been mobbed for wearing less, but not much less."

Virtually every underwear catalog published during the 1960s was produced for the homosexual consumer, who relished their images of elongated gay blades in skin-tight shorts and stuffed crotches leaning languorously in poses that advertised their sexual availability. The flamboyant early creations of the underwear revolution bear the hallmarks of a distinctly gay sensibility, from the "Wa La" jockstrap with its white satin pouch embroidered with a beaded flamingo and lined with natural mink to the Coat O'Male, a girdle for the upper torso equipped with foam rubber pectorals guaranteed to give you "that He-Man physique in a flash! Now, the secret of Hollywood super-stars can be yours." The blatantly epicene images in the earliest underwear catalogs, which helped accustom the heterosexual consumer to the notion that underwear could be fashion, reveal that an intimate part of straight male attire was shaped by the obsessions of gay men who laid the foundations for the pioneering work of Calvin Klein and Joe Boxer. The acceptance of the sexual function of men's lingerie by the general public was made possible by the gay subculture, which is as close to heterosexual men as their briefs. They are wearing right next to their genitals an article of clothing whose baroque modern forms come directly out of the masturbatory fantasies of the very minority that many of them profess to despise. These fantasies have contributed to the structural instability of underwear and have altered the language we use to talk about our briefs, the types of fabrics from which they are made, the size of the waistband, the position of the fly, the appearance of the laundry tag, and the alluringly exotic names of individual brands—like the Berry Basket, the Satin Dude, the Snappy Shortie, the Teaser, and the Skimp.

But it is not only the look of underwear that has changed since the 1960s but also the almost allegorical ways in which homosexuals have interpreted and, in a way, even *moralized* it. In the process of assigning new sexual meaning to our briefs, we have produced an enormous variety of contradictory "readings" that has made our involvement with this seemingly trivial artifact complex and problematic. The language that both the early catalogs and their contemporary equivalent, International Male, use to describe underwear reflects the abrupt change that it has experienced in its status as a commodity. The fanciful briefs and boxer shorts that these companies advertise don't simply "fit," "protect," "cover," and "support," they "sculpt," "mold," "contour," "chisel," "transform," "embrace," "accentuate," and even, in the case of the form-fitting "Body Brief," "kiss your every contour." The advertising copy in gay catalogs anthropomorphizes underwear, which it characterizes, not as a simple piece of fabric, but as a sculptor of flesh, an artist in residence who molds and chisels, kneading our bulges into youthful new forms. Compare, for instance, the description of a Balbriggan union suit sold for 42 cents in the 1908 Sears catalog with a description of the Pow-Briefs advertised in a mid-1960s Regency Square catalog or the Sheer Bodywear advertised in a 1994 catalog of the openly gay mail-order company H.I.M.:

The drawers are adjustable in the back with buttoned straps and have a large double seat which gives it thorough reinforcement. The buttons are sewed on to stay. . . . We can guarantee this garment will give satisfaction.

[The Pow-Briefs are] zowie-wow nylon briefs with mesh inserts that give you a zingy look.

Seductive, enticing, designed to embrace every inch, Sheer Bodywear is fashion's wearable aphrodisiac.

Whereas the Balbriggan union suit merely offers such unglamorous features as durability and convenience, the Pow-Briefs and the Sheer Bodywear not only interact with the consumer's body, "embracing every inch," but they grab the attention of an implied audience of admirers who have a strong physical reaction to the appearance of the underwear. The underwear in the Sears catalog, by contrast, has neither an implied audience nor any significant aesthetic qualities but hangs limply over the consumer's frame like a drop cloth that serves solely to warm the body and "absorb all perspiration and the vaporous exhalations of the skin."

As these examples reveal, in the course of a century, as homosexuals began to explore the erotic potential of men's lingerie, underwear has taken the ultimate step in the religion of consumerism and transcended its own inanimacy to become an active agent that shapes and rejuvenates our sagging flesh. The rhetoric of consumerism exaggerates the talismanic power of our briefs, which gay men don't so much buy in plastic packages, like other inert products, as recruit from a pool of prospective image consultants, intelligent collaborators to whom we assign the onerous task of maintaining an attractive appearance. The homosexual's obsession with underwear has revolutionized the very rhetoric with which we talk about it, transforming the sexless bloomers and baggy woolen drawers of the past into sacred vestments, a kind of Golden Fleece that electrifies the wearer with its own galvanizing energy.

Since the 1960s, homosexuals have revolutionized men's underwear by radically feminizing it, incorporating into its design sensuous fabrics like satin, lamé, and lace and drastically shortening it, shrinking it into overtly erotic cuts modeled on the sultry teddies and sheer negligees of women's lingerie. The gay catalogs of the 1960s were a hotbed of fashion subversiveness in which manufacturers openly set out to make underwear androgynous, to transform the blocky union suit, which at the turn of the century sealed men from their ankles to their chins in a sweltering kind of thermal body bag, into the micromesh G-string. Flitting about in billowing caftans, the hip swingers who modeled early briefs lounged around their bachelor pads in a constant state of semiundress, wearing such precious and unmanly costumes as the Plume Strap, which consisted solely of an ostrich plume suspended over the groin, or the Bugle Bead Fringe Posing Strap, which consisted of a tiny curtain of threaded bugle beads dangling over what was known as a "modesty patch." In this unapologetically homoerotic and effeminate world, which offered the lonely gay consumer both erotica and a reassuring glimpse of an illusory homosexual utopia, scantily clad hedonists whooped it up at all-male weenie roasts and drowsy, morning-after brunches where they are shown dishing with the girls, noshing on finger foods, and proudly sporting their London Scandals, Batik Lava Lava wrap-arounds, and terry cloth Tree Top togas. The feminized underwear fashions of the 1960s emerged out of the androgynous world of matronly caftans, gauzy tunics, and "provocatively [sic] sensual 'sin at home' lounge wear" which attracted the homosexual as a form of modified drag. In the thick of the counterculture's unisex frenzy, homosexuals felt no qualms whatsoever about gussying themselves up in the hilariously dated transvestism of such outfits as see-through nylon harem pants, fishnet leotards, and sheer "swim coats" that one catalog promises us "will make you look like a movie queen." The modern brief would look entirely different had the homosexual subculture not torn it apart at the seams, stripped it down to its most basic elements, and then remodeled it in accordance with gay sexual obsessions, the erotic fantasies that straight men in the 1990s now wear on their own bodies in the form of their Adidas stretch briefs and their Calvin Klein sport straps.

Homosexuals' fascination with men's lingerie has also added a new dimension of expressiveness to the basic model of the austere white brief, whose functional design contrasts dramatically with the rococo extravagance of such items as chiffon boxers embossed with swirling metallic patterns or gaudy bikinis made out of transparent lace or shimmering lamé. Unlike the bland styles of the past, contemporary underwear offers the gay man an unlimited repertoire of personae from which he can create imaginary characters and project emotional states, much as a "cute" dress makes a woman feel young and vivacious, or a slinky skirt foxy and adventurous. Clothing designers now encourage gay consumers to think of their briefs as individualizing accessories that play a communicative role, enabling them to perform the complex task of self-definition and to reveal to others their inner person, their mood and temperament.

Two images are central to the homosexual's fantasies about the transformative power of fashion: the contrasting personae of the virgin and the whore, the saint and the slut, characters that manufacturers create by reinforcing a geographically based distinction between underwear indigenous to the United States and exotic styles imported from abroad. The International Male catalog introduces narrative tension into the purchase of underwear by devoting separate spreads to the personality traits of these two major psychological types, to the demure and understated modesty of plain, pure, all-American white briefs, on the one hand, and the lasciviousness and whimsicality of European thongs and bikinis, on the other. Sultry foreign fashions include such racy outfits as "the Ribbed French Thong," the "Marseille Brief," the Italian "Palermo Mesh Bikini," the "Barcelona Brief," or the "Monaco Stripe Bikini," all of which come in a rainbow of colors and textured fabrics that are cut in provocative styles which often bare the entire thigh, as well as a large portion, if not all, of the buttocks. The French "Sheer Thong," for example, is the very embodiment of French hedonism, consisting solely of a small patch of "next-to-nothing nylon mesh" that comes in arousing colors identified as "midnight" and "passion." If the startling differences between these products and more traditional designs are any indication, the age-old Jamesian conflict between the naive American and the depraved continental voluptuary is still being waged in our briefs, which preserve our nineteenth-century sense of inferiority to decadent civilizations abroad.

What the geographic distinction between American and European briefs enables gay men to do with cultural differences, the distinction between traditional and modern briefs enables us to do with fashion history and the passage of time. One of the most recent developments in the use of underwear for purposes of self-expression is the rise of underwear nostalgia or retro-underwear. These garments explicitly evoke the gauche styles of intricately constructed, full-length body-suits, like those in Calvin Klein's new line of archaic loungewear, a set of literal facsimiles of Edwardian museum pieces. Designers are now even attempting to revive the gay man's interest in long johns or one-piece "step-ins," costumes that hark back to the Wild West and the Gold Rush. Underwear is changing so rapidly that gay men have begun to revisit obsolete fashions in the same playful spirit of allusiveness with which women now wear the horn-rimmed glasses of the 1950s or the bell-bottoms and beehive hairdos of the 1960s. Just as the underwear industry assigns characterological significance to the difference between indigenously American products, which connote wholesomeness, and exotic imports, which carry with them the taint of iniquity, so manufacturers have created another costume drama by forging a spurious opposition between "classic" and "modern" underwear. Designers impose on the gay man's briefs an apocryphal history, a melodramatic plot in which the gleaming white brief plays the role of the virtuous damsel, the embodiment of an old-fashioned tradition of innocence and purity, and in which the decadent modern G-string is cast as the femme fatale, the embodiment of contemporary jadedness and promiscuity. It is now possible to choose what was once the only choice, the perennial American "classic," and in making such a decision, one is essentially rejecting the gaudy extremes of recent underwear commerce. Capitalism thus provides the gay consumer with an avenue of protest against the invasion of our underpants by the vulgar marketplace, in all of its exhibitionistic eroticism.

The recent socialization of underwear and its emergence as an appropriate form of semipublic attire have prompted manufacturers to define various kinds of briefs by the particular situations in which they are most appropriately worn. As underwear is reclassified from an hygienic appurtenance to a fashion accessory, it experiences a significant loss of adaptability. Companies are inventing a complex new etiquette in order to persuade the gay consumer to diversify his underwear collection, to expand it so that it reflects the same hierarchies of style implicit in other more conventional sorts of fashion. Our briefs no longer come in one undeviatingly uniform model, a generic, all-purpose prototype perfect for every occasion, but in an array of disorientingly esoteric variations designed to meet the unique requirements of work, marital rituals, times of the day, or special events, much as an evening gown is worn to a ball, a suit to the office, or a party dress to a garden party. The International Male catalog has fulfilled this basic capitalistic mandate to create out of a single monotonous commodity a multiplicity of rarified choices by imposing a strict fashion code that differentiates the underwear we wear to work from the underwear we wear on a date, loungewear from sleepwear, gymwear from jokewear (e.g., the underwear that people give each other on birthdays or holidays, such as Joe Boxer's line of "graphic briefs" whose rear ends are stenciled with slogans like "Exit Only," "Honey Buns," or "I Love You, Butt . . ."). What the International Male catalog calls the "basics you can rely on every day" are carefully distinguished from underwear that has "sleek dramatic looks for after-hours drama," which is, in turn, distinguished from underwear in which you cuddle up to sleep and that in which you "wind down," "relax," or "just horse around."

If the primary strategy of the gay underwear revolution of the 1960s was to strip everything down to the barest minimum, to bikinis made of "almost invisible, next-to-nothing nylon" and briefs "so light and breezy you'll forget you even have them on," gay men have now taken the exact opposite approach and seek to cover up as much of the body as possible. The take-it-off tendency of the 1960s has collided with the put-it-back-on tendency of the 1990s. This impulse has inspired a craze among gay men for baggy boxer shorts, which we have begun to eroticize as the underwear of the lunk, the "guy," the negligent straight slob who is so hopelessly heterosexual that he is indifferent to the sex appeal of his underwear. After decades of wearing briefs that are tight and skimpy, many homosexuals now drool over the saggy knickers of the careless nebbish, whom we exalt as a symbol of masculine authenticity, as someone who has abstained from the orgy of commercialism in which gay men have been embroiled since the 1960s. Our fatigue with the enervating trends of underwear fashion has provoked a backlash among some members of the gay community, an attempt to undo the homosexualizing of the brief, to make it straight again, to restore it to its golden age of manly innocence, the unspoiled era of artlessness and naiveté that predates the rise of the gay subculture. The gay underwear renaissance launched in the 1960s is thus entering a second stage, that of a counterrevolution in which our fetishism is turning back on itself and rejecting its own mannerisms in an effort to decontaminate and purify what many now view as a morally compromised garment emasculated by its association with gay life. In the put-it-back-on tendency of the 1990s, we see gay culture reacting against its own manic sexuality which is leading "straight-acting" and "straight-appearing" gay men to rid themselves of any visible traces of the subculture and to aim instead for the bland invisibility that will enable them to merge seamlessly into mainstream heterosexual society.

The new self-consciousness that characterizes this second stage of the gay underwear revolution has also given rise to what might be called meta-underwear, underwear that is in some sense "about" underwear, that openly comments on its own structure, exaggerating all of its basic components, its waistbands, straps, seams, and flies. Engaging in a self-reflexive analysis of the "anatomy" of each particular design, manufacturers obsessively examine the garment for new sources of fetishistic appeal, singling out individual features and overstating them, putting them into a sort of visual italics or quotation marks.

Designers pursue this new spirit of underwear formalism by blowing up the brief's supporting elements to twice their normal size and eroticizing them with a myopic intensity that makes the products sold in the International Male catalog seem florid and overwritten.

Often needlessly complicated with laces, zippers, and snaps, underwear flies are no longer simply convenient openings but full-fledged codpieces. These distended pouches protrude from the crotch of the brief, offering at once an invitation, a door marked "please enter," and a prohibition, a locked door, one that is hard to open, equipped with complex latches that suggest a new degree of inaccessibility. Similarly, waistbands are no longer discreetly camouflaged but are now three and sometimes four inches wide, like that found on Tactics' Cross Trainer, a huge sash that encircles the abdomen like the belt of a jockstrap; or that found on Tactics' Hi-Top Brief, which is as wide as a cummerbund, composing virtually 50 percent of the garment. Straps now appear in superfluous places, criss-crossing the buttocks like scaffolding, or are elongated to preposterous lengths. Basix's Body Thong, for instance, is a jockstrap that involves the entire body, its spandex belts running all the way from the crotch to the shoulders and then plunging down the back, like the spaghetti straps of a woman's evening gown, only to disappear tantalizingly between the cheeks of the buttocks. The seams and elastic bands that once served a strictly utilitarian and unobtrusive function of shaping and defining the garment are now the objects of obsessive interest in themselves, the source of a formalist fixation or mania that designers express through a concerted strategy of overemphasis.

The rise of the designer label is another feature of the new formalistic self-consciousness of meta-underwear. As manufacturers trespass on once inviolable regions of our anatomy, they delve into the innermost recesses of the garment in search of new features of erotic interest. This systematic inquiry is so invasive that parts of our briefs that were formerly hidden away on the inside of the waistband, like the small tags identifying such companies as Jockey, Hanes, or Fruit of the Loom, are now flaunted and exposed, advertised in enormous letters on the outside of the waistband, like the underwear of Joe Boxer, whose logo is so ostentatious that it is the most distinctive feature of his creations. Not only is underwear itself coming out into the open and escaping the solipsistic confinement in which it was concealed up until the present, but hitherto unexplored parts of underwear are also being thrust into public view, inverted like a

glove by a creeping form of economic imperialism which is insinu-
ating itself into our bodies' most intimate "space." Far from being a
plain and unpretentious product, as it was in its unglamorous, utilitarian past, underwear now reenacts a kind of striptease in which
it shamelessly "exposes" *itself*, thereby achieving a further degree of
explicitness. As it is remade into a public spectacle, an open-air theater for communal recreation, even the inconspicuous company tag
and laundry instructions are turned inside out, sewn on like badges
for everyone to see.

The second stage of the gay underwear revolution also involves
an effort on the part of many manufacturers to broaden the appeal
of their products to heterosexual men who, up until the last two
decades, have resisted flashy trends in men's lingerie. Whereas the
earliest underwear catalogs appealed exclusively to gay men, betraying the sexual orientation of their readers in everything from drawings of strapping cowpokes by Tom of Finland to stationery that
featured naked boys wiggling their buttocks invitingly in the air,
recent catalogs are far more ambivalent and understated. As a gay
spokesman for International Male stated, his company now routinely
aims for that "grey area" that will continue to appeal to its core
homosexual market and yet also entice venturesome straight men
who would be repelled by open reminders of the link between gay
culture and the sluttish styles of the manufacturer's merchandise. As
companies attempt to sell their products outside of the narrow market niche in which they were largely trapped before the 1970s, they
have undertaken a process of de-gaying underwear, remasculinizing
it, and carefully suppressing its disreputable origins in homosexual
fetishism. It is one of the major ironies of the underwear revolution
that gay liberation did not enable the consumer to acknowledge the
homoerotic appeal of men's lingerie but drove our briefs back into
the closet, with the paradoxical result that the gayest underwear catalogs appeared before Stonewall and not, as we would have expected,
after it.

Nowhere is this de-gaying process expressed more clearly than in
the evolution of Ah Men catalogs from the 1960s to the 1970s. In its
first issues, Ah Men was awash in camp. In addition to describing a

set of debonair if garish ascots as an accessory that is "guaranteed to make you look like that TV star with only eighteen months to live," it pulled such stunts as photographing a line of laughing gay men in bikinis next to a guffawing fag hag in a leopard-skin bathrobe who seems to be playing the role of the lead Rockette of the Ziegfeld Follies, an impression confirmed by the accompanying caption which reads, "now boys, it's one, two, three, kick!" As time passed, however, its catalogs became much more subdued. Among other things, a major change took place in a stock character that recurred in Ah Men's pages, the token female, who, in early issues of the catalog, was dressed as scantily as the male revellers who rallied around her but nonetheless looked like someone's sister camping it up, not with a muscular group of dashing lady killers, but with a gaggle of flustered queens. By the late 1970s, this perennial fruit fly had become a buxom blonde beach bunny whom gargantuan body builders hoisted on their shoulders, staring lecherously at her cleavage and swooning in the sand dunes as she paraded disdainfully by. Although Ah Men continued to sell such gay products as vibrators and books entitled *Asses* well into the 1970s, it significantly toned down its campy sense of humor in an obvious bid to broaden its appeal to straight men, who would undoubtedly have been mystified, if not appalled, by swim coats that "make you look like a movie queen" or miniskirts that are advertised as perfect either for a female friend "or for Halloween."

The evangelical mission of contemporary manufacturers to reach beyond the faithful gay brethren of the underwear religion to the straight laity has also led companies to deny outright the sexual function of their briefs. For all of the sensuality of the gorgeous young hunks who revel in their voluptuousness in the garish photographs of the International Male catalog, an unmistakable note of reticence, even embarrassment, can be found in the advertising copy that accompanies the gauzy "jock socks" and full-length "unitards" in which the models strut and swagger. As homoerotic as the company's merchandise appears, International Male describes its briefs in lackluster and clinical terms, as if the most gratuitously decorative elements of the garment—sheer fabrics, massive pouches, strapless thighs—functioned solely to eliminate unsightly panty lines or, in the case of the "U.S. Jock Brief," to offer something rather inscrutably described as "natural vertical lift support without uptight pullback." The International Male catalog also ascribes such prosaic, nonsexual qualities to the "Support Bar Brief," which, like a padded brassiere, is equipped with a foam rubber cushion clearly designed to enlarge the bulge of the genitals but is justified as serving to "support and lift."[1] Utilitarianism thus becomes a justification for fetishism, a ready-made excuse or alibi that allows straight men at once to indulge obscenely in their erotic obsessions and falsify or gloss over the homosexual hedonism that the International Male catalog celebrates with such wild abandon in its photographs. A publication inspired by the rapturous self-indulgence of Southern California is in fact riddled with inhibitions and pruderies that suffuse the catalog's semipornographic pages with the rhetorical equivalent of a maidenly blush, a self-consciousness that surfaces in this dissonant relation of text to image. This surprising lack of candor stems from both the discomfort straight men feel about allowing themselves to be admired as sex objects and from a deliberate attempt to conceal from them the origins of underwear fetishism in gay culture. In this way, the influence of homosexuality on the whimsically homoerotic appearance of International Male's briefs is disguised by language that transforms even the most screamingly meretricious codpieces and G-strings into garments as dowdy and serviceable as corsets. The marketing of underwear to heterosexuals since the 1970s provides a clear instance of how the translation to mainstream straight culture of an artifact or ritual that originates in the gay community, from men's lingerie to disco to Voguing, necessitates an act of neutralizing self-erasure. Just as underwear must be laundered of the effeminate taint it has acquired after decades of gay experimentation, so the cooptation of gay culture

---

[1]Compare the pseudo utilitarianism of International Male with the real utilitarianism of turn-of-the-century Sears and Roebuck catalogs, which describe their underwear in the plainest terms possible, telling us that "the short, stout suit is made . . . to fit short stout men" and that their black underwear is "in great demand by miners, farmers and workingmen who want underwear that will not show the soil and who during the hot weather work in their undershirts."

in general involves the systematic elimination of its most distinctive features, which must be sanitized if they are to be absorbed by the mainstream. The commercialization of gay culture thus inevitably leads to its disappearance.[2]

---

[2]The paradoxical prudishness with which International Male describes patently gay underwear stands in marked contrast to the way in which it discusses swimming suits or gymwear, even though these outfits are often identical in appearance to underwear, revealing as much, if not more, of the flesh. The "Slicker String Bikini," which consists solely of an elastic thread that slips invisibly between the buttocks and a black vinyl patch that flops over the groin like a tiny plastic loincloth, is characterized as "ultra-sexy," perfect for exposing "a winning sculpted physique." The "Freedom Hot Short," in turn, "serves up outspoken sex appeal in body-conscious poly and spandex," while the bold pattern of flamboyant polka dots on the "Dot Buns Bikini" "pinpoints some of your best attributes" and is so "sexy" that it is "sure to attract more than your share of admiring glances!" Although we can admit that swimming suits and gym shorts serve a social and erotic function, we become extraordinarily circumspect when we describe underwear, resorting to dainty euphemisms about comfort and support that exhibit a peculiarly old-maidish modesty about garments that have clearly been designed for purposes of display. (Note here the complex euphemism "body-conscious." This expression is a code word for "sexy" and is used throughout the advertising of contemporary men's lingerie and swimwear. Not only does the expression animate our briefs by attributing to them a "consciousness"—the ultimate form of consumeristic flattery—but it recasts a synonym for sex appeal in such a way that it sounds less self-indulgent. The word carefully disguises the erotic nature of underwear by making our briefs seem as if they were a crucial part of a healthy lifestyle, a wholesome promoter of our physical well-being as salubrious as bran flakes, granola, and oatmeal.)

Just as underwear and swimming suits are subject to a double standard, so men's and women's lingerie are advertised in remarkably different ways. There has, for instance, never been any need to disguise the sexual function of women's underwear. In the woman's section of a mid-1960s Regency Square catalog, the products the company advertised are described in language free of the cant of "supporting" and "lifting" found in advertisements for men's underwear. The Fallen Angel, for instance, promises that "you'll smoulder and bewitch in this boudoir gown of clinging desire. Sheer lace spreads a provocative veil over you to almost reveal your secrets"; and the transparent lounge set the Veiled Threat offers "a fatal illusion of you veiled in a whisp of a secret. Only a mirage of what is, shows itself. It's devastating and you're devine [sic] in a veiled cloud of fantasy." Similarly, a lacy creation called Dangerous is said to provide "rippling boudoir allure sheathed in breathless excitement," while the stretch nylon Boudoir Britches are "fantasy bedroom favorites ... that give excitement to languid luxurious moments." Only in the 1994 gay catalog H.I.M., which tells the reader to "steam up your wintery nights with the enticingly sheer Glimmer Thong" and "undress to thrill in the Tear-Away bikini," do descriptions of men's underwear finally break through

The anxiety that characterizes the later stages of the underwear revolution, as men's lingerie passes out of the hands of the subculture and into those of a more broadly based heterosexual market, is also expressed in the friezelike frontalism of underwear ads. In most catalogs, the butt is, so to speak, the dark side of the moon, unseen, enigmatic, unrepresentable. With very few exceptions, companies are reluctant to let the model turn his back to his audience but insist that he stand face forward, looking in the general direction of the viewer, perpetually on guard against the lurking sodomite who might sneak up on him unawares, launching an assault against this most vulnerable region of the male anatomy. In part, the relative absence of butt shots reveals how incompletely our culture has eroticized the male body, which, unlike the female body, can never be the passive recipient of someone else's gaze, appraised and evaluated as a sex object, but is always frozen in genitally centered images so the model can look back at the viewer, meeting his stare head on. But perhaps just as importantly as the at best partial nature of the objectification of the male body, the refusal to turn the model around also represents a protective gesture, an act of coyness, an expression of discomfort with the traditional audience of underwear, the horny

---

their reserve and overtake the vampish excesses of purple prose that endow women's lingerie with their fatally magnetic attraction.

Whereas the slinky froufrou sold in such stores as Victoria's Secret is obviously designed to appeal to the senses of a male audience, the bizarre concoctions of contemporary men's underwear are said to appeal solely to the senses of the wearer, who dons his Pointelle Boxers and strapless Sock-Its, not for exhibitionistic purposes, but only because of their silkiness, their softness, their sensuality—in short, for what they do to *him*, not what they do to *her*. While the woman who wears sexy lingerie is a temptress, a bewitching coquette, the man who wears sexy lingerie is a hedonist, a selfish voluptuary who thinks exclusively of his own pleasure, of how the satin caresses his thighs, and not how his partner will pant over the projecting bulge of his genitals and the shapely contours of his buttocks. We have always been able to admit that women's lingerie serves the social and sexual function of seducing her partner, but in the case of men's underwear, we retreat into a spurious solipsism in which the underwear serves a distinctly self-indulgent function, catering to the senses of the wearer who enjoys his briefs purely for the pleasure of their gossamer softness and well-ventilated "breathability."

gay men who devour the model's body with their eyes, assessing the
value of his attributes as if he were a slave girl on an auction block.
In the fiercely defended frontal nudity of the contemporary underwear ad, we see an implicit acknowledgment of the presence of the
homoerotic gaze, a bashful awareness that the homosexual is looking,
that it is he who sits in the front row of this never-ending striptease,
relishing every bump and grind. No matter how hard manufacturers
attempt to suppress the origins of the underwear revolution in gay
culture, the homoerotic history of men's lingerie keeps emerging,
shining through the pretense of utilitarianism, and haunting the tormented fashion awareness of the self-conscious straight consumer
who finds himself wearing a costume that emerged from the sexual
fantasies of this most troubling of minorities.

The unusual problems involved in the sale of men's underwear to
the general public provide a perfect example of the usefulness of gay
consumers as a bridge market. We help companies to introduce products that heterosexual men would have been reluctant to buy if homosexuals had not first demonstrated that such a drab, utilitarian
piece of clothing, seldom seen outside of gyms or bedrooms, could
serve aesthetic and erotic functions. Homosexuals have helped break
the male market wide open and allowed manufacturers to commercialize aspects of men's lives that were formerly closed to them,
barred by the strictures of machismo, the taboos that made the heterosexual's body an impregnable fortress against the economic incursions of manufacturers. Gender-based inhibitions about the vanity
of primping and the self-indulgence of bodily adornment once prevented companies from selling men their facial creams and Jock
Socks, thus protecting the male body from the rampant commercialism that has taken over women's bodies, from their eyelashes to
their toenails, from their panty hose to their cross-your-heart bras.
Because the tribal imperatives of masculinity were somewhat weaker
in gay men, we helped suppress our gender's natural immunity to
the marketplace and thus invited Madison Avenue into parts of the
male anatomy from which it had been previously excluded but that
it now took by storm in an effort to create the same multi-billion-

dollar industry that it had already created out of women's physical insecurities.

Just as gay magazines sanitize the image of the homosexual in order to attract national advertisers, so underwear needs to be thoroughly laundered of the stain of the subculture if such a heavily homoeroticized commodity is to be marketed to straight men, who are naturally self-conscious about wearing a garment that constitutes the flamboyant uniform of a world that repels them. But it's not just straight men who want to disassociate themselves from the architects of recent underwear fashion. Many homosexuals also want their briefs dehomosexualized, restored to their spotless, utilitarian innocence, as in the case of baggy boxer shorts which some gay men wear in an effort to mimic the heterosexual male's manly indifference to the slovenly appearance of his shapeless underthings. The de-gaying of underwear provides a metaphor for the assimilation of the subculture into mainstream society, which is willing to accept the homosexual only when he is stripped of his subversive, erotic identity and remade in the wholesome image of the straight man, a process that will ultimately destroy the gay sensibility, eliminating its distinctive characteristics.

The history of another ideologically problematic commodity, leather, provides a more complicated example of the way in which an unacceptable aspect of gay culture has been cleansed and sterilized in an effort to bring it in line with public opinion. In the course of the last 30 years, the leather community has submitted to a process of banalization that has rendered it harmless in the eyes of the heterosexual majority, who will tolerate this seemingly sinister underground only when it has abandoned the very qualities that initially gave it its dangerous edge. If the change from "special friend" to "husband" provides a way of gauging homosexuals' assimiliation over the past three decades, so the changes in terminology and sexual practices seen in the before and after picture of the leather subculture in the following chapter show how gay men willingly submit to a destructive campaign of self-editing.

The Death of Kink:

Five Stages in

the Metamorphosis

of the Modern Dungeon

B EFORE WORLD WAR II, the closeted practitioners of S/M did not have access to the vast selection of chastity belts, slings, body bags, and meat hooks now sold at such erotic retailers as Good Vibrations, the Crypt, Fetters, and the Pleasure Chest. There were no mail-order companies selling the esoteric stock-in-trade of the contemporary sadist, the bullwhips, the butt plugs, the manacles, the adjustable alligator tit clamps—instruments of torture readily available today everywhere from shopping malls and dirty bookstores to upscale boutiques. Even the ceremonial vestment of the religion, the leather jacket, was a rare commodity before the 1940s. Because this most crucial item of S/M regalia could be purchased in America only in police equipment outlets, which refused to sell to civilians, hard-core fetishists were forced either to scrape by with the riding crops and braided whips offered by equestrian suppliers[1] or to make do with a belt, a pair of leather gardening gloves, and some cord from a clothesline.

By the late 1960s, the entire situation had changed. It was no longer necessary to pose as a cowboy or a jockey in order to secure the requisite paraphernalia for one's sexual fantasies. Mail-order companies that specialized in rigging out the modern dungeon had

---

[1]Samuel Stewart, *Leatherfolk* (ed. Mark Thompson) (Alyson, 1991), p. 83.

sprung up across America featuring everything from leg irons called "love bracelets" and cock rings called "ring-a-ling ding-dong napkin holders" to rawhide belts called "meat tenderizers" ("bring back that color to his cheeks!") and handcuffs with extra sets of keys ("don't dial 'Operator' with your tongue"). In a single catalog from the early 1970s of the S/M supplier Leather Forever, one finds no less than 11 types of body harnesses, 12 types of dog collars, at least 20 types of "ball mauls" and cock rings, and 22 types of dildos in a capricious array of odd shapes and sizes, from pencil-thin corkscrew phalluses no longer than one's pinkie finger to deadly battering rams, from the Erecto Squirmy and the Deluxe Double Dong to the Big Fricket and the Giant Man-o-War. In less than 40 years, leather and S/M have come out of the closet to produce a thriving cottage industry of novelty businesses that feature such items as Christmas cards with naked Santa Clauses thrashing with candy canes the red bare bottoms of disobedient elves or—for the aesthetically inclined—do-it-yourself kits that teach the Japanese art of ornamental bondage.

Although the practice of S/M clearly predates its two founding fathers, the Marquis de Sade and Leopold von Sacher-Masoch, the leather community as we know it today originated in the early 1950s with the rise of the first gay biker clubs, which also became the sartorial birthplace of the clone look, a style of fashion that eventually changed the appearance of virtually the entire gay community in the 1970s. These underground organizations were formed to defray the hospital expenses of members injured in accidents and to stage competitions and brief recreational excursions into the countryside for drunken weekend getaways. Straight motorcycle gangs of disaffected youth, the macho precursors of the beatnik and the hippie, had formed as early as the late 1940s and had immediately caught the attention of a renegade sector of gay men, who soon began to impersonate them, imitating their snarling, contemptuous masculinity and disdain for middle-class respectability.

In 1954, the first gay biker club, the Satyrs, was established in Los Angeles only a year after the appearance of a movie that served as one of the major inspirations of the early gay leather scene. Marlon Brando's cult classic *The Wild One* depicted a gang of grungy heterosexual teenagers who barreled down the open highway on their Harleys and roared into the midst of the bewildered residents of a placid, sleepy hamlet, which they proceeded to terrorize. Based on a supposedly true incident, which the film's menacing epigraph warns us "it is a public challenge never to let...happen again," the story focused on the Black Rebels who violate the mores of a town as quaint as a Currier and Ives print by making disrespectful remarks to members of the law enforcement, damaging the hair driers of a beauty parlor, and dancing openly with licentious women in eye makeup and skin-tight sweaters while snapping their fingers and uttering such comments as "you gotta make some jive." Brando looked so magnificent in his lowering sunglasses and his leather cap cocked rakishly over one eye that he quickly became the sullen mascot of the fledgling gay leather movement, which revolved, not around leather per se, but around the motorcycle, a piece of heavy equipment that functioned as a countercultural symbol, the embodiment of unfettered individuality as well as of adolescent America's nihilistic worldview. It was only in the 1970s that leather was finally liberated from the motorcycle, and the focus of the fetish shifted from this prohibitively expensive mode of transportation to the less costly but equally masculine accessories of the uniform—the studded belts, eagle insignia, and stenciled images of skulls and crossbones. Gang members' leather jackets, gauntlets, and boots eventually upstaged the mythic image of the gleaming Harley, which receded completely into the background of this oddly cultish vehicular religion.

While the gay motorcycle clubs of the 1950s and 1960s were in most respects simply social groups, they did play a pivotal role in the burgeoning gay liberation movement. The implicit purpose of such organizations as the Satyrs was to subvert the prevailing stereotypes of effeminate homosexuals by creating a hypermasculine environment in which members could cultivate the machismo of their heterosexual heroes. An S/M manifesto from 1965 stated that "in leather and its rites, gay men find an escape from the marshmallow, soft, cloying sweet" culture of the "nelly queen," whom they abhor, fleeing "the over-feminized present into a past where men of strength and muscle, power and determination, men like Achilles and Hercules, Galahad and Lancelot, Davy Crockett, Daniel Boone, the Spanish Conquistadors were admired and emulated." "The men who love leather," it goes on to say, are entirely different

> from the image that society usually holds of the homosexual: the mincing, effeminate queen whom leather men regard with a contempt stronger and more bitter than that they feel toward women. What they admire is the hardest, strongest, most violent qualities in their own sex.[2]

In order to counter the straight world's expectations that all gay men were lisping poufs with bouffant hairdos and loud perfumes, leathermen strove to express their butchness in every aspect of their lives—even in the decoration of their bars, which were stripped of the baby grands and gilt mirrors of traditional cocktail lounges and adorned instead with dented chrome fenders and rusty exhaust pipes cannibalized from abandoned motorcycles. The owner of the earliest leather bar in San Francisco, the Toolbox, which opened in 1962, stressed what he called "the anti-feminine side of homosexuality" by displaying a cluster of tennis shoes dangling from the ceiling before a sign that read DOWN WITH SNEAKERS!, a potent symbol of effeminacy as despised as angora sweaters.[3] The leather trappings that often accompanied the cult of the motorcycle therefore provided gay men with an answer to a very specific image problem. Some homosexuals solved the dilemma of effeminacy through an elaborate form of transvestism that involved putting on the bogeyman costumes of a new social threat to the bourgeois heterosexual world, the roving gangs of surly punks that began to appear in large numbers during the 1950s. In a flamboyant act of impersonation of these social pariahs, who emanated lawlessness and danger, some gay motorcyclists went so far as to incorporate a violent new style of lovemaking into their political rejection of the desexed eunuch, whose vilification became crucial to the agenda of the early gay pride movement.

---

[2]*Leather* (Guild Press, 1965), no page numbers. Anonymous introduction.
[3]"Homosexuality in America," *Life*, June 26, 1964.

Behind each of the major changes that has occurred in the leather community since the 1950s lies what might be called an implied dungeon, a metaphorical space that provides the social context for sadomasochistic sex, which often advanced larger political aims entirely separate from the sensual pleasures of the individual acts themselves. If the history of gay men's involvement with leather is interpreted as a succession of dungeons, the first dungeon was not a woodshed where bad boys were spanked or a damp oubliette where disobedient prisoners were left to rot in chains, but a comfortable dressing room in which homosexuals took off the sneakers and the angora sweaters of the swish and stepped into the rugged dungarees and leather jackets of Marlon Brando. In the 1950s and 1960s, S/M sex was not about pleasure and pain, about the allegory of domination and submission; it was about gay liberation, about creating an alternative image of the subculture. For most of the early participants in the leather phenomenon, rough, unsentimental S/M sex was less a means of erotic fulfillment than a political affectation.

But the rejuvenating effect of S/M on homosexuals' compromised virility was far surpassed by the social amenities offered by this new sexual demimonde, which quickly began to resemble a high-spirited Masonic Lodge whose members behaved, not like connoisseurs of cruelty, but like Shriners or Knights from the Rotary Club; during the 1960s and 1970s, they even organized slave auctions to benefit such charitable organizations as the SPCA, Easter Seals, and Toys for Tots. From its beginning in the 1950s, the so-called kinky community has underplayed its public image as a hellish underground full of diabolical satanists and potential serial killers and posed instead as a frolicking philanthropic society that holds bake sales for injured cyclists or comes to the rescue of its persecuted brethren by bailing them out of jail or paying the retainer fees for their defense attorneys. The vibrant social dimension of the leather world, with its endless circuit of "bootblacking" competitions, bullwhipping demonstrations, and "Buns R Us" benefits, is not a by-product of the S/M fetish but one of its primary incentives, the motivating factor that continues to attract teeming hordes of gay men who disingenuously claim to share the same fascination with violent sex. Just as the wide-scale practice of S/M was originally motivated by the need to masculinize the image of the homosexual in the eyes of straight society, so its eventual triumph as a "lifestyle," with its dizzying social calendar of beer busts and "Pin the Clothespin on the Slave" parties, was a result of the intense isolation homosexuals experienced in the atomized world before Stonewall, which gave rise to urgent social needs to establish connections with other gay men.

Since the inception of the S/M movement, the cult of leather has served as a way for the gay man to identify himself to others and only incidentally as a means of fulfilling overpowering erotic urges to engage in ostensibly illicit practices that, far from representing an epidemic of sexual pathology, have become simply a pretext for a perverse act of networking. For most homosexuals, in other words, S/M has never been the psychological fetish of the lone pervert guiltily salivating over whips and groveling on the cold dungeon floor while eagerly awaiting the crack of his master's riding crop or the stomp of his hobnailed boot. Instead, in the case of the vast majority of homosexuals who engage in S/M sex, leather is a *social* fetish, an "acquired" or "learned" fetish that has little to do with an inherently kinky predisposition for alternative erotic practices.

This intense spirit of camaraderie is still regularly expressed in one of the house organs of the leather movement, *DungeonMaster*. In 1981, the magazine announced in all seriousness the establishment of an emergency relief fund for the S/M victims of a devastating firestorm that had swept through San Francisco's South-of-Market district, reducing their well-appointed playrooms to rubble, incinerating irreplaceable collections of historic whips, and melting down whole treasure troves of marital aids and dildos. Rather than asking them to send money, the author urged readers to scour their own dungeons and rifle through their toy chests for harnesses "you never use, your duplicates, the things you've outgrown," box them up in Care packages, and send them off to a specific S/M group in San Francisco that, like the Red Cross or the Save the Children Fund, would make certain "they are forwarded to the men in need."[4]

---

[4]*DungeonMaster*, July 1981, p. 5.

Throughout the twentieth century, gay men have established group allegiances in a number of odd, unexpected, and often circuitous ways that allowed them to communicate with other members of the tribe, much like prisoners rapping in code on the pipes of their cells. Some men, as we have seen, created community through movies, through fandom, through the worship of stars, and others, just as ingeniously, fostered cohesiveness through the cultivation of sexual fetishes. As different as they might at first appear, fandom and fetish have served the exact same function in gay society, that of providing us with a collective identity. In precisely the same way that the love of actresses sounded a rallying cry that helped us overcome our solipsistic insularity, so leather and uniforms became a banner uniting large numbers of isolated homosexuals, who experienced their first taste of solidarity through marathon bike runs, clubhouse initiation rites, red-hanky parties at the local leather bar, and Friday night Dungeon-Dance fund-raisers. The movement even has its own gossip columnists; for over 20 years, the irrepressible "Mr. Marcus" has written the equivalent of the leather community's parish letter in the San Francisco gay newspaper the *Bay Area Reporter*. In his weekly round-robin, he acts as a kind of public-service samaritan, offering rewards for information leading to the capture of the thief who stole Mr. 1993 Deaf Leather's sash or relaying flash bulletins about "local leather personages," such as adorable Darrell who, smitten with the Eagle's jacket checker, abandoned his job and eloped to Albuquerque. In the early years of the leather movement, a second implied dungeon appeared simultaneously next to the dressing room: the clubhouse where gay men use sexual theater much as frat boys use hazing rituals or Shriners use fezzes and scimitars.

While the leather fetish helped some homosexuals solve the problem of effeminacy, it nevertheless created a new difficulty: it unleashed a wave of criticism from both the psychiatric establishment and from sexually squeamish members of mainstream America who interpreted S/M as further evidence of the homosexual's innate perversion. In an effort to achieve a new kind of legitimacy as a macho clan of menacing hoodlums, gay men only succeeded in reinforcing the prevailing belief in the homosexual's unsavory status as an unbalanced psychopath who slaked his bloodlust on innocent victims while prowling through a seamy underworld of rapists and child molesters.

One of the most extraordinary examples of the straight world's willingness to believe even the most apocryphal stories about the leather community occurred in Los Angeles in 1976 when two busloads of riot police raided a charity slave auction organized by the S/M club the Leather Fraternity. While two heavily armed helicopters circled above, their searchlights raking the area for fugitives fleeing the scene, 65 commandos from the LAPD stormed the hall where the benefit was being held and triumphantly liberated the slaves chained to the auction block, arraigning the guests in attendance on charges that they had colluded in the sale of human beings for personal gain. Immediately after the success of this brilliantly orchestrated rescue operation, the reactionary *Orange County Register* ran the headline POLICE FREE GAY SLAVES, a story they reported as a literal emancipation of imprisoned hostages, praising the police for cracking this dangerous ring of Mafia kingpins engaged in the lucrative white slave trade.[5]

In order to counteract such enormous perception problems in the eyes of a gullible public ready to believe anything about the S/M underground, leather apologists in the late 1960s and 1970s began a process of self-reconstruction that profoundly altered the practice of S/M. Writers refuted accusations of depravity not only by denying the abnormality of S/M sex but by holding up erotic experimentation as a surefire method for promoting a preeminently *healthy* lifestyle, one its practitioners advertised as a kind of miracle cure, an anomalous form of therapy that accelerated the process of "personal growth" and "self-discovery." Virtually every book that has come out of the leather community in the last 25 years placates the public's sensitivity to violence by turning S/M into a wholesome form of self-actualization that allows both the master and his slave, through merciless sessions of flogging, to achieve such goals as formulating "a

---

[5]"Dummer Goes to a Slave Auction," *Drummer* 1 (6), May/June 1976, p. 12.

more positive image,"[6] discovering "their own potential," and acting
on the "universal desire for people to express their individuality and
'do their own thing.' "[7] In 1972, Larry Townsend, a psychotherapist
and world-renowned sadist, derided the "first enemy" of the leather
fetishist, "the psychiatric establishment," by claiming that, after participating in the sweaty exhilaration of kinky sex, "your uninhibited
leatherman [emerges] in much the same emotional condition as a
client after a successful hour on the couch of catharsis."[8]

At the very moment that leathermen had succeeded in portraying
themselves as a disreputable pack of pirates and thieves, they backed
away from this butch stereotype and began instead to rebut their
characterization as degenerate outlaws. They attempted to rehabili-
tate their images in the eyes of mainstream America by accommo-
dating themselves to its criticisms and adopting the therapeutic
jargon used to condemn them, setting themselves up as the very
paradigm of mental health, the summit of self-actualized stability
and well being. Rather than accepting their illicitness and welcoming
their reputation as a subversive fringe element that skirted the mar-
gins of respectable society, leathermen engaged in a self-betraying act
of bad faith. Even today, a calculatedly defensive rhetoric constructed
out of the clichés of the human potential movement colors S/M literature, as can be seen in books by leather therapist Guy Baldwin,
who insists that all masters develop "top person-to-person skills" and
that bottoms experiencing too much pain "consult [their] inner 'traf-
fic light.' " "Don't take your wounded inner child into the playroom," Baldwin admonishes, shaking his finger like a psychiatric
social worker, "SM is for consenting adults and is no place for children, especially an injured one that may be inside you . . . leave your
kid at the door when you walk in."[9]

If the implied dungeon during the early years of the biker movement was either a clubhouse or a dressing room in which timid

---

[6]Guy Baldwin, M.S., *Ties That Bind* (Daedalus, 1993), p. 52.
[7]*PFIQ*, 1, 1977, p. 2.
[8]Larry Townsend, *The Leatherman's Handbook* (Le Salon, 1972), p. 173.
[9]*Ties That Bind*, p. 207.

pansies draped themselves in leather trappings, the implied dungeon of the 1970s was a therapist's office in bland pastels. In this sterile consultation room, clinicians with pencils and legal pads challenged the bigotries of the American Psychological Association by asserting that S/M helped people to achieve "empowerment on a personal level,"[10] to "channel their unconscious urges,"[11] and to "recoup some long-lost creative expressiveness."[12]

At the same time that the human potential movement was providing ammunition against right-wing zealots who portrayed the S/M world as a dangerous breeding ground for pedophiles and murderers, for John Wayne Gacys and Jeffrey Dahmers, pop psychology actually fueled gay men's interest in leather. It not only convinced them that S/M would make them healthier individuals, but it disseminated a set of metaphors that allowed them to rationalize the often startling contradictions between their recreational activities and their careers, between their undercover aliases as raunchy bikers in leather chaps and jockstraps and their public identities as staid businessmen with conservative, white-collar jobs as CEOs, bank presidents, and systems analysts. Although pop psychologists would have us believe their adherents lead integrated and "holistic" lives, the view of the self implicit in their literature is that of a disintegrated and compartmentalized hierarchy of inner beings, a hodgepodge of alter egos neatly divided into "sides," "halves," "facets," "parts," "levels," and "layers." The human potentialized self is fractured into a Sybil-like conglomeration of multiple personalities including "the warrior side of myself," "the bottom side of myself," "the professional level of myself," "the leather/SM/fetish parts of myself," and "the masculine facet of my personality." Such language has enabled the S/M community to justify the extraordinary act of self-dismemberment involved in living the leather lifestyle, which requires its followers to erect impenetrable barriers between their

---

[10]Interview with Don Ed Hardy in *Re/Search no. 12: Modern Primitives* (eds. V. Vale and Andrea Juno) (Re/Search Publications, 1989), p. 51.

[11]*Re/Search no. 12,* p. 53.

[12]*Re/Search no. 12,* p. 52.

careers and their professionally damaging private fetishes, every trace of which must, by necessity, be banished from the boardroom, the staff meeting, and the job interview.

Without the basic concept of the desirability and even healthiness of the compartmentalization of the personality, the explosion of interest in S/M since the early 1970s would have been impossible. The rhetoric of the disintegrated self gave gay men the theoretical framework that enabled them to live comfortably with the schizophrenic contradiction of being, by day, a primly dressed controller at a law firm and, by night, a bootlicking slave into duct-tape mummification, latex body bags, and bare-bottom woodshed discipline. Far from fostering the integration of one's sex life and one's daily life, human potential psychology ensures that leathermen can keep them safely apart by relegating their activities to what it is now fashionable to call a "play space." As Larry Townsend explains, in this infantilized hybrid of a nursery room and a torture chamber, the S/M practitioner can express "those portions of his personality . . . [and] that part of his inner self that society forces him to conceal at any other time."[13]

But although the rhetoric of human potential was invaluable to the leather community, its application to S/M is, as we will see, as inappropriate as the palliatives it offers to the victims of the AIDS epidemic. One of the major ironies of the leather movement is that the therapeutic jargon used to legitimize it runs entirely counter to the true spirit of S/M sexuality. The pop psychologist's religion of free will simply does not jibe with sex that is based on physical restraint and even literal imprisonment. The human potential movement stresses the importance of untrammeled self-expression and individuality, exalting self-determination and independence, whereas S/M denies free will, encourages relationships of servile dependence, and glorifies the most despotic forms of external control, from handcuffs and gags to anonymous hoods that reduce the masochist to little more than a gaping orifice, a dehumanized mouth slit, a warm wet hole at his master's disposal. A form of sex that involves physical

---

[13]*Leatherman's Handbook*, 1972, p. 11.

immobility and punishes the slave for the slightest assertion of independence is paradoxically described as a celebration of emotional freedom, a sensitive and fulfilling interpersonal experience that provides a supportive and nurturing environment in which the individual can find "an outlet for self-expression" and "an avenue for self-exploration." In the course of the 1970s and 1980s, the profound conflict between this jargon of independence and the physical and psychological realities of S/M, which categorically preclude autonomy and delight instead in duress and captivity, began to shape the very nature of kinky sex, which underwent a succession of dramatic self-corrections as its proponents attempted to reconcile the contradictions between theory and practice.

The first of these were instituted in the 1970s after a second wave of criticisms, quite different from the alarmist jeremiads issued by the psychiatric establishment, inspired even more vigorous attempts to bring S/M practices in line with the reigning pieties of the time. Rather than coming from outside of the gay community, this new barrage of criticisms came from within, from the left wing itself, from feminists who reviled S/M as a transparent allegory of patriarchal fascism and recoiled from both the heterosexual and homosexual fetishist's extreme objectification of the body; from antiwar activists who decried violence and were troubled by leathermen's undisguised fascination with military paraphernalia—dog tags, camouflage fatigues, and army boots; and, just as significantly, from conservative gay men who preached the gospel of assimilation and strove to present a rosy-cheeked, choirboy image of the homosexual to mainstream America. All of the disparate forces of the counterculture teamed up with the most hidebound of society's moral leaders to form an unlikely alliance that backed the S/M community into a corner and extorted concessions that ultimately eroded its members' confidence and forced them to soft-pedal their once defiant rhetoric. The publication of *Against Sadomasochism: A Radical Feminist Analysis* (1982) constituted one of the strongest attacks against the leather community. In this collection of vitriolic essays, Robin Morgan argued that, for most women, books praising S/M were what books entitled *Why You Know You Like It on the Plantation* were to blacks or *How to Be Happy in the Showers* were to Jews.[14] Similarly, Diana Russell asserted that S/M is not only "incompatible with feminism" but betrays "monumental insensitivity to black people" who were forced to endure centuries of real slavery and who therefore could not accept the idea of sexual role playing as a form of recreation.[15]

To understand the tension between the left and the S/M community, it is important to remember that, despite its original disdain for effeminacy, leather culture was one of the first forms of gay liberation, a highly confrontational method through which a small minority of gay men invented for themselves an unconventionally masculine image of a militarized homosexual, a bellicose G.I. Joe. In the 1960s and 1970s, however, these early gay liberationists were swept into the same movement with peaceniks, flower children, and feminists, passionate proponents of leftist crusades who disapproved of the sexual practices and reactionary posturing of leathermen, which many viewed as nothing more than fodder for right-wing sensationalism. After over a decade of being sealed off from both gay and straight society as a solitary club of biker renegades, S/M fetishists suddenly found themselves in league with a group of ill-matched bedfellows, ideologically inflexible reformers who had diametrically opposite political agendas, which, far from ignoring, leathermen absorbed and took to heart. The gay liberation movement after Stonewall was not a uniform and monolithic consensus of like-minded agitators who shared the same platform and priorities. Instead, it comprised a volatile mixture of contradictory forces that maintained a precarious balance, forming a fragile coalition that, in the case of something as ideologically objectionable as S/M, could be preserved only through urgent efforts on the part of leathermen to explain and excuse their behavior. These apologies ultimately changed the entire nature of their sexual practices, as they undertook a massive PR blitz, an all-out snow job in which they caved in to the critics in order to recover their legitimacy in the eyes of the rest of the subculture. Just as leathermen absorbed the rhetoric

---

[14]*Against Sadomasochism* (ed. Robin Ruth Linden) (Frog in the Well, 1982), p. 109.
[15]*Against Sadomasochism*, p. 177.

of their psychiatric critics, so they now recharacterized aggression as affection, sadism as tenderness, cruelty as kindness.

Even today, they continue to insist that "true S/M is not cruel; it is a loving fulfillment of a partner's needs";[16] that "the giving and taking of abuse" is not an act of violence, "it is an act of love";[17] that "fascism is in no way implicit in sadomasochism";[18] and even that a bottom suspended from a meat hook "is not merely a piece of meat. He is a human being."[19] Nothing dramatizes more clearly the whole-sale emasculation of everything the leather community once stood for than a simple change in terminology: the shift from the word *leathermen*, which was used in the 1970s, to the word *leatherfolk*, which has become popular in the 1990s. This expression conjures up images, not of the Marquis de Sade flogging French milkmaids and deflowering innocent children, but of a quaint tribe of macrobiotic vegetarians in tie-dye caftans singing protest songs at peace rallies. If, as we will see, drag was paradoxically masculinized in the course of gay liberation, leather was paradoxically feminized, becoming a defanged movement of starry-eyed soul searchers who, while beating their lovers black and blue, delivered "every stroke [as] an act of love" that left them "warm with the feeling of having created this ecstasy in another man's life."[20]

This process of mitigation and compromise eventually led S/M apologists to draw attention away from the actual fantasy of sado-masochistic sex, from its symbolic allegory, and direct it toward its reality, the sensual element of the experience, which they no longer describe as an abstract "plot" involving a set of time-honored sce-narios. Such perennially favorite subjects for S/M sex "scenes" as the warrior and his captive, the Spanish Inquisitor and his heretic, the Nazi guard and his Jewish internee, and the fraternity brother and his rush-week pledge were, for some people, problematic.

---

[16]Arnie Kantrowitz, "Swastika Toys," in *Leatherfolk* (ed. Mark Thompson) (Alyson Publications, 1991), p. 207.
[17]*Leatherman's Handbook*, 1983, p. 24.
[18]*Leatherfolk*, p. 207.
[19]*Leatherman's Handbook*, 1983, p. 29.
[20]Geoff Mains, *Urban Aboriginals* (Gay Sunshine Press, 1984), p. 48.

The new breed of politically correct leathermen resolved the troubling ideological issues raised by these improvised dramas by excising the suspect narrative from the S/M scene altogether or at least toning it down, concentrating instead on the pleasurable sensations of kinky sex acts. By the 1980s, writers had begun to discuss S/M in such exclusively sensual terms that some leaders of the leather community called for a reinterpretation of the very initials *S/M*, which they said referred, not to "sadism" and "masochism," but to "sensuality" and "mutuality" or even "sex magic," a linguistic trick that enabled them to disassociate themselves from the hotly contested narrative of domination and submission.

The deallegorizing of S/M sex emerges in a comparison of the first and second editions of Larry Townsend's pioneering work, *The Leatherman's Handbook*, which was originally published in 1972 and then reissued in an expanded version in 1983. In the course of only 11 years, Townsend, who is considered by most to be a stodgy and somewhat dated representative of the old school of rugged bikers, shifts away from discussions of the symbolism of the leather sex scene to specific recommendations for heightening its sensory pleasures, which are described with an almost scientific understanding of the nature of erotic response.

The second edition of the book is like a clever home economist's encyclopedia of old family recipes and grandmotherly tips. It includes everything from advice on how to hard-boil the smoothest and firmest eggs for rectal stuffing scenes to instructions for pumicing calluses off the soles of your feet for the gentlest possible acts of foot fucking; from what to soak your gags in to eliminate latex aftertastes to how to use vitamin B with a high yeast content to turn your urine "a nice, bright yellow"[21] for water sports; from the dangers of using Fels Naptha enemas to the advantages of using Saran Wrap for mummification (it cuts down on "the wrapping time and effort [and] it also sticks to itself thus eliminating the need for fasteners"[22]). One of the most revealing additions to the 1983 version of *The Leather-*

---

[21]*Leatherman's Handbook*, p. 152.
[22]*The Leatherman's Handbook II* (Carlyle Communications, 1995), p. 219.

man's Handbook is Townsend's lengthy discussion of how to create the right atmosphere in the dungeon, a room he characterizes, less as a dingy prison cell lined with hobbles, muzzles, and cat-o'-nine-tails, than a darkened theater in which a master illusionist stages awe-inspiring feats of prestidigitation. In his analysis of the fine art of decorating the playroom, Townsend strips S/M of its intellectual fictions and concentrates on the sheer physiology of pleasure and pain. He describes the sadist torturing his slave as if he were a surgeon operating on a patient, inducing sharply defined sensations whose effect has been calculated in advance through careful preparation. He advises the reader to plan out the smallest details, from the impact of the cold tile floor on the slave's bare feet to the room's odor, which he suggests that masters concoct like perfumists, using an olfactory recipe that includes generous doses of amyl nitrite, grass, urine, beer, cigarettes, burnt hair, candle wax, sweat, and the smell of old boots—anything but the sickly sweet stench of Lysol![23]

What we are witnessing in Townsend's fascinating descriptions of his rigorous science of atmospherics is the rise of S/M aestheticism, a bedroom philosophy that resembles nothing so much as that enunciated by the decadent and neurasthenic narrator of Huysmans's *À Rebours*, who built complex contraptions containing the distilled essences of liqueurs and perfumes with which he created synesthetic symphonies of tastes and smells. Although Townsend remains one of the old-line diehards of the S/M community, its venerable grey eminence, he too is clearly moving away from the ideologically prob-

---

[23]Similarly, the lighting should be more than just a low-watt bulb dangling from a cord but should be bright enough to enable the master to thread the tiny holes of a harness and, moreover, should create "a 'warm' aura," a hypnotizing ambience of subtle hues achieved through a combination of red and blue. (These "warm" colors are, coincidentally, "flattering since they tend to obscure skin blemishes and wrinkles.") The music, by the same token, should never include vocal selections, because lyrics to such songs as Donna Summer's "MacArthur Park," Charlene's "I've Never Been to Me," or Abba's "Dancing Queen" could potentially distract the slave from the scene, a miscalculation Townsend suggests you avoid by confining yourself to film scores or orchestral pieces like Ravel's *Bolero*, Wagner's *Ride of the Valkyries*, Shostakovich's *The Human Comedy*, or even the music for *2001: A Space Odyssey* (although it is important to remember to edit out the section from the "Blue Danube Waltz").

lematic fictions of sadomasochistic sex, from the allegory of servitude, and concentrating instead on how bondage and domination *feel* as opposed to what they *mean*. In the 1980s and 1990s, a fourth dungeon has arisen in the long succession of metaphorical dungeons: the laboratory of pure sensations, a magic chamber in which the ecstatic eroticism of deallegorized S/M sex is filling the vacuum created by the gradual collapse of the narrative of submission, which ultimately will not be able to withstand the vigorous objections being raised to the sexual politics of humiliating power games.

The erosion of the S/M allegory and its replacement by the contemporary leather aesthete's doctrine of raunch-for-raunch's-sake is also evident in a change that has occurred in the very dynamic of the scene. In traditional accounts of sadomasochistic sex, the burden of sexual responsibility rested squarely on the shoulders of the slave; it was his duty to wait hand and foot on the sensual needs of his master, who, in some cases, professed disdainful indifference to the erotic fulfillment of the contemptible creature stretched out like a doormat before him. In more recent accounts, however, the source of erotic pleasure has moved from the bottom to the top, so it is now the master's responsibility to arouse his slave, to assume the role, not of a callously detached torturer, but of an empathetic sensory engineer who plays on his subject like a musical instrument until he cries out in ecstasy, with billions of firing neurons inducing in him a trancelike state of sensual intoxication. Such how-to books as Race Bannon's *Learning the Ropes: A Basic Guide to Safe and Fun S/M Lovemaking* (1992) or Jack Rinella's *The Master's Manual* (1994) describe the scene as if the master's pleasure were strictly subordinated to the voracious needs of the bottom, whom the top must satisfy and serve with thankless devotion, selflessly catering to his inert subject's every sensual whim, loosening the manacles chafing his wrists or massaging his prickly feet during crucifixion scenes. In one of his weekly columns for the *San Francisco Sentinel*, Rinella even launched a blistering attack against the Marquis de Sade on the grounds that he demonstrated an unpardonable lack of loving concern for his bruised and battered slaves by failing to inquire if the scene was meeting their needs and to solicit emotional "feedback" while torturing and raping them.[24] The sexual politics of domination and submission have become so complex and so closely scrutinized by the feminist sex police that the inequities of power in the traditional scene have swung in the opposite direction. The top has swapped roles with his bottom, who, in an extraordinary act of manumission, is actually gaining ascendancy over his supposed master.

The leather community's attempts to present a more egalitarian front to its primary critics have not only relocated the center of sexual attention in the S/M scene, producing an imbalance of power as lopsided as that found in the dungeons of the ancien régime, but they are contributing to the collapse of sex roles themselves, which are losing their sharp resolution. Leathermen now routinely switch positions at will according to the impulse of the moment, often in the middle of the same scene, where, out of a spirit of good sportsmanship, they take turns, spelling off like cooperative teammates, the one pitching, the other catching. One of the major developments in the leather community during the last 25 years is the increase of versatility and the dissolution of the formerly prescriptive labels of top and bottom, which men once adopted and adhered to for their entire lives, accepting them like Hindus accept their castes, the Brahmins reveling in their privileges, the untouchables resigning themselves to their humble station. As Larry Townsend laments in the second edition of *The Leatherman's Handbook*, sexual ambidextrousness is now so commonplace that it has created a crisis for old-fashioned bottoms whose touching plight he memorializes in a nursery rhyme that casts a wistful glance back to the good old days when masters were masters and chattel chattel:

Poor little upside-down cake
Your troubles never stop;
Because little upside-down cake,
Your bottom is on your top.[25]

---

[24]*San Francisco Sentinel*, July 14, 1993, p. 39.
[25]*Leatherman's Handbook*, 1983, p. 83.

For Guy Baldwin, who recklessly transgresses the sexual precepts of his S/M elders, roles are not absolute and unchanging categories deeply embedded in the personality or entwined in the DNA like the X and Y chromosomes of one's gender. Instead, they are "situational" and vary according to the mood of the participant, who must be allowed "the freedom to express" both sides of himself, dominating his partner when he is "feeling Toppy" and wants to satisfy his "non-slave needs" and then submitting when he chooses to "turn his bottom side on."[26] This debonair treatment of roles that were once viewed as basic ontological classifications, like "left" and "right" or "inside" and "out," reveals that the very structure of the S/M scene is finally succumbing to the concept of personal liberty implicit in the human potential movement, whose cult of free will has, over time, destabilized the basic divisions of top and bottom. These two diametrically opposite categories are giving way to the philosophy of personal initiative, choice, and self-actualization, to an ethos of relativism that refuses to tolerate inflexible sex roles dictated by some unalterable aspect of the participant's character, a personality trait that refuses to conform to the assertion of the will. In other words, the human potential movement has had both a stimulative effect on the spread of S/M, in that it has encouraged the acceptance of practices condemned by the psychiatric establishment, and a corrosive effect, in that it has eaten away at the fundamental narrative of domination and submission, which becomes increasingly tenuous and unconvincing as sex roles are reduced to little more than "lifestyle choices." In the S/M community of the future, sex roles will have evaporated entirely, killed off by both their political inconvenience and the rhetoric of free will. All that will remain is a series of elaborate techniques for creating intense sensations, an abstract aestheticism that will replace the exaggerated dramas of control and dependence.

If critics of S/M have dealt this narrative a significant blow, they have also encouraged the invention of a brand-new and far less objectionable story line. For many members of the leather community,

---

[26]*Ties That Bind*, p. 62.

S/M is no longer about tying people up or crawling worshipfully on one's belly before figures of masculine authority who force their hungry slaves to chow down on Milkbones or eat Alpo and Gravy Train out of dog dishes. Rather, it is about inflicting pain to achieve higher levels of consciousness and to induce a state of ecstatic mysticism, which the S/M avant garde uses to escape the onus of Western culture, reenacting ceremonies loosely based on American Indian O-Kee-Pa suspension rituals and ancient Hindu Kavandi piercings.

One of the most recent developments in the history of S/M is the rise in the late 1980s of the so-called modern primitives, a group of gay men, lesbians, and even heterosexuals who cover themselves with piercings and tattoos, often during masochistic New Age gatherings that, according to one "pagan priest," enable the participant to "slip into the primal" and become nothing less than "a raging beast."[27] The spiritual leader of this new movement is not, in fact, a homosexual, although he is closely aligned with the San Francisco S/M community: Fakir Musafar, the shamanistic pseudonym for a former advertising executive in Menlo Park who, for many years, led a dual existence as the CEO of a multi-million-dollar PR firm and the grand wizard of Northern California's gay "Magic Faerie Circles." The star of such cult films as *A Man Called Horse* and *Dances Sacred and Profane*, Fakir is a kind of *Ripley's Believe It or Not* circus sideshow who regularly impales himself on meat hooks through his "trapeze tits" and frolics on his own private jungle gym of iron maidens and homemade racks. In this well-equipped torture chamber, he lounges on beds of nails or parallel rows of razor-sharp cleavers in an effort to induce the endorphin highs of what are commonly referred to as "OBEs," or "out-of-body experiences." Although few followers of the modern primitive movement are as committed as this extraordinarily supple contortionist who bends and twists himself like Gumby into any number of anatomically implausible poses, he and others like him have launched an entirely new fashion among young gay people for multiple facial piercings and abstract tattoos that coil and snake over the entire body, forming occult designs

---

[27]Joseph Bean, Interview of Fakir Musafar, *Drummer* 133, Sept. 1989, p. 53.

that suggest the inscrutable symbols of alchemists and astrologers.

In order to downplay the objectionable elements of S/M sex, the leather community has begun to recharacterize the act of being handcuffed to headboards and lashed with nettles both as a form of Eastern meditation and a way of demonstrating deep respect for the casualties of American imperialism in the Third World (as exemplified by such non-Western cultures as the Micronesians, who have tattooed themselves for hundreds of years, or African tribes, who puncture and distend their lips and earlobes with objects as large as tin cans). S/M sex has thus been transformed from an exaltation of patriarchal fascism into an educational foray into multiculturalism, a method of creating out of the body itself a politically correct artifact that advertises the wearer's disdain for Western culture and his admiration for the quaint customs of noble savages. In this way, S/M practices have been profoundly banalized, rendered innocuous by the efforts of one key sector of the leather community to circumvent the problematic politics of submission and replace them with a more acceptable narrative in which, as "leathersex faerie" Joseph Bean puts it, sadomasochists take "a rebel's stand against the ethos of the . . . Judeo-Christian world."[28]

In the modern primitive movement, a fifth disguise for the dungeon emerges next to the dressing room, the clubhouse, the therapist's office, and the laboratory: that of the temple, the ashram where flabby Westerners, living in a decadent and devitalized culture of white-collar automatons, smear their faces with war paint, don grass skirts, dance rain dances, and burn incense to the Great Medicine Man in the sky in order to reestablish their connection with the primordial forces of nature. Leather was first psychologized, then sensualized, and now at last, in an effort to create a kinder, gentler S/M, it has been spiritualized. What began as a satanic movement has become an angelic one; behavior that was once immoral and transgressive has become righteous and pure. Whereas leather emerged in the 1950s as a form of rehabilitation for gay men, a way of getting in touch with their masculinity, it is now, in the 1990s, purging itself of

---

[28]*Leatherfolk*, p. 259.

these archaic patriarchal rituals and becoming a form of theater through which middle-class homosexuals, who enjoy all of the privileges of an affluent, commercialized life, discover a "spiritual pathway to enlightenment."[29] As the founder of what has been called the "asshole consciousness" movement has put it, "for me a day without cosmic erotic ecstasy is like a day without sunshine."[30]

When it started in the 1950s, the leather movement represented the consummate expression of the Western worldview, a cult that revolved around technology, a machine. In the early gay biker clubs, studded leather jackets were the ceremonial vestments of a vehicular religion whose central totem was an unlikely god, a mode of transportation, a device manufactured by a highly industrialized culture. The leather fetish in its earliest forms was rooted in the body of iconography that grew up around heavy equipment and the internal combustion engine, a symbol of industrial power that gay men used for deeply psychological purposes. In the 1970s, as we have seen, the cult of leather detached itself from the motorcycle even as the costumes of the old religion displaced the original object of worship and acquired the status of fetishes in their own right. In a strange twist of fate, by the 1980s and 1990s, a movement that began as an erotic tribute to industrialism, an homage to an icon of Western technology, has mutated into its very opposite, a religion that exalts the preindustrial world of the primitive savage who lives in mud huts in the rain forest, far away from the mechanized environment of contemporary consumeristic culture.

The efforts to normalize S/M sex, to address the nitpicking criticisms of its enemies, to assuage all of their fears and prejudices, and to disguise the leather scene as a healthy, self-affirming lifestyle, as wholesome as Mom and apple pie, will ultimately lead to its disappearance. When kink stops being kinky and becomes as salubrious as vitamins and prune juice, it will lose its appeal for vast numbers of leathermen who thrive on their marginalized status as sexual outcasts, clinging to the glamor of practices that, far from being really

---

[29]*Leatherfolk*, p. 295.
[30]*Leatherfolk*, p. 293.

and truly illicit, have become an almost respectable form of behavior. The campaign to clean up the leather community's image has been so successful that even the most bizarre forms of S/M sex now lie well within the precincts of normality, the very realm in which sadomasochism cannot survive, depending as it does on a strong sense of its own impermissibility. This delicious conviction of wickedness and impropriety is already being undermined by the innocent gregariousness of "Bun-Warming Fund Raisers" at a dollar a whack, four-day intensive retreats that provide hands-on workshops for cock-and-ball torture, and leather weekend roundups called "Bound by Serenity" for recovering leathermen in 12-step programs. The dungeon has gone from being a charnel house, a place where forbidden desires are fulfilled, to a cozy parlor where prayers are said and emotional nourishment is prepared and consumed by men who "find their activities liberating, educational and rewarding."[31] In seeking the legitimization of kink in the eyes of mainstream society, leathermen are committing a very slow act of suicide, a process of self-eradication in which sadists the world over are engaging in the deadliest form of S/M possible, a snuff scene—their own.

The changes that have occurred in the practice of S/M sex and in the propaganda used to rationalize it can be seen as a perfect example in microcosm of both the cooptation of the entire subculture and the obliteration of the gay sensibility, which must be turned into hygienic pabulum if homosexuals are to be accepted by mainstream America. Just as the human potential movement played an instrumental role in the sanitization of the straight majority's image of the homosexual by sanctioning nonmarital relationships, so, too, does the pop psychologist's fractured view of the self, of the healthy divisions between the gay man's erotic pursuits and his professional aspirations, help soften the image of leathermen by enabling them to relegate their questionable preferences to a safe "play space," the dark attic of the gay libido where homosexuals wrestle in private with their internal demons. Here, socially unacceptable primal urges are kept under

[31]Geoff Mains, *Urban Aboriginals*, p. 121.

close guard, quarantined in a murky, nighttime realm of recreational perversions, far removed from the high-powered careers they could potentially jeopardize. If gay liberation helped integrate our jobs and love lives (and produced in the process the economically invincible secret weapon of assimilation, the DINK), the human potential movement helped drive a wedge between them, banishing sexual practices that were too marginal to be accepted by the mainstream. It thus succeeded in insulating our livelihoods from the most subversive aspects of the subculture, from the raunchy games of the torture chamber. The metaphors of selfhood generated by the human potential movement have performed an essential task of preserving the homosexual's economic viability by devising for him an undercover identity that allows him to keep socially unacceptable elements of the subculture out of public view.

Like the new glossy magazines, leather once served to dehomosexualize the homosexual, to cancel out the traditional image of the flamboyant swish with a defiant new countericonography derived from the rebellious fashions of urban street gangs, with their tattoos, tight blue jeans, biker boots, and leather jackets. Two seemingly contradictory aspects of gay culture, leather and drag, often serve the exact same function for homosexuals, that of flouting the prevailing image of the limp-wristed gay man. It is precisely this stereotype that many drag queens rebel against by building into their night lives a satiric ritual ridiculing old styles of feminine behavior, the queeny mannerisms that the modern homosexual flatters himself he has outgrown. In the before and after picture of the subculture presented in the following chapter, I explore how assimilation and nostalgia for the vanishing gay sensibility have redesigned the appearance of the costumes many of us now wear during the annual high jinx of Halloween.

The
Aesthetic
of Drag

I N THE POPULAR IMAGINATION, drag is often mistakenly conflated with transvestism. While many people may believe its primary purpose is to enable men to "pass" as women, verisimilitude has never been the guiding aesthetic principle at work when gay men dress up as bearded nuns on roller skates, topless baton twirlers with rhinestone pasties, or whorish prom queens in fuck-me pumps and beehive hairdos. Only in a minority of cases is naturalism the gay man's first consideration when he chooses the squalid frocks and sensible shoes of dowdy frumps or the resplendent sequined gowns and turkey-feather boas of femmes fatales, outlandish getups that bear only a vague resemblance to what women really wear in their daily lives.

Even in much of the scholarship on the subject, drag and transvestism are discussed as the same phenomenon and romanticized by the politically correct academic in particular as aspects of a single fashionable heresy. This approach flies in the face of the fact they are entirely dissimilar, both aesthetically and psychologically. Suffused with self-deprecating irony, drag is a farcical prank, a laughable hoax for Halloween, while transvestism is the ultimate swindle, the calculated and desperately earnest imposture of an accomplished illusionist who undertakes an act of sexual self-effacement. The stylistic ideal of the transvestite, who attempts to blend seamlessly into the general public, is the understated look of the cautious centrist who prefers unobtrusive clothing that is tastefully subdued and un-assertive and therefore unlikely to draw attention to the inevitable imperfections of his disguise, his suspiciously masculine jaw, husky voice, and square shoulders. The stylistic ideal of the drag queen, on the other hand, is screaming vulgarity, the overstated look of the balloon-breasted tramp in the leopard-skin micro-mini skirt who strives to be loud, tawdry, and cheap. The transvestite, in short, tries to tone it down; the drag queen, to tone it up. Unlike the lone fetishist who, in an effort to "pass," squeezes into corsets and tapes his breasts together to create the illusion of cleavage, the drag queen doesn't flee from his gender but actually incorporates it into his cos-tume. Nor does he fear disclosure as the transvestite does; he invites it. A gesture of electrifying revelation is often central to the comedy of his strapless ball gowns, bulging panty hose, and plunging neck-lines: the startling exposure of the prosthetic breasts, the impulsive removal of the wig, or even more brazen acts of exhibitionism, as in the time-honored drag convention of the floor-length cape which, like a flasher's raincoat, can be flung dramatically open to reveal the flat-chested and scantily clad male body beneath.

While the styles of transvestites have evolved in strict accordance with the seasonal fluctuations of women's fashions, the aesthetic of drag has evolved according to an entirely different set of historical and political factors that have increasingly distorted its relation to women's clothing, thus contributing to its high degree of stylization. Far from being simply a debased form of female attire, drag is an autonomous fashion phenomenon.[1] Its "fright" wigs, fringed bustiers,

---

[1]The distinction between drag and women's clothing also derives from the fact that the earliest public forms of drag were linked with types of entertainment that blunted its subversive impact at the same time they increased its irresistibly vulgar panache. In the late nineteenth and early twentieth centuries, the illegality of cross-dressing gave rise to ingenious schemes to outwit public authorities by disguising gatherings of men in women's dresses as masquerades or Mardi Gras–like carnivals, acceptable public events in which the costumes were already stylized, thus providing protective camouflage for those guests who wanted to appear in dresses. (See George Chauncey, *Gay New York: Gender, Urban Culture, and the Making of the Gay Male, 1980–1940*, New York: Basic Books, 1994, p. 295.) The heavily mannered aesthetic of drag thus emerged out of a politically expedient melting pot of Halloween parties and Bourbon Street parades,

and eight-inch platform heels look as surrealistic as they do in part because drag originally took its cue, not from the streets but from the
stage, from the gaudy, overstated fashions of the actresses and singers
who starred in minstrel shows and vaudeville, the two major varieties
of mass entertainment in which female impersonation flourished. The
architecture of theaters—their cavernous auditoriums—still conditions the appearance of drag: the costumes of early female impersonators, like Liberace's shimmering jumpsuits and jewel-encrusted
smoking jackets, were meant to be viewed from a distance under the
glare of the footlights and thus were designed to sparkle with blinding
flashes of light that made the performer herself seem literally radiant,
framed in a dazzling halo. Just as entertainers had to project in order
to be heard in the furthest corners of echoing theaters with poor acous-
tics and balconies placed at dizzying altitudes, so they had to wear
clothing that would make them stand out for spectators seated hundreds of feet away. Long after drag moved off of the stage and onto the
streets, the most popular fabrics that men use for their costumes come
straight out of the wardrobes of Central Casting, the sequins, rhine-
stones, satins, and lamés that capture and intensify the light, contributing to the drag queen's glittering aura. The interjection of theatrical
costumes into real-world situations involves an enormous displacement of context that makes the drag queen, in her greasepaint and ostrich plumes, a perpetual refugee, a wandering expatriate in search of
her native homeland, the dinner theaters in Las Vegas and the burlesque palaces on Broadway.

But an even more important factor has complicated the relation
of drag to the actual clothing of women. Since the first recorded

---

drunken festivals whose unorthodox dress codes left a permanently flamboyant mark
on a forbidden activity for which they provided a kind of alibi, a legal fiction, lending
it a spurious air of respectability. Even today, the ruse of misclassifying drag under the
rubric of a masquerade continues to influence men's outfits, as can be seen in the highly
conventionalized typology of permissible period costumes that many people still wear
at major gay celebrations where they impersonate such safe drag heroines as Spanish
señoritas in mantillas, marcelled flappers, Queen Elizabeths, Madame Pompadours, and
Marie Antoinettes. The result is that drag is haunted by a kind of phony antiquarianism,
a tendency to recreate anachronistic styles of vintage clothing.

drag balls in the nineteenth century, its primary viewers have always consisted of disproportionate numbers of idle curiosity seekers anxious to experience firsthand the forbidden pleasures of decadent urban nightlife. Embedded within the aesthetic of drag is the sensibility of the heterosexual tourists who constituted the first dumbstruck audiences for which drag queens camped it up, succumbing to the self-dramatizing impulse of turning themselves into theater for voyeuristic onlookers. To borrow from feminist theory the metaphor of the so-called male gaze, the "gaze" of drag is a heterosexual gaze. In fact, it is more like a "gawk" than a gaze, the gawk of the slumming sightseer whose uninformed preconceptions about homosexuality gay men vividly reinforced in a strange act of self-exoticization achieved through clouds of luscious marabou feathers, immense trailing veils, and billowing layers of petticoats and flounces. Far from being a literal imitation of women's clothing, drag was the stylized way that the marginalized members of an emerging subculture sought to present themselves to the mainstream. Pandering to heterosexuals' often callow myths about gay men, the denizens of this beguiling underworld exaggerated the distance and incommensurability between the straight viewer and the ostentatious drag queen, whose feathered headdresses, fluttering scarves, and ruffled parasols echoed the audience's alienation from this inconceivably romantic and unfamiliar world. The unnaturalistic aesthetic of drag is the concrete manifestation of the straight audience's fascinated revulsion from this seamy demimonde whose unthreatening remoteness the drag queen magnified in order to keep these two worlds reassuringly separate.

This exhibitionistic delight in the lurid artificiality of the basic drag wardrobe also presupposes a second, entirely different sort of gaze than that of the heterosexual gawker. This gaze involves, not the naked eye, but the lens of a camera. The drag queen's strangely agitated gestures and grotesque facial expressions make sense only when understood as part of a fantasy central to the whole enterprise of dressing up: he is not just a woman but a celebrity, a great actress greeting her fans, extending her arms in a warm, maternal embrace of gratitude or hurling them triumphantly into the air. Like Divine in *Female Trouble*, he primps and preens in a frenzied dumb show of stagestruck poses that presume the presence of an audience that functions as one of the hidden subtexts of drag, its second gaze: the penetrating scrutiny of the media, the jostling throng of invisible paparazzi snapping away with their magnesium-flash cameras as the imaginary star runs the gauntlet of her hysterical admirers, blowing sloppy kisses and cradling votive offerings of enormous floral bouquets. In gestures reminiscent of those of performers basking in the homage of a standing ovation, the drag queen lives out our deepening obsession with Hollywood and Broadway, a religion that assumes almost fanatical proportions in the strange, ventriloquistic rites of lip synching and in the reverential impersonations of such prima donnas as Bette Davis, Joan Crawford, and Marlene Dietrich.

Modern drag is thus rooted in the culture of mass celebrity, which did not exist before the twentieth century. It is an eccentric by-product of our increasingly intense involvement with popular entertainment, an obsession caused by the role that actresses and cinema played in unifying the gay community. The cross-dresser's gaudy aesthetic, which was stimulated by television and film, presupposes the existence of unprecedentedly vast audiences fixated on a limited pantheon of superstars, who are thus invested with a charismatic mystique far more powerful than that of any celebrity in the past. Drag can, in some respects, be seen as a tribal expression of gratitude to the mass media. Gay men became aware of themselves as members of an oppressed minority, scattered throughout the entire country, only when the United States emerged out of agrarian provinciality and acquired, through radio, television, high-speed travel, and national newspapers, a high degree of centralization and homogeneity. Drag is a celebration of the forces that helped us overcome this fragmentation, a deranged jubilee in honor of the telecommunications industry that contributed to the subculture's collective consciousness. Throughout most of history, cross-dressers imitated women's clothing in general. In the course of the twentieth century, however, drag became something much more specific and complex, not merely the imitation of *a* woman, *any* woman, but an imitation of *the* woman, the star, the Mae Wests, Judy Garlands, and Marilyn

Monroes whose glamorous auras as legendary icons brought us together as fans. If drag was not rooted in the media that helped unite and nationalize the subculture, its aesthetic would almost certainly have been more naturalistic, closer in appearance to the dresses of the transvestite, taking as its models the clothing that ordinary women wear on the streets rather than the sumptuous raiments that cinematic goddesses wear on the screen.

The influence of the culture of mass celebrity on the aesthetic of drag has been intensified by developments within the fashion mainstream, where rigid differences between men's and women's clothing are collapsing into unisex styles that, while liberating women from the inconvenience of traditionally feminine outfits, are subtly eroding the very conditions that make drag possible. In all but the most formal contexts, the distinctions in clothing between the sexes have become so amorphous, so ill defined, that it is almost impossible to do drag of contemporary women's daily wear, which consists of such genderless staples as blue jeans, T-shirts, leather jackets, sweatshirts, khaki pants, backpacks, baseball caps, and tennis shoes. The entire aesthetic of drag has thus been thrown into a state of crisis by the drift toward androgyny in modern fashion where the emergence of a single emasculated prototype for both men's and women's clothing is starving drag of its customary sources of inspiration.

In order to sustain her own precarious illusion of caricatured femininity, the drag queen must therefore reject the interchangeable fashions of the present and restrict herself to styles of dress in which the differences between the sexes are more clearly demarcated. As a result, drag is haunted by nostalgia, by a homesick longing to roll back the leveling developments in contemporary clothing that are fueling the retrospective orgies of dated fashions that form the basis of the whole look of contemporary drag. Dismissing the drearily neutered sporting wear of a society in which both sexes now dress in the drag-unfriendly costumes of jeans and corduroys, gay men resurrect, in a spirit of dizzy antiquarianism, such obsolete museum pieces as white kid gloves, pillbox hats, flapper headbands, mod go-go boots, fox furs, opera-length evening gloves, and cascading blond falls. Only by mimicking archaic styles can the drag queen artificially reinvent the once impassable boundaries between the sexes that have become increasingly permeable as more and more people shop at such stultifying bastions of androgyny as L.L. Bean and The Gap. Modern drag, which has never been literally verisimilar of women's clothing, has thus become even less so. It has such a complex and indirect relation to the actual styles of current dress because it refuses outright to imitate them and is thus driven further and further back into the past in search of outfits that provide the necessary quotient of cartoonish femininity on which it thrives. In short, fashion progresses; drag devolves.

Contrary to the notion that drag fosters experimentation with sex roles and blurs oppressive distinctions between masculinity and femininity, it is in fact sexually reactionary and all but allergic to androgyny. It is far surpassed in its radicalism by what is happening in the arena of everyday fashions, where gender distinctions are indeed being obliterated by the desexualizing revisionism of such unlikely vehicles for change as Adidas sneakers, Levi jeans, and J. Crew sweaters, articles of unisex clothing that are as "transgressive," as destructive of sexual discrepancies, as the gay man's ball gowns, mink stoles, stilettos, and rhinestone chokers are regressive and nostalgic. In other words, drag is not a liberating event in which one breaks out of the sartorial prison of one's gender. The sartorial prison has already been unlocked. We have escaped it. Drag knocks to be let back in.

The aesthetic of drag also underwent enormous changes after the Stonewall riots in 1969 when a handful of grieving drag queens mourning the death of Judy Garland struck back against an inept group of policemen. In the wake of this historic brawl, drag was embraced by large sectors of the gay community as the ceremonial costume of the new militant homosexual and thus the uniform of the burgeoning gay rights movement, which suddenly invested an innocuous camp pastime with enormous ideological significance. As one of the founding members of STAR, the Street Transvestite Action Revolutionaries, reminisced, drag queens were in "the vanguard of the revolution . . . the front liners [who] didn't take no shit from nobody."[2] This statement bristles with the spirit of defiance that made post-Stonewall drag something more than just a gimmicky spoof but an improbable symbol of our dissident heritage and a provocative challenge to the status quo. After 1969, drag became the ultimate impersonation, the impersonation of the female impersonators at Stonewall who were exalted, by a fluke of history, into subcultural Freedom Fighters. Going out in public in women's clothing was transformed into an act of solidarity, a form of civil disobedience that celebrated the gutsiness of a new gay rights heroine, the warrior drag queen.

The flaming assertiveness of this quasi-militaristic figure ironically began to masculinize a hyperfeminine aesthetic, exaggerating its already extravagant mannerisms. The politicizing of drag had a concrete visual impact on the nature of the costumes men began to wear as they came to see themselves as saber-rattling cross-dressers, insurgents in the trenches who proudly displayed hairy legs, hairy chests, and hairy faces, often appearing with neither blouses nor boobs in the surrealistic, fuck-you drag of a figure that constituted a bizarre hybrid, half transvestite, half man. The aesthetic of self-exoticization with which gay men once hammed it up in order to seduce straight gawkers gave way to the aesthetic of the outrageous, a style that actively strives to talk back and antagonize, assaulting and intimidating as vigorously as older forms of drag once mystified and titillated. As a camp institution was elevated into a vehicle for gay rights, men began to subvert the studied loveliness of the old-fashioned drag queen's beguiling getups, her faded sables, yellowing ermines, foot-long cigarette holders, and trains of ruffled froufrou, and cultivated instead a look of angry hideousness, at once abrasive and confrontational. Drag took on the increasingly unfriendly appearance of the "gender fuck," a belligerent, almost gladiatorial look best seen in a uniquely modern form of drag, the bearded nun in a sequined habit, clown-white face,

---

[2]Eric Marcus, *Making History: The Struggle for Gay and Lesbian Equal Rights* (New York: HarperCollins, 1992), p. 195.

and fishnet stockings shrieking obscenities like a snarling pit bull straining at her leash.

Even the facial expressions of drag queens changed in the aftermath of Stonewall. The ecstatic, open-mouthed look of the heavy-lidded goddess languorously licking her lips gave way to the famous drag screech, which involves a ferocious baring of the fangs, as if the drag queen, who often seems to be frozen mid-scream like a Francis Bacon painting, were poised to attack her admirers rather than to embrace them, to frighten them with predatory growls and menacing glares. Politics have now become so integral to the style of drag that aesthetic terms have actually taken on political meanings, as in the word that the drag queen still uses to describe how she looks when she is wearing her dress—namely, "fabulous," an expression that ostensibly refers to her appearance but in fact refers to her rising sense of political empowerment. To look "fabulous" is to feel "fabulous." It is the rallying cry of the effeminate homosexual, an entirely ideological expression signifying his full self-acceptance in the face of social bigotry.

While Stonewall gave new political meaning to what was previously merely a quaint folk custom of a hidden underworld, gay liberation also made the existence of drag more problematic by masculinizing the subculture, which now sought to purge itself of effeminate mannerisms and adopt instead the virility of the ersatz cowboy in chaps and Stetson or the icy detachment of the marine in army fatigues and reflective glasses. Although many gay men began to espouse drag as their own personal credo, touting its medicinal properties as a vehicle for "consciousness raising," dressing up in women's clothing nonetheless challenged the normalized culture of humorless machismo that developed in an era that produced its own peculiar sort of drag, the cowboy boots and bomber jackets of the new paramilitary G.I. Joes who set the fashion agenda during the disco era.

If Stonewall radicalized drag, the new cult of masculinity had the opposite effect; it introduced into men's costumes an entirely incompatible element, the smirking sarcasm of the self-conscious clone whose newfound fear of compromising his manliness clashed with the political belligerence of the warrior drag queen. The rise of the gay ghetto produced an aesthetic that smacks of condescension and embarrassment, of the blushing awkwardness of the new mainstream homosexual, who, frightened by the negative implications of drag, has transformed it into a howling travesty. Unable to experience the kittenish delight in femininity that men used to bring to their outfits, assimilated gay men now deck themselves out in the tasteless scarecrow drag of rainbow-colored wigs, earrings made out of Christmas tree bulbs, hats made out of hubcaps, and breasts as large as watermelons. This new breed of drag queen is so ambivalent about the stereotypically effeminate behavior of the old-style swish that he attempts to deflate his costume, turning it into a knee-slapping farce, undercutting it with such items as towering ancien régime wigs or breasts made out of plastic funnels containing flashing lights. The already tenuous relation of drag to women's clothing became significantly more so as men lampooned what they viewed as a contemptible charade by wearing the wacky costumes of goose-stepping drum majorettes, vengeful Sissy Spaceks in blood-soaked prom dresses, or murderous Joan Crawfords brandishing coat hangers and chasing terrified Christinas in knee socks and pinafores.

Two opposite impulses—one from the left, the other from the right, the one boldly iconoclastic, the other timidly conformist—have thus ironically had the same effect on the aesthetic of drag. On the one hand, the romance of the drag queen as the bottle-throwing insurrectionist in four-inch spikes and laddered stockings clobbering cops with bar stools distorted the relation of drag to women's clothing by contributing to the rage that now seethes in men's outfits, the undercurrents of indignation that poisoned the ethereal daintiness of the old drag queen, who was meant to be both absurd and enticing rather than contemptuous. At the same time, a reactionary impulse stemming from the new normalized culture of wholesome masculinity has produced a style of hyperventilating silliness that provides many homosexuals with comic insulation from the curse of effeminacy. Drag has become part of a ritual of disownment in which we disassociate ourselves from the effeminate behavior of the past through a public act of disavowal, a repudiation of the old stigmatized costumes of gay oppression which we burn in effigy, lynching our predecessors in absentia. Just as the evolution of our pornography, hygiene, underwear, and personal ads resonates with hostility toward the subculture, so the evolution of drag shows the eradication of the gay sensibility. Contemporary homosexuals preserve their masculinity by making a willful effort to sabotage the transformative illusion of drag, to make certain that its basic purpose—to give them the appearance of women—doesn't work, that it is discredited, punctured, invalidated, that the wearer is encased in a protective sheath of irony. Drag is suddenly at war with itself, and has once and for all been released from the burden of verisimilitude to become an hallucinogenic collage of mismatched hand-me-downs and tattered rejects, of trinkets and gewgaws whose dazzling meretriciousness has widened the gap between drag and women's fashions.

After the 1960s, ideology also tightened its grip on the aesthetic of drag when gay men began to use their costumes to reevaluate the whole concept of normality and thus carry out a crucial part of the cross-dresser's agenda: revenge. Contemporary drag performs a wicked dissection of the tastes of the mainstream and thus functions, like the diva's bitchiness, as one of the weapons in the modern homosexual's arsenal of resistance against the homophobia that has condemned him to the marginalized status of an outcast, persona non grata in a society dominated by a highly prescriptive standard of respectable behavior. Just as modern drag is haunted by nostalgia, so it is dominated by kitsch, by the bitch flips and fringed cropped tops of a culture whose intolerance of difference the drag queen gleefully derides by incorporating into her costumes the tackiness of a world of asphyxiating conventionality. When gay men design their costumes, they rifle through the closets of Middle America in search of the fashion atrocities for which drag provides an exhaustively comprehensive showcase, a kind of perma-press, ready-to-wear encyclopedia of JAPishness, a living archive of the egregious tastes of the homosexual's bigoted opponents. The drag queen catalogs these fashion faux pas with a connoisseur's relish for the minutia of suburban shabbiness, creating on her own person a scathing montage of Americana, of gold slippers, polyester pants suits, leather bolero jackets, green monkey muffs, and leopard-skin, stretch stirrup pants. Drag involves a ritual descent of the proverbial tastemakers of our society, gay men, into the morass of American vulgarity where we remake ourselves into funhouse-mirror images of everyone from mall rats to trailer trash, from Moral Majoritarians to Miami socialites. If traditional forms of drag tended to dress upscale, aiming to achieve the glamor and elegance of the inaccessibly remote celebrity, more contemporary forms of drag dress downscale, revolving around the absence of glamor and elegance, around the barbaric and the crude, the beer-can curlers, bunny bedroom slippers, and ratty negligees of bedraggled housewives. It is perhaps because kitsch plays such an important political function in the aesthetic of contemporary drag that many feminists mistakenly believe that drag queens are misogynistic, when in fact they are taunting, not women in particular, but complacent heterosexuals in general. The drag queen orchestrates a brilliant stylistic reprisal against the leisure-suited chauvinists sitting in the Naugahyde La-Z-Boys beneath the velvet paintings, exacting an eye for an eye, a clutch purse for a clingy tube top.

This new satiric function of drag marks a clever inversion of the entire aesthetic of dressing up. Throughout the first half of the twentieth century, drag embodied the way gay men were perceived by the heterosexuals who pressed their noses up against the glass, feasting their eyes on the rare species of marine life that drifted about in their scarves and veils like mysterious deep-sea creatures, fully aware of the tourists staring into this glass house with no exit, this tropical aquarium that was all windows and no doors. But whereas the drag queen was accustomed to being looked at, she has now begun to look back, to gawk in turn, to appraise maliciously the preposterous costumes of the very pillars of our society, who suddenly find themselves the subject of the same patronizing scrutiny they once directed at gay men. No longer does the drag queen accept unquestioningly the role of the exotic exile, the fascinating specimen who staged an elaborate pageant dramatizing her foreignness. Instead, she has now turned the tables and treats the heterosexual world, the ostensible insiders, as freaks and monstrosities. The aesthetic of drag has thus come full circle, so that the traditional spectator of drag, the heterosexual, becomes its new subject, and the drag queen herself becomes the source of the "gaze," the one gawking at the circus sideshows, the stodgy and respectable members of the mainstream whom gay men interpret as the real deviants, the real perverts, the ones most deserving of being ogled and spied on.

If the subject of drag has changed, so has its primary audience. Whereas the spectators of drag used to include large numbers of straight people, drag shows held in gay ghettoes now consist predominantly of other homosexuals who actively strive to exclude the gawkers, the "lookie Lous," as they are called, who are invariably attacked in the gay media as prurient witnesses of a spectacle some gay activists would prefer to keep in house, under wraps, among friends. For many gay men, drag has become a largely subcultural rite intended for a limited band of the initiated, who jealously insist on drawing the curtains and tossing out the riffraff, the heterosexual snoops whose morbid curiosity gay men once welcomed but now find politically suspect, tainted by homophobia, by ghoulish voyeurism. In our efforts to transform a ritual that at one time embraced members of the mainstream—indeed, insisted on their presence— into an event that appeals solely to the sisters of the sorority, many have tried unsuccessfully to transform drag into a sheltered festival cut off from society at large, hidden from the prying eyes of the gate crashers who seek to participate in a ceremony that we hold hostage in the snug, insular world of the ghetto.

This change of audience has proven to be one of the most important factors in the evolution of the aesthetic of drag. When the old-style drag queen was deprived of the audience that once goaded her on to devise ever more extravagant images of the exotic nature of gay life, she was drafted into serving the mundane function of subcultural hygiene, providing a way of disinfecting ourselves of effeminate stereotypes and simultaneously caricaturing the world of prescriptive normality. The result is that, while the aesthetic of drag was in part originally formulated as an aphrodisiac, a means of arousing the tourist with sexually alluring images of a mythic world of lush sensuality, it has now been entirely voided of its erotic content and is used instead as a form of first aid, of therapy, of triage for the survivors, the fag-bashed victims emerging shell shocked out of the wreckage of the homophobic culture that is only slowly granting us our basic civil rights. The homosexual no longer uses drag for purposes of self-exoticization because he is addressing other homosexuals who do not respond erotically to his feminine appearance, to the heavily mascara-ed goo-goo eyes that he once fluttered at straight men, who were enthralled by these moony, lovelorn overtures. As the relation between the man in drag and his audience changes from that of an insider addressing an aroused outsider to that of an insider addressing another unexcited insider, drag is neutered, stripped of its sexual appeal, of its coquettishness, becoming instead a ridiculous travesty staged by lumbering gym queens teetering on stiletto heels.

But even as drag is de-eroticized, it paradoxically becomes more obscene. Men now wear such sexually explicit outfits as ball gowns with prosthetic breasts sewn on to the outside of the dresses, black nighties with gigantic strap-on dildos, and transparent vinyl miniskirts that reveal lacy panties with strategic rips and telltale stains suggestive of deflowerment. The less drag is meant to allure, the bawdier it becomes, with men openly massaging their breasts, squeezing the bulges of their G-strings, sticking out their rear ends and tongues like porn stars in heat, and lying spread-eagled on their backs on parade routes with their helium heels flung into the air and their virginal prom dresses thrown over their heads. Far from seeking to arouse viewers, the contemporary drag queen is in fact precluding this very possibility from the outset through an absurd sexual demonstrativeness that parodies the erotic content of old styles of drag, gutting them of their glamor and thus ensuring that they evoke, not hard-ons, but guffaws, belly laughs, and snickers. Bawdiness destroys eroticism. It is the new prophylactic of drag. Through the low comedy of this aesthetic, we have initiated a kind of subcultural reclamation project in which we attempt to reappropriate a ritual that arose in conjunction with straight people but that we now treat as the exclusive property of gay men. By undermining the aesthetic of self-exoticization that provided the very foundation of modern drag, we are snatching it out of the hands of the tourists whom we once tantalized but whom we now spurn, repelling them with the vulgarity of drag rather than seducing them with its loveliness.

*   *   *

Two different elements of gay culture have responded in two diametrically opposite ways to the phenomenon of assimilation. On the one hand, the leather community made a series of extraordinary compromises that has turned the subversive theater of S/M sex into a safe if somewhat unconventional form of therapy, an acceptable method of self-discovery sanctioned even by the human potential movement. Drag, on the other hand, is becoming less respectable. At the very moment this colorful pastime appears to be on the brink of being embraced by the heterosexual mainstream, as can be seen in the success of such pop icons as RuPaul or such films as *The Birdcage,* many gay aficionados of drag are attempting to stave off the assimilation of this venerable artifact of classical gay culture. Drag has become what it is now fashionable to call a "site of contention," an arena in which curious heterosexuals are forced to lock horns with the stalwart defenders of the vanishing gay sensibility, who are now engaging in a fierce tug of war, a dispute as politically charged as Greece's fruitless campaign to reverse centuries of cultural imperialism by reclaiming the Elgin Marbles. The acrimonious debates in the gay community over its territorial rights to drag reveal the subculture in the act of resisting assimilation, of protesting against the construction of the vulgar theme park that television and Hollywood are building around this endangered bit of camp wildlife, which the most fanatical of gay ecologists want to preserve in a pristine state of unobserved innocence.

The passions raised among politically conscious gay men over the issue of drag provide a gauge of how rapidly our integration into mainstream society is progressing. As the gay sensibility begins to collapse, a tremendous amount of nostalgia is generated among certain homosexual purists who want to protect their ethnic heritage from cooptation, from the pillaging of grave robbers. They cling sentimentally to relics of their history like curators and archaeologists bent on salvaging indigenous subcultural rituals from their destruction at the hands of careless tourists. Sentimentalization is a symptom of the subculture's decline. It represents the wistful longings of a group witnessing the sunset of a sensibility, seeking to intervene in its preservation long after the irreversible process of its absorption by straight society has been set into motion, as we have also seen in the case of gay pornography, which attempts to recreate artificially, through the clumsy convention of the false maiden, the conditions of shame that have all but disappeared from our lives. Our exasperated cries of protest are a requiem for gay culture, an elegy composed by a community in mourning for itself, lamenting its own passing, beating its breast and tearing its hair as stately pallbearers carry the casket into the mausoleum.

The passing of the gay sensibility has also been accelerated by another more literal form of death, AIDS. This is not because AIDS has made a significant impact in the actual number of homosexuals living in America, but because the epidemic has helped push the selling of the subculture up the economic food chain, from the Mafia and the sex industry to respectable corporations, which have discovered in the sympathy generated by the illness a way of appealing safely to an enticing but previously reviled market, now insulated from its illicitness by compassion. AIDS has perversely legitimized the gay community as a group of consumers, making us an object of pity that can be openly addressed through advertising and thus welcomed into the fold of conventional shoppers. What the fight for gay rights has been unable to accomplish in the legislatures, a micro-organism has achieved in the hearts of the American public. The HIV virus has become one of the most important agents, not only of the commercialization of the subculture, but of its acceptance by a society whose once obdurate and closed minds have been softened by the exercise of mercy.

The Kitschification

of AIDS

A CLOUD OF PERFUME as overpowering as a bathroom deodorizer wafts up to our nostrils as we thumb through an issue of *Vogue*. Flipping the pages, we come upon a photograph that, in its inappropriateness, screams out as an incomprehensible non sequitur in the middle of a magazine so deadeningly uniform that it is often impossible to distinguish its advertisements from its articles. In violent contrast to tips on hair types and earnest warnings about the perils of liposuction or of yo-yo dieting, a two-page color spread lies marooned amid ads for Maybelline's Moisture Whip and Clairol's Ultimate Blonde "gel colourant," a curious context for the skeletal figure of a man obviously dying of AIDS. Stretched out in a hospital bed beneath a cheap print of Jesus Christ beckoning from the Great Beyond, he is surrounded by his sobbing father, who clutches him like a rag doll, and his grief-stricken mother, who sits crumpled in despair. Scanning the image for an explanation of the presence in a fashion magazine of this astonishing deathbed scene, our eyes drift to the far left-hand corner of the photograph where several words sit quietly like unbidden guests maintaining respectful silence in the face of the family's anguish; they read, "United Colors of Benetton. . . . For the nearest Benetton store location call 1-800-535-4491 anytime."

An advertisement disguised as a public service announcement, the photograph would seem to represent a magnificent gesture of social goodwill on the part of a company that has long experimented with multiculturalism as a marketing technique, plastering the sides of buses with a frolicking group of teenagers as racially diverse and brightly pigmented as the hues of the manufacturer's own clothing. In fact, however, the image is a public relations stunt that, much as the Wizard of Oz endowed the Tin Man with a heart and the Scarecrow with a brain, attempts to endow the corporation with a political conscience.

When a tragedy as devastating as AIDS is turned into a vehicle for advancing the economic interests of a manufacturer as prosperous as Benetton, the result is a highly compromised form of self-advertisement, a way of flaunting a company's credentials for corporate samaritanship. Since the disease was first identified, a handful of American businessmen have not hesitated to use it to make money. These uses range from the straightforward pitches of morticians (like the one who advertises on the obituaries page of the gay newspaper the *Bay Area Reporter*, promising to tell you "everything you wanted to know about funerals but were afraid to ask") to the more subtle techniques of clothing manufacturers who exploit AIDS in order to sell their products to young, socially conscious consumers who are easily convinced that the act of shopping constitutes a form of philanthropy toward oppressed minorities.

In little over a decade, AIDS has become so thoroughly commercialized that the marketing of compassion now sustains a number of flourishing cottage industries, such as those represented in Under One Roof, the gift store housed in the San Francisco headquarters of the Quilt. This upscale boutique carries an expensive selection of merchandise on the cutting edge of the epidemic: "Cuddle Wit" teddy bears that sport tasteful red ribbons, Keith Haring tote bags, T-shirts stenciled with the words "We're cookin' up l♥ve for People With AIDS," and Wear With Pride's "Awareness Watches," whose dials are decorated with red ribbons. Filled with browsing yuppies beaming with good intentions, this posh yet vaguely sinister retail store, which peddles mementos mori as ghoulishly as tourist traps sell souvenirs, even stocks a unique line of AIDS-specific sympathy cards. One of the most popular features a photograph of a seductive

ACT UP clone leaning inconsolably against a tombstone angel. This baroque image is accompanied by a message that seems as sincere as an undertaker's condolences: "I wonder at times why some are chosen to leave so soon. Then I remember who has left, and I know. God must have wanted them home because he missed them." The crowning jewel of this ingenious entrepreneurial enterprise, which testifies to the increasingly intimate alliance of commerce and death, is a macabre coffee-table book of the Quilt itself. This lavishly illustrated hardcover is meant to be displayed in living rooms, presumably for bored guests to casually thumb through, unaware of the morbidity of exhibiting this monument of carnage as a political knickknack, as innocuous as an album of Impressionist paintings.

Under One Roof, or the "Shop for AIDS Relief," as it is facetiously nicknamed, is just one example of a phenomenon that is affecting AIDS activism on a far wider scale. AIDS has become a veritable playground for kitsch, from rap songs to safe-sex brochures, from the panel in the Quilt representing an enormous airmail envelope addressed to "A Better Place" to Andre Durand's painting *Votive Offering*. The latter depicts an ethereal Princess Di surrounded by saints, placing her hands on an emaciated PWA while dying men in the hospital beds around her strain at their dripping IVs like lurid scarecrows pleading to touch the hem of her skirt. Sentimentality has eroded conventional portrayals of the disease in ways that suggest that, to a far greater extent than other illnesses, the current epidemic is intrinsically vulnerable to the abuse of yellow journalists, celebrities, New Age healers, pop psychologists, holistic chiropractors, and Hollywood producers—to name just a few of those who have transformed it into a trite melodrama, a cozy bedtime story narrated in a teary singsong for the edification of the American public.

Just as food manufacturers add sugar to their products as a way of enhancing their comestibility, so the manufacturers of kitsch employ gaudy cosmetics and stagy lighting to make the pathetic more pathetic, the sad sadder. They use the gentle art of overkill to turn actual events into TV docudrama designed to tug on the heartstrings of sedentary thrill seekers who live vicariously through pity. The outrageously stylized images of the theater of misfortune supply perfect emotional fodder for such public relations extravaganzas as Elton John flying Ryan White to Disneyland to meet Brooke Shields, or Miss America of 1992 haunting the hospital wards where, before an entourage of camera men, she consoles dozens of victims like a princess appearing among lepers. Even Whoopi Goldberg has turned up at displays of the Quilt pushing around a man in a wheelchair, an image that serves as the perfect allegorical emblem of the kitschification of AIDS: just as politicians dandle babies while stumping on the campaign trail, so the epidemic has provided celebrities with men in wheelchairs who serve as paraplegic props for photo opportunities that dramatize their generosity and humanitarianism. An entire social circuit of well-advertised benefits, like the dusk-to-dawn dance-a-thons held by New York's Gay Men's Health Crisis, is now providing celebrities with unlikely venues for careering, for shoring up their credentials for tolerance, and administering a shot in the arm to their flagging reputations. In a bizarre chapter in the social evolution of the illness, movie stars and pop singers now routinely decide which of the bewildering number of fund-raisers they will attend on the basis of who's on the guest list and how much coverage the event will receive in the press—serious considerations for people terrified by the prospect of appearing at a heavily hyped washout shaking empty donation cans in rooms bereft of cameras. AIDS has led to the creation of a new philanthropic elite, consisting not of the dour, religious benefactors of the turn of the century, but of the hip iconoclasts of an entirely secular demimonde, a circle of glamorous hedonists like Madonna, who have discovered in the epidemic a clever method of appealing to their impressionable constituencies, the young, sexually active group that is most at risk.

But there is another, more legitimate reason for the prominent role that celebrities have played in AIDS activism. Hollywood assumed the responsibilities for fund-raising and education that Washington systematically refused to accept during the Bush and Reagan administrations when meager federal support for AIDS research and social outreach was snarled in the red tape of an inefficient bureaucracy. Movie stars—with one notable exception—became the epidemic's unofficial statesmen, glamorous panhandlers who were forced to seek alternative sources of funding, not from the government, but in the marketplace, at charity balls, rock concerts, and fashion benefits where they went hat in hand, scrounging for every nickel and dime that Reagan and Bush were unwilling to allocate.

It was at least in part because of the government's failure to act that AIDS has been heavily commercialized. With inadequate sources of federal funding, the epidemic had to be "sold," marketed to the public like the red ribbon paperweights and the "rose thé" eau de toilette available at Under One Roof. Desperate for private contributions, activists turned the disease into a commodity, into what might be called the AIDS "product," which they introduced onto the market through a media blitz consisting of kitschy public appeals designed to elicit pity. By packaging the epidemic in clichés, they reduced potential donors to a state of maximum susceptibility to the plight of the disease's victims, who were paraded before us like mistreated animals at a carnival.

While all terminal illnesses are prone to sentimentalization—who can forget *Love Story* or *Brian's Song?*—AIDS propaganda has been particularly heavy handed because of the unusual circumstances in which activists were initially forced to raise money to pay for the enormous costs of research, treatment, and education. In the earliest stages of the epidemic, doctors, as well as leaders of the gay community, had to convince the private sector to bear the financial burden of hospital costs, a task they undertook by devising representations of AIDS that appealed to the broadest possible audiences. Because the American public was at best ambivalent, at worst actively hostile, to the first casualties of the disease, it had to be wooed, seduced, and placated with kitsch which activists used as the detergent in which such forbidden topics as anal sex, promiscuity, "bodily fluids," and recreational drug use were laundered. The need for kitsch was a direct consequence of the need for funding, and the more money that was needed, the kitschier the disease became. This vast new philanthropic machine achieved its own self-sustaining momentum, which continues to raise millions of dollars long after the government finally increased federal support and thus ostensibly lessened the need for the sentimentality that opened the floodgates of the American public's generosity. Had the Republican administrations of the 1980s funded AIDS research from the beginning, the epidemic would not have spawned nearly so many outlandish images specifically constructed to overcome consumer resistance and prime the pumps of charitable contributions.

Given the ideological complexity of the disease, which has ravaged entire communities of marginalized groups, the marketing of the AIDS "product" to the American public has involved considerable ingenuity on the part of those who have had to perform one of the most extraordinary revisions in human history of the image of critically ill people, at least some of whom are suffering from a sickness that was sexually transmitted. Unlike less controversial illnesses, such as multiple sclerosis, whose wholesale destruction of the central nervous system has few, if any, political repercussions, AIDS is overwhelmed by kitsch because of our urgent need to render its victims innocent. In order to thwart the demonization of gay men by neo-conservatives, we have attempted to whitewash sexual practices that mainstream America finds socially unacceptable and thus combat bigotry and discrimination with a countericonography that has the unfortunate side effect of turning the victim into a beseeching poster child. Because such characterizations provide an almost impenetrable defense against opponents of AIDS funding, the infantilization of the epidemic's victims has come to play a more and more important role in AIDS propaganda, as can be seen in the mawkishness of the songs of HIV-positive children on the album *Answer the Call* in which choruses of quavering sopranos sing such plaintive lyrics as "We need love/We need compassion to live/We've got hugs/We've got kisses to give."

Of all of mainstream American magazines, *People* has responded most strongly to the political imperative to provide morally simplistic portraits of AIDS victims in an effort to foster an atmosphere of tolerance and understanding. It played a pivotal role, for instance, in what amounted to the beatification of Ryan White, whom they transformed into a living Hallmark sympathy card through shameless literary touches reminiscent of Dickens's Tiny Tim wasting away on the hearth, racked by chills and a hacking cough. Milking his story for its pathos by including in their reports scenes of mother and son kneeling beside his bed in prayer, the magazine seemed to relish his tragic decay, which they described in great detail, from his dainty feet in his "huge, furry 'Bigfoot' slippers" to "his tiny blue fingers,"[1] which he was continually warming over the burner on his mother's electric stove. Although written with the best of intentions, *People*'s frequent profiles of White characterized him as an anachronistic piece of Victoriana, a poetic wraith who reportedly enjoyed wandering in and out of the tombstones of his future burial place, the cemetery in Cicero, Illinois, which he preferred to the cheerless plots of Kokomo, the town of despicable bigots who essentially railroaded him from their ranks because of his HIV status.

From the beginning of the epidemic, AIDS propagandists have found themselves in a peculiar moral bind. On the one hand, they attempt to elicit compassion from the American public by turning the victims of the disease into seraphic innocents, as the mother of one AIDS victim does in her book about her son's death; after returning to Florida from his funeral, she imagines that she sees him soaring like an angel outside of the window of the plane, waving his hand and saying "Hi Mom! Hi Dad! Don't Worry! Be Happy!"[2] But the epidemic's salesmen are, at the same time, just as anxious to avoid using psychologically demeaning rhetoric that portrays HIV-positive people as powerless charity cases, bedridden invalids incapable of lobbying for their own interests. The result is that propagandists must struggle to meet two conflicting ideological requirements by balancing their impulse to render the victim weak, pitiable, and thus guiltless with the image of the triumphant PWA, an indomitable superhero whose life is constantly being held up as a model of unshakable resolve and optimism—a punitively high standard of behavior, it should be noted, for people suffering from a deadly disease. Those who die from the epidemic are almost uni-

---

[1]"24 Hours in the Crisis That Is Breaking America's Heart," *People*, Aug. 3, 1987, p. 61.
[2]Sylvia Goldstaub, *Unconditional Love: "Mom! Dad! Love Me! Please"* (Cool Hand Communications, 1993), p. 19.

versally embalmed in their obituaries in heroic clichés and exhibited to the public like taxidermic displays, waxen, dehumanized "foot soldiers in the war against AIDS" who perish after "beautiful battles" and "long and courageous struggles," exhibiting "tenacious spirits" and a "brave refusal to surrender." The representation of the AIDS victim is thus torn between two extremes of stylization, between the childish image of the guiltless martyr, clutching his teddy bear and warming "his tiny blue fingers" over the stove, and an "empowered" image of the stouthearted hero, whose gutsy brinkmanship in the face of death is deliberately designed as an antidote to the maudlin victimology that lies at the very heart of AIDS kitsch.

In addition to blurring our perception of AIDS with the rhetoric of fearlessness and innocence, activists have invented another propagandistic device to manipulate the way the epidemic is judged by uninfected outsiders. One of the most haunting and yet problematic means by which we have undermined potentially bigoted images of homosexuals and IV drug users is the Quilt, the acres of fabric, embroidered with sentimental mottoes like a vast sampler, that serve as the store-shelf wrapping in which the AIDS "product" has been sealed for immediate public consumption. Just as activists attempt to make the disease economically appealing to the consumer by counteracting homophobic stereotypes with desexed images of AIDS martyrs, so the Names Project covers the epidemic's infantilized victims in what amounts to a macabre security blanket, an immense ideological shield that makes them invulnerable to the attacks of right-wing fanatics. According to Cleve Jones, the Quilt's founder, this embodiment of "pure good,"[3] which emanates "coziness, humanity and warmth,"[4] "touch[es] people's hearts with something so pure and so clear in its message"[5] that it creates an outpouring of compassion that helps fight discrimination.

Despite the hushed tones of reverence with which we are supposed to discuss this unassailable artifact, the Quilt represents the very pin-

---

[3]*The Quilt: Stories from the Names Project* (New York: Pocket Books, 1988), p. 19.
[4]*The Quilt*, p. 12.
[5]*The Quilt*, p. 18.

nacle of AIDS kitsch. It evokes the archaic innocence of nostalgic folk traditions straight out of a pastoral world of buggies and butter churns. "From our earliest days," the jacket copy of the coffee-table book *The Quilt* explains, "the quilt and the quilting bee have been part of American life" and thus constitute a quaint, old-fashioned pastime that Jones, "his eyes glisten[ing] with both sadness and pride," describes as "a way for survivors to work through grief in a positive and creative way."[6] As such comments reveal, those in charge of marketing the disease have attempted to place its primary commemorative monument within the context of a wholesome tradition of American history, to turn it into a kind of faux antique, an artifact from a phantasmal Arcadia. In this mythic, prelapsarian America, AIDS is stripped of its stigma as the scourge of depraved homosexuals and endowed instead with the integrity of a bucolic community in which good-natured rustics of unspoiled simplicity produced their handicrafts in a utopic atmosphere of democracy and cooperation. Appropriately enough, the Quilt, which was designed to encourage consumers to buy a "product" that the government itself refused to purchase, attracts us by exploiting one of the fundamental methods of consumerism: the sentimentalization of handmade goods. For a heavily consumerized society like our own, dependent on the assembly-line manufacture of commodities, the Quilt exudes a spurious aura of artsy-craftsyness, of kindly old grannies in bifocals and bonnets stitching up a storm, plying a trade that harks back to the naive primitivism of the era of *American Gothic*. Nostalgia is thus a fundamental ingredient of AIDS kitsch, the longing for a legendary American wilderness, a disease-free never-never land that preceded the current crisis.

Another reason the actual appearance of AIDS propaganda is often modeled on the pictorial conventions of folk art is that folk art can conveniently substitute for the iconography of the Christian church. Kitsch is the necessary outcome of the politics of AIDS imagery, which is couched in rhetoric associated with therapy rather than in the more conservative rhetoric of religion. Almost from the

---

[6]*The Quilt*, p. 12.

beginning of the 1980s, the image ecologists of the epidemic have urged us to ventilate our pent-up grief as part of a regular program of mental hygiene, as well as a way of bringing the tragedy to the attention of ever wider constituencies, thus rallying new supporters to the cause. Rather than using the venerable Christian ceremonies with which people used to honor their dead, however, many of us have turned away from religion and have sought out in the marketplace new models for *secular* get-togethers, for healing circles and die-ins that are closer in spirit to sensitivity groups or counseling sessions than wakes or masses. This shift from sacred to secular paradigms for AIDS ceremonies has come about in part because of our culture's reverence for the psychotherapist but just as importantly because of the spirit of anticlericalism that permeates the gay community. Many gay people rightly perceive the church as a bastion of homophobia and persecution and therefore as an inappropriate vehicle for implementing the psychological agenda of the new politics of grief.

The most obvious manifestation of this need to invent nondenominational forms of grieving is, of course, the Quilt. When a subculture as intensely secular as the gay community repudiates religion and seeks out new models for therapeutic rituals in which we can purge ourselves of our sorrow, we skirt around the ceremonies available to us in the church and plunder instead an improbable new surrogate for religion: folk culture and pop psychology. The nostalgia of consumerism, the homesickness of an industrialized culture for an agrarian one, threatens to subvert this unprecedented effort to invent from scratch a mourning ritual that appeases both our distrust of religion and our adoration of therapy, a dilemma we have solved by creating this sacramental shroud that reeks, not of ecclesiastical incense, but of the inauthenticity of a shopping mall's Yarn Barn.

There is another more literal way in which AIDS has been sold to the American public. If the propaganda of AIDS activists and the Names Project is addressed to the housewife in Topeka, a second major variety of kitsch is addressed to the AIDS victim himself. It is he who buys this distinct and highly "niched" line of the AIDS "product," which is sold by marketers who exploit, not the lucrative emotion of pity, but the fabulously profitable one of panic.

The staggering blow that AIDS has dealt to our illusions about the power of traditional medicine to resolve every health crisis has unleashed legions of New Age healers, who have rushed into this ideological vacuum like carpetbaggers, unprincipled entrepreneurs who cash in on the desperation of people grasping for straws. AIDS has been overrun with kitsch, not only because of the economic expedience of commercializing the disease, but also because it has breathed new life into moribund New Age fads whose representatives have now encroached on territory that the failures of medical experts have left vulnerable to blatant examples of charlatanry. There are now even channelers who serve as conduits for the pronouncements of ancient "Beings of Disincarnate Intelligence,"[7] "higher spirits" who, in certain circles, are touted as leading experts in AIDS.

The backlash against conventional medicine and the subsequent bonanza of economic opportunities for a new breed of spiritual mercenaries has produced a superabundance of kitsch for two reasons. First, the current crisis has generated another variety of nostalgia, in this case for a premedical era of witch doctors and medicine men who lived before the rise of scientists and their empirical methods, which we have rejected in a regressive fit of pique, a tantrum held against conventional Western authority figures. Contemporary internists have been defrocked in a popular uprising against rationalism and in their place we have set up absurdly anachronistic figures decked out in the trappings of modern medievalism, the magicians and alchemists who perform primitivistic rituals expressive of our disenchantment with medical techniques. One of the masterpieces of AIDS kitsch, the film *Men in Love*, is suffused with longing for an edenic world without science. Retiring from the city to a peaceful land of docile lotus eaters, a group of

---

[7]Jason Serinus (ed.), *Psychoimmunity and the Healing Process: A Holistic Approach to Immunity & AIDS* (Celestial Arts, 1989), p. 225.

grieving Californians, the ideological castaways of a secular society, spurn traditional medicine for moonlit healing circles in Maui where they don grass skirts, mutter incantations, and dance ecstatically around bonfires, repudiating the basic scientific tenets of Western civilization.

But even more productive of kitsch than this frustration with science is the fact that the mindless optimism of the self-help and human potential movements, which have also profited from the paralysis of the medical establishment, is grotesquely unsuited to the fatalistic realities of the epidemic. The bleak prognosis for the victims contrasts dramatically with the happy-go-lucky, "can-do" attitudes of pop psychology's demoralizingly euphoric followers. The result is a whole slew of testimonials by gay men who deny the imminence of their deaths and even claim that AIDS is, as one Bay Area PWA put it in a profile in the *San Francisco Examiner*, "the most wonderful thing that ever happened in my life." This flabbergasting statement is echoed in a letter that a disciple of Louise Hay, the reigning messiah of alternative medicine, wrote to an anthropomorphized image of his disease:

Dear AIDS,

For so long now I've been angry with you for being part of my life. I feel like you have violated my being. The strongest emotion thus far in our relationship has been anger!!

But now I choose to see you in a different light. I no longer hate you or feel angry with you. I realize now that you have become a positive force in my life. You are a messenger who has brought me a new understanding of life and myself. So I thank you, forgive you, and release you.

Never before has anyone given me such great opportunity. . . . Because of you I have learned to love myself, and as a result I love and am loved by others. I am now in touch with parts of my being that I never knew existed. I have grown spiritually and intellectually since your arrival. . . . So again I thank you for giving me this opportunity to have insight into my life. How could I not forgive you, when so many positive experiences have come from your visit.

But you have also led me to the realization that you have no power over
me. I am the power in my world . . .

With love,
Paul[8]

In *Immune Power*, a self-help treatment guide, Dr. Jon D. Kaiser
even advises his clients to initiate a regular correspondence with their
virus which, in a bizarre game of role playing in which the patient
assumes both parts, writes back. Like a pen pal or a well-bred guest
schooled in the etiquette of Emily Post, the virus thanks its "hosts"
"for sharing your feelings with me" "[that I] have overstayed [my]
welcome," adding that "I appreciate your thoughts and I am not
offended by the bluntness of your attitude towards me."[9]

The AIDS "product" sold to the HIV community infuses the
tragedy of the epidemic with an incongruous and quixotic perkiness.
Such exuberance flies in the face of medical realities, as becomes
especially clear when prophets like Hay attempt to incorporate their
clients' illnesses into their upbeat programs for self-actualization, as
if the epidemic were simply another hurdle to be overcome, another
opportunity for growth. The euphemisms of pop psychology, which
also strike a dissonant note in their application to S/M, have turned
much of the self-help literature written for victims of the epidemic
into black comedy full of inadvertent gallows humor, an ideological
self-parody that reveals our culture in the very act of willfully ignoring something that challenges its fundamental ethos: that we
alone are in charge of our destinies and that our bodies, as well as
the world around us, are mere physical extensions of this infinitely
plastic sense of self, this ebullient confidence in the inevitable triumph
of progress. The work of the demagogues of what might be called
the "empathy industry" is premised on the belief that we have full
control of our lives, that no problem is so overwhelming that a simple
act of self-assertion will not ultimately lead to its resolution, and that

---

[8]Louise Hay, *The AIDS Book: Creating a Positive Approach* (Hay House, 1988), p. 30.
[9]Jon D. Kaiser, M.D., *Immune Power* (New York: St. Martin's Press, 1993), p. 108.

nothing can impede our inexorable march onward and upward toward the realization of ever higher forms of spiritual growth. The
modern therapeutic paradigms from which AIDS profiteers derive
their methods thus fail spectacularly to acknowledge the possibility
of tragedy and refuse to admit that anything could evade the re-
sourcefulness of the human will, much as leatherfolk describe bondage and coercion as celebrations of the masochist's autonomy and
liberated selfhood.

Given the outrageous falsifications and ideological deformities that
stem from AIDS profiteering, it is somewhat surprising that the very
place one would expect to find kitsch is in fact relatively free of it:
fiction, one of the chief commodities produced by the disease. It is
not as if such authors as David Feinberg, Edmund White, Paul Mo-
nette, Robert Ferro, John Weir, or Christopher Coe are (or were)
actually all that good but simply that they avoid so assiduously being
all that *bad*. They conscientiously refrain from indulging in tearful
bedside farewells and shocking expulsions of ailing children by heartless parents, all of the schmaltzy, yet appetizing tidbits that the
American public finds so alluring. The fear of sentimentality haunts
fiction about AIDS, serving as a constant brake that keeps writers
from slipping into self-pity, from striving to be poignant yet falling
into bathos. The literary depictions of the epidemic are therefore
often case studies in authorial restraint, in the finicky refusal to drop
one's guard and walk briskly over the eggshells that lie strewn in
the path of this treacherous subject. In fact, the phobia of kitsch is
so strong in AIDS fiction that contemporary literature is in many
ways immune to AIDS, inoculated against it by a tendency toward
flippant ironizing. In John Weir's compulsively jocular *The Irreversible Decline of Eddie Socket*, for instance, the dying protagonist struts
and poses through his disease, striking theatrical attitudes he self-
consciously plagiarizes from Hollywood B films, like the addled
femme fatale in Manuel Puig's *Kiss of the Spider Woman*.

But where AIDS novelists fear to tread, journalists and docudra-
matists go without hesitation, spellbound by the narrative richness of
the disease, which they evoke as a combination of a police procedural
and a James Bond thriller, a tale of cloak-and-dagger intellectual

espionage. Despite their self-righteous posing as staunch advocates of the downtrodden, journalists take pride of place as the ultimate AIDS profiteers, in that they exploit the theatrical nature of the epidemic to advance their own professional interests as entertainers. From Dominique Lapierre's "epic story" *Beyond Love*, a French pot-boiler that turns the history of AIDS into a soap opera, to Randy Shilts's *And the Band Played On*, nonfiction about the epidemic is paradoxically far more fictional than the fiction. Journalistic report-ing on the epidemic has been swamped by narrative, by the need to invent scenes, overhear conversations, tap internal monologues, create suspense, devise artful foreshadowings, and evoke menacing atmos-pheres. The mainstream media have found these literary devices so irresistible that their need to novelize the disease has prevailed ir-responsibly over their obligation to document it.

Nowhere are the kitschifying effects of narrative seen more clearly than in the HBO movie *And the Band Played On*, which adapted for the screen Shilts's New Journalistic history, itself a tissue of recon-structed dialogues and internal soliloquies. Common sense would tell us the book should have been interpreted as a straightforward rep-ortorial documentary with footage from newsreels and interviews, but in fact Hollywood created a fictional reenactment with an all-star cast including a soulful Richard Gere, an earthy Lily Tomlin, and a brooding Ian McKellen. The movie thus novelizes a noveli-zation, so that watching this skillfully plotted sci-fi film, which un-furls before us like *The Andromeda Strain* or *Alien*, we completely lose sight of the fact that it was based on a piece of journalism rather than on fiction.

This strange confusion of genres was made possible by the fact that AIDS journalists adopt an approach that, in its improbably in-timate point of view, allows us to study the human tragedies of the epidemic at close range, as if we were viewing the scene through a hidden camera, in such thrilling proximity that we are actually seeing the events as they occur on the page. Assuming the perspective of omniscient third-person narrators, reporters minimize our awareness of the necessarily secondhand nature of the facts they provide by in effect transforming the reader himself into the witness or source of the report. We are positioned in such a way that we are literally in the hospital when the grief-stricken wife profiled in the article in *Ladies' Home Journal* entitled "AIDS & Marriage: What Every Wife *Must* Know" paces frantically up and down the echoing corridor keeping "a silent and solitary vigil"[10] before her dying husband's quarantined room. Likewise, we become eavesdroppers in the very mobile home—indeed, in the very *mind*—of the victim of the bigoted southern town profiled in *U.S. News & World Report*'s article "Outcast" who prayed as a teenager for God to make him straight: " 'Please, dear Lord, change me,' Steve prayed nightly as he lay in bed as a youth in his father's trailer."[11]

The ethical justification for these vivid recreations of scene, which induce in the reader the feeling of what might be called "presence," of "being there," an ideal that constitutes the highest aim of contemporary journalism, is that the reporter is trying to bring the disease alive for us, to make it "real" and thus awaken our sense of moral responsibility to its victims. The danger of this approach is that, in packaging AIDS as a spectacle the American public can accept and thus fund, journalists have turned the epidemic into a kind of medical theme park where their audiences are treated to the thrills and chills of a shocking peep show that gives them direct access to the most intimate details of the victims' everyday tragedies. The kitsch of AIDS journalism resides in the fact that this transparent rationale of throwing us into the mythical front lines of the disease justifies the most extraordinary invasions of privacy, with the didacticism of an orchestrated series of expertly staged visualizations and tableaux vivants becoming the perfect disguise for prurience. Our roving reporter has carte blanche to probe into subjects as intimate as the little boy who asked to be buried with his favorite stuffed animal, and the mother who lovingly combs the hair and kisses the corpse of her son in the secluded chapel of a funeral parlor. The pose of the responsible reporter simply provides cover for the ambulance chaser who rummages around amid the smoking debris of the crash site in search

---

[10]Katherine Casey, *Ladies' Home Journal*, May 1987, p. 151.
[11]*U.S. News & World Report*, Oct. 12, 1987, p. 64.

of some sufficiently morbid piece of picturesque gore, a touching
exhibit of human misery that camouflages what is in effect the gloating and wallowing of pure voyeurism as a socially redeeming effort
to inform and instruct his readership. In this way, reporting on AIDS
has been upstaged by storytelling, journalism by kitsch, and the tragedies of real individuals turned into circus sideshows in a bustling
fairground where we trample over other people's sufferings amid the
ice cream vendors and the hot dog stands that have sprung up right
in the middle of our hospital wards.

The gay market is so appealing to manufacturers not only because
homosexuals are psychologically predisposed to shopping as a means
of redressing social inequalities through displays of tastefulness, or
because we can be easily exploited as a bridge market, but because
the current health crisis has afforded a convenient solution to a re-
current image problem affecting corporations. In a world sensitized
by the consumer-protection campaigns of Ralph Nader and scandals
about the potentially life-threatening dangers of defective products,
from exploding gas tanks to leaking silicon breast implants, the
American public is all too ready to believe that manufacturers are
unscrupulous, price-gouging capitalists who have no social conscience
whatsoever. Given this atmosphere of mistrust, it would be naive to
interpret the outpouring of corporate support for AIDS research as
an entirely disinterested act of philanthropy. Instead, the rush to
attain a place on the honor rolls of America's most generous companies must be seen as a calculated attempt to correct a major perception problem and foster a kinder, gentler image of the
conglomerate as a team player, a responsible member of society willing to do its part for the good of the country. Since the 1980s, homosexuals have become useful in helping CEOs improve public
relations by allowing them to create the appearance that they are
contributing to the solution of the most urgent health crisis of our
time, either through advertisements disguised as public service an-
nouncements, as in the case of Benetton, or through hefty corporate
grants to AIDS organizations, as in the case of such companies as—
to name only a few of the most charitable—IBM, American Airlines,

Chevron, and Levi-Strauss. The assimilation of the gay market into the economic mainstream has thus found an unlikely ally in the epidemic. Our transformation into a pretext for evincing compassion, for displaying corporate good samaritanship, has ironically strengthened the bonds between the gay community and the business world, which now work together in a synergistic new relationship that will undoubtedly grow even more intimate as companies begin cashing in on the potential of this eager new market.

Just as glossy magazines, which also decommercialize shopping through the politics of economic clout, sanitize the image of the homosexual for their advertisers, so activists and journalists have sanitized the image of the AIDS victim in order to ensure that the American public will respond compassionately to his plight. This process is emblematic of the way in which the entire minority must be stripped of its subversiveness if it is to be integrated into society at large. Assimilation necessitates the destruction of the gay sensibility and its replacement with a benign image of the desexualized, Teflon homosexual who pays a high price for his moral redemption: namely, the elimination from his behavior of unsavory reminders of the outlawed subculture in which he lives. In the kitschification of the AIDS victim, we can actually observe mainstream society in the very act of absorbing a troublesome minority into the fold of conventional Americans by neutralizing its distinctive features, weeding out its morally unacceptable qualities, and fabricating for it a wholesome identity. This process only reveals how provisional and disingenuous our society's acceptance of ethnic differences really is.

In other chapters, we have seen how one of the primary forces behind this process of assimilation, the human potential movement, advanced the cause of gay rights by legitimizing relationships other than traditional marriages. But although the pop psychologist's philosophy of personal fulfillment helped immeasurably to improve the image of homosexuals in the eyes of the American public, a religion that celebrates choice and self-initiative, that urges its adherents to take control of their lives and actualize their full potential, made gay men particularly vulnerable to the ultimate impediment to the personal freedom and unfettered individuality he extolled. The AIDS epidemic triggered, not only a medical emergency, but an ideological crisis in a subculture whose intellectual foundations left its members unprepared to be thwarted in any way, deprived of life, liberty, and the pursuit of happiness, the very things they had been taught were available to them merely by asserting themselves as virtually omnipotent free agents capable of achieving whatever goals they set. The human potential movement deprived us of the sense of fatalism that might have allowed us to face the disease more stoically, resigning ourselves to it by embracing an almost medieval belief in the fickleness of fortune and the uselessness of fighting something well beyond our control. Had we not been so thoroughly indoctrinated in the superficially genial precepts of self-actualization, we would have been more prepared to accept the reality of our powerlessness, of our inability to triumph over a biological catastrophe by sheer force of will. Our failure to accept this fact becomes disturbingly evident in our susceptibility to the charlatanry of spiritual healers, who try to convince gay men that they can destroy the virus simply by writing it a polite, businesslike letter of dismissal and telling it in no uncertain terms, like a lawyer reminding the defendant of a lawsuit of a contractual obligation, "that you have no power over me," that "I am the power in my world." A subculture strengthened by this joyously optimistic philosophy of self-assertion was pathetically ill equipped to accept a cruel necessity of life that contradicted one of the chief intellectual tenets of gay liberation.

In our discussion of drag, we saw how the spread of nostalgia is both a tribute to traditional gay culture and a symptom of its decline. Our zealous overprotectiveness of this key institution, which some men attempt to seal in a time capsule as an irreplaceable souvenir of a lost era, stems from the fact that homosexuals have begun to sentimentalize historical features of the gay sensibility as a protest against the inexorable process of their acceptance by society. The same sort of nostalgia emerges in the before and after image of gay propaganda drawn in the following chapter. As assimilation progresses, the literature of the gay pride movement becomes more and more antiassimilationist, with the ironic result that the less marginal we become, the more we romanticize our marginality as an outlawed group, a status that is now largely the self-flattering fiction of a minority well on its way to achieving complete social integration. When we cease to experience oppression, we grow intensely fond of the sensibility that grew out of this oppression, the rituals that can be admired for their own sake only when they no longer serve the same function for which they were originally invented. Their increasing lack of utility is the prerequisite for their enshrinement as museum artifacts.

Glad-to-Be-Gay

Propaganda

THE FIRST MEETINGS OF the Mattachine Society in 1952 were anything but raucous blowouts. Wearing neatly tailored suits, solemn dignitaries, as lugubrious as church elders, performed such monotonous duties as electing board members and voting on amendments to the corporate charter in a room so funereally free of camp that one exasperated participant recalls that she finally exploded, "For God's sake! You're acting like directors of Chase Manhattan Bank!"[1] Early gay liberationists were not dangerous radicals conspiring to overthrow basic social institutions but cautious centrists who waved the flag and pledged "allegiance to church, state and family," a sentiment espoused in the society's official slogan "evolution, not revolution."[2] Through this painstakingly slow process of allaying fears and subverting stereotypes of gay men and women, they sought to reassure society that "an organization of homosexuals is capable of being responsible and conservative."[3] To secure the sympathies of hostile outsiders, One, Inc., another early "homophile" organization, told its membership that it must not wait "for the

---

[1]Betty Berzon, Ph.D., and Robert Leighton (eds.), *Positively Gay* (Celestial Arts, 1979), p. v.
[2]Harold Sylvester, "Why I Am a Member of the Mattachine Society," *The Mattachine Review*, Mar./Apr. 1955, p. 30.
[3]Lyn Pedersen, "A Forgotten Commonplace," *The Mattachine Review*, Nov./Dec. 1955, p. 26.

heterosexual to strew your path with roses [but must] do a little rose strewing yourself,"[4] sprucing up its tarnished public image through a propitiatory act of Uncle Tomism that involved "carry[ing] ourselves in an acceptable manner"[5] and ostracizing as lepers what one reader called "the obvious painted bitches."[6] During the 1950s, gay liberation lacked the one crucial ingredient that defines it to this day, its association with leftist politics, with the revolutionary posturing that was entirely absent from the archaic homophile movement, which was led by what the post-Stonewall gay liberationist dismisses as conformist quislings intent solely on mollifying the prejudices of an intolerant society.

Far from romanticizing their minority status as a colorful ethnic identity, early gay liberationists exhibited very little of what is now such a key provision of the activist's agenda that it is almost impossible to imagine a gay rights movement without it: "gay pride." The Mattachinists explained homosexuality as a biological accident, whose stigma they sought to eliminate through wholesale integration into a society they hoped would soon find their sexuality, not glamorous, but utterly transparent, as morally insignificant as being color blind or left handed. To accomplish this, they deliberately strove to de-exoticize homosexuality, to portray gay people as harmless, hardworking citizens with mortgages and school loans, as dutiful sons with aging parents and veterans with war wounds, "human beings very like their neighbors working at dull jobs with inadequate wages, struggling to meet the payments on furniture from Sears for the sixty and seventy-a-month apartment on unromantically-named streets like Sixth or Central or Main."[7] Gay propaganda from the 1950s and 1960s is characterized by what might be called the Shylock argument, the assertion that a homosexual is not a freak of nature, a dissolute libertine well beyond the pale of respectable society, but "a creature

---

[4]Sal Makis, "How to End Hostility Towards Homosexuals," *One*, Aug./Sept. 1956, p. 13.
[5]"The Fifth Freedom," *One*, Oct. 1955, p. 26.
[6]*One*, July/Dec. 1967, p. 15. Letter from reader.
[7]David I. Freeman, "Literature and Homosexuality," *One*, Jan. 1955, p. 15.

who bleeds when he is cut, and who must breathe oxygen in order to live."[8] Early gay rights propagandists and those of the post-Stonewall era can be best differentiated by their contradictory attitudes toward the issue of assimilation: while the former sought the destruction of homosexuality as a defining trait of the gay person's character and indeed eagerly anticipated the obliteration of his minority status, which had none of the cachet it has now acquired, the latter sought the exaltation of homosexuality as the central element of their personalities. They actively instilled in their audiences a sense of ethnic patriotism and team spirit, as well as an almost smug complacency about the privileges of being gay.

As repugnant to the post-Stonewall activist as this indifference to the glamor of ethnicity were the ways in which early writers attempted to gain pity for homosexuals by likening them to the maimed and the crippled, to "men with a kidney or lung removed"[9] or to "Peg-Leg Bates," a talented Negro who, to the delight of cheering crowds of white onlookers, danced spasmodic ditties on a prosthetic limb while his appreciative audience pelted him with coins.[10] Writers for the *Mattachine Review* didn't hesitate, even at the risk of depicting themselves as bizarre curiosities, to tug on heterosexuals' heartstrings by conjuring up images of gay men as the scorned dregs of humanity reduced to their miserable condition by virtue of an hereditary flaw. As time went on, however, activists became increasingly uncomfortable with the arguments of writers who pleaded for tolerance in articles that read like Dickensian sob stories bewailing the unhappy fate of a ragged army of deformed beggars, of the blind and the paraplegic, each of whom "was born that way. He cannot change even if he wants to. . . . Why, then, is he punished for something he cannot help?"[11] Writers who asked such questions as "must

---

[8]Ward Summer, "On the Bisexuality of Man," *Mattachine Review*, July/Aug. 1955, p. 16.

[9]Luther Allen, "Homosexuality . . . Is It a Handicap or a Talent?," *Mattachine Review*, July/Aug. 1955, p. 8.

[10]Allen, "Homosexuality," p. 10.

[11]Anonymous, "New Deal for Deviates," *One*, Oct. 1955, p. 14.

we beat the cripple because he had polio as a child?"[12] turned the homosexual into a congenital reject who merited, not acceptance and equality, but the compassion and clemency of selfless straight altruists who were encouraged to exercise noblesse oblige and "look down in mercy"[13] on those who suffered from nothing more than an ignominious biological condition.

By the mid-1960s, the propaganda of powerlessness seemed almost repulsively archaic, and gay ideologues recoiled from the efforts of the early Mattachinists to milk the homosexual's plight for its pathos. Instead, by 1965, gay newspapers like *The Vector* stated that "we want to get rid of . . . feeling sorry for ourselves. We are *not* helpless"[14] but rather are determined and powerful. So powerful were they in fact that, unlike the first gay activists, who claimed the homosexual had no control over his desires, many of the new gay liberationists claimed they actually *chose* their sexual orientation, that they embraced it as a positive aspect of their identity rather than stoically endured it as a disastrous genetic affliction. As the gay rights movement gathered steam, writers thumbed their noses at the straight establishment by asserting that, far from being the involuntary behavior of a pitiable victim, homosexuality was a blessing, "a conscious choice in human living."[15]

Within the context of the history of gay propaganda, however, this proud assertion of one's sexual preference represented a fatal miscalculation. Once gay men emphatically stated that their homosexuality was an "option" they had selected from a whole range of possible sexual behaviors, they placed themselves in an extremely untenable position vis-à-vis the homophobic American public, who now came to believe that their sexual orientation was indeed—to use the noxious shibboleth of the evangelical right—a "lifestyle choice." It is one of the paradoxes of progay literature that, in many instances, the arguments of activists did not counteract and neutral-

---

[12]"New Deal," p. 14.
[13]*One*, Apr. 1955, p. 23. Letter.
[14]*Vector*, Mar. 1965, p. 1.
[15]R.O.D. Benson, *What Every Homosexual Knows* (The Julian Press, 1965), p. 7.

ize antigay propaganda but in fact fueled it, giving religious moralists the ideological loopholes they needed to attack a segment of the population once protected by the mawkish, if effective, rhetoric of powerlessness.

For a brief period before and after Stonewall, the tone and content of gay propaganda changed dramatically. While gay activists often misrepresent the riots as the dawn of a national movement that erupted into existence during a single flash of defiant anger, it is far more accurate to view the 1969 disturbances and the mountains of revolutionary slogans and brash socialist manifestos they inspired as a temporary detour in the history of gay politics. What sets the political rhetoric and style of activism typical of the Stonewall era apart from the quiet and orderly picketing engaged in by the first gay organizations (which were so determined to convey the "right" impression to the public that they forced their members to attend rallies dressed in conservative business attire) is the conflation of the gay rights movement with the counterculture. In the late 1960s, gay liberation, which had hitherto been led by a self-deprecating group of conciliationists, merged with both the civil rights movement and feminism to form a militantly left-wing coalition of oppressed peoples struggling against a single, monolithic enemy, the white patriarchy, the so-called Pig Class (which such organizations as the Gay Liberation Front and the Street Transvestite Action Revolutionaries dubbed "the Establishment," "the carnivorous system of Capitalism," "straight white Amerika," the "Ruling Elite," "the Brotherfuckers," and "the Mastah Man"). New Left firebrands rejected the conservative, assimilationist propaganda of the Mattachinists, whom they dismissed, with some justification, as "Uncle Toms and Aunt Marys," "weak-willed apologists and wishy-washy do-gooders" who groveled before "their straight puppet-masters," indulging in a "contemptible Pollyannaism [that] is like a cancer rotting out the very vitals of the gay liberation movement."[16] The political propaganda of the homophiles was so patently *un*radical until the mid-1960s that contem-

---

[16]Justin Raimondo, *In Praise of Outlaws: Rebuilding Gay Liberation* (Students for a Libertarian Society, 1979), p. 42.

porary activists tend to discount the contributions that such organizations as the Mattachine Society and One, Inc. made to gay liberation, as if Stonewall were an act of spontaneous combustion entirely without precedent, a coup d'état from which gay politics sprang up overnight, emerging fully formed from an ideological vacuum. In a deliberate act of oversimplification motivated by their contempt for their timid political forebears, they designate 1969 as ground zero of the struggle, the beginning of a brand-new era, a millennium that divides gay rights into a "before" and an "after," a B.C. and an A.D., a Dark Ages of obscurantism, slavery, and cowardice and a blinding Enlightenment of emancipation, courage, and rebellion.

Before Stonewall, gay propaganda was aimed at two distinct audiences: the straight majority, who had to be prodded into a recognition of the error of their ways, and homosexuals themselves, who needed to be pampered and cajoled into self-acceptance through a constant barrage of uplifting affirmations of their self-worth. For a brief time after Stonewall, however, gay propaganda had only one audience, gay people, while straight society was demonized into an unaddressable enemy, a brutally repressive regime of stuffed shirts who, safely ensconced in the boardrooms of corporate "Amerika," needed to be overthrown. The radicalizing of gay politics thus immediately severed a once vital link with an audience that the unradicalized Mattachine Society, which was so bashful that it assiduously avoided the word *homosexual* in its mission statement, had taken great pains to cultivate through what they called their "public relations and educational project." An early antidefamation league, this far-flung national network of outreach programs, seminars, and public lectures was intended to influence not only heterosexual citizens but political officials as well.

How completely many post-Stonewall gay liberationists cut off dialogue with the straight establishment can be seen in a passage from an article that at first sight appears to address heterosexuals directly, although it becomes immediately apparent that its author, Martha Shelley, a member of the Gay Liberation Front, had little intention of winning converts to the cause:

Look out, straights! Here comes the Gay Liberation Front, springing up like warts all over the bland face of Amerika, causing shudders of indigestion in the delicately balanced bowels of the Movement. Here come the gays. . . . We are the extrusions of your unconscious mind—your worst fears made flesh . . . we are the sort of people everyone was taught to despise—and now we are shaking off the chains of self-hatred and marching on your citadels of repression. . . . Are you uneasy? . . . We want you to be uneasy, to be a little less comfortable in your straight roles. . . . You will never be rid of us, because we reproduce ourselves out of your bodies.[17]

What is interesting about this passage is that, while it claims to be addressing heterosexuals, its reader is in fact a pure fabrication, a straw man who is forced to bear the brunt of the author's aggression, a human dartboard at whom she hurls barbed socialist slogans. The use of the second person is a rhetorical ploy that dehumanizes the enemy for the malicious entertainment of the passage's real audience, other homosexuals, who are meant to chuckle with glee at the spectacular discomfiture of terrified members of the "Pig Class" quaking in their boots at the frightening prospect of an imminent bloodbath.

In the years immediately following Stonewall, the gay propagandist and the heterosexual majority became so polarized that the latter was transformed into a grotesque chimera at whom the gay activist did little more than shout revolutionary platitudes, savoring the unprecedented opportunity of treating the heterosexual outsider as a dastardly cartoon villain. Although we have been conditioned to regard Stonewall as the starting point for real progress in gay rights, the propagandist of the 1950s ironically had a far closer and more pragmatic relationship with his straight audience than the post-Stonewall propagandist, who, after discovering leftist politics, withdrew from his enemy into a self-enforced state of belligerent insularity. For a short time during the 1970s, this isolationist radicalism ghettoized our propaganda, turning it into revolutionary gibberish muttered in a soundproof room.

---

[17]Martha Shelley, "Gay Is Good," in *Gay Flames*. (New England Free Press, 1972), pp. 3–6.

The demonization of the heterosexual enemy went hand in hand with the apotheosis of the homosexual and the sentimentalization of our minority status, the second major development in gay politics after Stonewall. Whereas in the 1950s and early 1960s, homosexuality was usually viewed as a distinct handicap, after Stonewall it became an inestimably valuable privilege, an enriching character trait that activists enshrined as the source of a subversive "ethnic" identity. Suddenly, gay was not only good, it was *better*, an asset that freed gay people from the shackles of conventionality, from the drudgery of a mortgage, a two-car garage, and a nine-to-five job. Carried away by the enthusiasm that followed the riots, gay liberationists began to describe homosexuals, who are "more advanced than straight[s],"[18] as the chosen people destined to lead benighted heterosexuals out of their enslavement to the nuclear family and into the promised land of total sexual equality, "the free society of the future,"[19] a communal paradise inhabited by androgynous flower children who dropped acid and read Carlos Castaneda. Not only was assimilation no longer the goal of the gay rights movement, but the very idea of forfeiting one's marginality was ridiculed as the naive and insulting integrationist fantasy of activists who did not seem to recognize that, given the dilapidated state of capitalism, "it is highly questionable whether we can or want to integrate into the present system."[20]

Stonewall, in short, did not mark the beginning of gay liberation but simply its redefinition as a revolutionary, countercultural movement whose anarchistic thrust can be seen in the battle cry of the gay magazine *Come Out!*, which warned conservative Americans that "you better start shakin'—today's pig is tomorrow's bacon!"[21] Although the political aftermath of the riots allowed many homosexuals to be more open about their sexuality than they had ever been before, the combination of the new separatism and the self-congratulating

---

[18]*Gay Liberation Front Manifesto*, 1971, p. 11. No author.
[19]*Gay Liberation*, p. 11.
[20]*Stonewall Means Resistance* (Stonewall Organizing Committee, 1978), no page numbers. No author.
[21]Rodger Streitmatter, *Unspeakable: The Rise of the Gay and Lesbian Press in America* (Faber & Faber, 1995), p. 133.

excesses of ethnic pride had a somewhat ambiguous effect on the progress of gay rights, at once contributing to the homosexual's isolation from mainstream society and providing an impediment to the very reforms that Stonewall is mistakenly credited with inspiring.

The demonization of the enemy was kept alive by the publishing industry that catered to gay readers following Stonewall. Within years of the riots, an enormous groundswell of interest in books and newspapers specifically devoted to conveying "positive" images of homosexuals produced a class of professional propagandists who, unlike the selfless volunteers of the early gay rights movement, derived a substantial portion of their income either through their writing or their appearances at liberal universities where they received princely honoraria for delivering lectures and hosting pep rallies. The late gay business magnate David Goodstein, the multimillionaire owner of the *Advocate* and the author of *Superliving: You Can Have the Life You Want*, added significantly to his already vast wealth by barnstorming across the nation promoting his "Advocate Experience," a cultish self-help program for homosexuals based on Werner Erhard's est; journalist Merle Miller became famous after publishing an article on being gay in the *New York Times Magazine*, a piece that enabled him to hit the talk-show circuit, chatting regularly with Dick Cavett about "what it means to be a homosexual"; and Troy Perry, the nondenominational pope of gay Christians, took the country by storm by preaching glad-to-be-gay sermons from the pulpit of his Los Angeles–based Metropolitan Community Church. Small gay presses like Alyson Publications, Gay Sunshine Press, the Gay Presses of New York, and Persona Press sprang up from coast to coast, bombarding gay readers with fiction as tendentious as Stalinist tracts, from the novels of Richard Hall and N.A. Diaman to those of Felice Picano and John Preston. For the first time in history, it became possible for writers to earn a living by writing books for an exclusively gay readership, as in the case of such lavender blockbusters as Rita Mae Brown's *Rubyfruit Jungle*, Gordon Merrick's *The Lord Won't Mind*, Armistead Maupin's *Tales of the City*, Larry Kramer's *Faggots*, and Andrew Holleran's *Dancer from the Dance*.

During the 1970s, the propaganda industry consolidated its economic base. It ultimately employed a significant number of people who had a vested financial interest in maintaining the conditions most favorable to their careers and in keeping alive for the public a vivid sense of the service they performed as a bulwark against the encroachments of the homosexual's ever-vigilant enemies. Once it became possible for authors and publishers to make money by supplying a newly organized market with both uplifting messages about our glamorous marginality and dire warnings about the schemes of our enemies to establish theocracies and deport us to concentration camps, gay propagandists essentially fell in love with the very thing they professed to despise: the oppression that provides the industry's rationale.

The holocaust fantasies of Don Clark, one of the most widely read of the glad-to-be-gay propagandists of the 1970s and 1980s, exemplify the alarmist jeremiads with which a well-established industry reinforces the fears and insecurities of its market. Writing in the late 1970s, Clark obsessively imagines what it would be like if the country were wracked by a homophobic backlash that would imprison homosexuals in their desolate ghettoes like the Jews in Warsaw, policed at gunpoint by bloodthirsty National Guard troops equipped with tear gas and attack dogs. If such a genocidal nightmare should come to pass, Clark advises that we either go into exile and eke out a hard-scrabble existence abroad living hand to mouth "washing dishes" ("keep your passports up-to-date . . . and have an escape route planned"[22]) or go underground, banding together in terrorist brigades of resistance fighters who, donning olive drab and shouldering bazookas and grenade launchers, "must defend ourselves by the most aggressive and efficient means available."[23] It is also important to remember, Clark tells us, already poring over maps of the front lines, that we are "not preparing for a picnic. A holocaust is no fun."[24] He is so taken with this vision of the mass carnage that would ensue during the homosexual Final Solution that he even imagines the

---

[22]Don Clark, *Living Gay* (Celestial Arts, 1979), pp. 140–141.
[23]*Living Gay*, p. 137.
[24]*Living Gay*, p. 142.

formation of the gay equivalent of Israel. This unconditionally receptive homeland would be governed by the Law of Return and located, not in the Middle East, but in California, which we would take over through strategic purchases of real estate, ultimately enabling us to "offer safety to escapees from other states."[25] Clark's hallucinatory ravings about the brutality of the sexual fascists of the future do not reflect real fear about the hurdles facing the gay rights movement but a more palpable fear about the loss of the primary tool of the propagandist's trade, the enemy, a figure that becomes ever more demonic the less of a threat he poses. When this rhetorical device subsides into a state of relative harmlessness, as he inevitably will in real life, the writers who depend on him for their living will be led to invent ever more alarming bogeymen, who while bearing little relation to reality, will successfully remind their readers of the value and necessity of their creators' increasingly obsolescent work.

When propagandists are not demonizing the enemy, they are re-making themselves in its image. One of the most enduring creations of the early gay rights movement was the Good Gay, a dutiful patriot, a practicing Christian, an irreproachably high-minded civic leader. This mythically pure homosexual made its debut as an instrument of propaganda during the first major crisis in the history of gay activism: the witch-hunts of the House Committee on Un-American Activities. During Senator McCarthy's reign of terror, the Mattachinists became acutely conscious of how susceptible homosexuals were to accusations of being seditious parlor pinkos à la Burgess and Maclean, crypto-communist members of all-gay spy rings that, out of financial self-interest, callously jeopardized national security. In order to refute such allegations, gay writers frequently wrapped themselves in the flag and took every opportunity to express civic pride in speeches couched in distinctly jingoistic terms, as in the following passage from an anonymous response to a red-baiting Republican senator entitled "Open Letter to Sen. Dirksen":

---

[25]*Living Gay*, p. 141.

> Our hearts do not beat less fast [than your hearts] at the excitement of a
> political rally. . . . Our tears do not flow less freely than yours at the loss of
> husbands, sons and brothers in warfare with Communism because we are
> homosexual. Our hearts are not less full of pride and honor at the sight of
> massed American flags because we are homosexual. We do not work less hard
> for America, or love her less, or support the Republican administration and
> policies less wholeheartedly because we are homosexual.[26]

The passage functions as a sort of self-administered loyalty oath
meant to reassure the American public that the homosexual is a true-
blue patriot. Moreover, because it adheres to the conventional format
of the Shylock argument, the heterosexual "you" it appeals to is a
literal "you," not the trumped up "you" of Martha Shelley's evil
phantom, whom she degrades into a mere biological host from which
"we reproduce ourselves," exploiting the heterosexual, as in the film
Alien, like a fertile organism necessary for completing our generative
cycle.

While early gay activists at first used the figure of the Good Gay
as the equivalent of an ethical scarecrow, an all-American embodiment of xenophobia and Cold War paranoia specifically designed to
frighten away rabid McCarthyites, it has proven to be a remarkably
resilient public relations device and is useful even today in disarming
the criticisms of such homophobic organizations as the Christian Coalition and the Moral Majority. It operates like a decoy, masquer-
ading in the very image of the right wing. The Good Gay subscribes
to many of the same opinions held by conservative Americans: he
disapproves of sexual excess, he is pious to the point of being reli-
giose, he develops nurturing monogamous relationships, and he projects a homely, unassuming love for the domestic, the pedestrian, and
the unexotic. Brian McNaught, a gay journalist and public speaker
who describes himself as a "recovering perfect person,"[27] is one of
the shrewdest of contemporary Good Gays, having parlayed his conservative Irish Catholic upbringing and bright-eyed-and-bushy-tailed

---

[26]*The Mattachine Review*, Jan./Feb. 1955, p. 14.
[27]*On Being Gay* (New York: St. Martin's Press, 1988), p. 39.

Ivy League demeanor into a full-time career as a "facilitator" for therapeutic workshops. This puritanical "sex educator," who confesses to still feeling guilty about masturbation, strives to be so unintimidatingly normal that he proudly announces he took "the phone off the hook during the *Waltons*" and cried during the final segment of the *Mary Tyler Moore* show. This behavior, we are encouraged to believe, is typical of a man who, as "a loyal and loving son and citizen," claims to "smile a lot, say please and thank you and give money to people in need."[28] McNaught's syndicated columns in gay newspapers consist of carefully worded displays of Middle American wholesomeness, of the unthreatening conventionality of a loyal Cub Scout who, in the course of an exemplary life, has been "patrol boy of the year,"[29] a successful basketball player, the senior class president, the editor of the Marquette University yearbook, a gardener whose "flowers are the envy of the neighborhood,"[30] and a talented homemaker who plies his husband with "Wilma Koslowski's recipe for coffee cake."[31] If powerlessness was once the ultimate propagandistic state, mediocrity has proven to be far more useful, as well as far less ideologically problematic. Gay activists like McNaught devote enormous amounts of time and energy attesting to homosexuals' averageness, to the lackluster tedium of a parade of faceless nonentities who exemplify all that is run of the mill and commonplace about the subculture.

While the figure of the Good Gay has been extremely effective in winning the hearts of conservative Americans, its repeated use has ultimately had a destructive impact on gay culture. The tyrannical specter of sanitized and desexed homosexuals who bake coffee cakes and potter around flower beds has placed a lid on the gay sensibility, a brake that has slowed down our creativity, reining in our sardonic sense of humor, cramping our outrageous sense of style, and even discouraging us from indulging in camp, which McNaught belittles

---

[28]*On Being Gay*, p. 164.
[29]*On Being Gay*, p. 5.
[30]*On Being Gay*, p. 164.
[31]*On Being Gay*, p. 15.

as "pathetic, self-deprecating and pessimistic."[32] Over the past few decades, the mantra of mediocrity has even contributed to the dissolution of the gay sensibility, to its gradual loss of shape, its homogenization, to the fading of its once vibrant colors into anemic shades of acceptable averageness. In the last 25 years, the subculture has been ravaged by an unlikely enemy, the gay activist himself, whose political agenda is strangling a sensibility that homosexuals are asked, in the name of acceptance, to muffle and tone down, modeling themselves on images of staid heterosexuals. Gay liberation has thus paradoxically played an instrumental role in the decline of the gay sensibility and not, as we would have expected, in its growth and dissemination throughout American society.

As important to the spread of gay liberation as the sexual revolution was the popularization during the 1960s of the work of human potential psychologists, whose emphasis on individuality and nonconformity, on actualizing one's full potential and being true to oneself, regardless of how different one is from the majority, not only excused deviation from the norm but celebrated it as a hallmark of authenticity and personal fulfillment. The pop psychologist encouraged us to cultivate our uniqueness and take pride in our idiosyncrasies as evidence of the fact that each of us is "our own special creation," as Brian McNaught put it during a "celebration" of his homosexuality that he performed at a religious retreat. The ceremony involved a group sing-along of the theme song of *La Cage aux Folles*, "I Am What I Am," a musical interlude that concluded with the distribution of long-stemmed roses to the audience, which greeted this proud assertion of selfhood with thunderous applause, their eyes "puffy with tears." As the music rose to a crescendo, he and the other weeping participants engaged in a kind of human potential orgy, liberally dispensing "good, long hug[s]" until they collapsed into each other's arms "in one intergenerational embrace of affirmation,"[33] sobbing together to the accompaniment of the words "I bang my own drum/Some think it's noise,/I think it's pretty." Be-

---

[32] *On Being Gay*, p. 23.
[33] *On Being Gay*, p. 39.

ginning in the 1960s, many Americans had fallen so completely under the influence of the new self-help psychologists that they no
longer viewed nonconformity as a symptom of maladjustment and
teenage angst but considered it a manifestation of psychological
health, of the ability to "express oneself" and ignore the strictures of
a society intolerant of abnormality. The cult of individuality fostered
by the human potential movement was profoundly useful to gay
liberation, in that it infused with courage homosexuals who would
otherwise have remained in the closet had the pop psychologist not
glamorized rebelliousness, thus giving us the license to defy the repressive sexual orthodoxies of our time. The rhetoric of human potential still forms the very foundation of glad-to-be-gay propaganda,
whose language remains a patchwork quilt of the slogans of the
"Me" generation. The heavy debt that the gay rights movement owes
to the work of such figures as Abraham Maslow and Rollo May,
who championed the individual and decried the oppressive status
quo, is discernible in everything from McNaught's insistence that
gay people learn "to say boldly, 'Hey, world, I like myself' "[34] to Bob
and Rod Jackson-Paris's self-help video *Be True to Yourself*. In this
educational tape for gay teenagers, the former Mr. Universe and his
ex-consort, a humongous blond bombshell and *Playgirl* centerfold,
teach a group of eleventh and twelfth graders to "love yourself and
be true to yourself," a point they underscore with songs by soulful
folk singers who croon out such lyrics as "listen, listen to your heart,
listen to the voice inside."[35]

   The gay liberation movement is unique in the history of political
activism because it fuses two completely unrelated forces, politics and
therapy. As a result, it has produced a richly ideological literature
that rallies the gay community together in the fight against bigotry
while it assuages the damaged egos of oppressed homosexuals. Just
as the major leaders of the civil rights movement came from the
church, which was the only institution in the black community capable of mobilizing the rank and file, so the leaders of the gay rights

---

[34]*On Being Gay*, p. 43.
[35]Rod and Bob Jackson-Paris, *Be True to Yourself* (21st Century News, 1991).

movement have often come from the mental health clinic, an institution that has played a critical role in giving homosexuals enough
self-esteem to organize into an effective political group. The gay
propagandist has always worn several hats. He has fulfilled the functions of at least two distinct roles, that of the hard-nosed lobbyist
campaigning for tough legislative reform and that of the compas-
sionate therapist ministering to the psychological needs of his emotionally scarred followers by reassuring them that "there is nothing
wrong with being homosexual,"[36] that you must *never* let your parents . . . make you ashamed of who you are,"[37] that "a same-sex orientation is not sick, dangerous, or evil,"[38] and that we must say into
the mirror every morning "I'm gay and I love myself."[39]

Gay politics has overlapped and blurred with therapy, just as black
politics has overlapped and blurred with religion. This odd alliance
of the shrink and the militant can be explained by the fact that gay
liberation has always involved more than just the nuts and bolts of
preventing job discrimination and combating prejudice: our progress
as a minority depends on our ability to perform an initial act of self-
acceptance, without which there would be no movement whatsoever,
no unified bloc of voters and activists to provide the thorn in the
side of reluctant legislators. Gay liberation is as much a psychological
phenomenon as it is a political one, as much an internal event as it
is an external social "cause," as much a therapeutic cure as it is a
revolution. It takes place simultaneously on the level of the homosexual's consciousness and on the level of the oppressive social structures that determine the way in which he lives. The two are so
inextricably linked that glad-to-be-gay literature has become a
strange hybrid of political statements and human potential bromides,
of brass-tacks statesmanship and self-help boosterism that serves both
to inspire direct legislative action and instill personal confidence by
administering emotional first aid to the traumatized victims of ho-

---

[36]*Young, Gay & Proud!* (Alyson Publications, 1980), p. 52. No author.
[37]*Young, Gay & Proud*, p. 49.
[38]Mary V. Borhek, *Coming Out to Parents* (The Pilgrim Press, 1983), p. xi.
[39]Jackson-Paris, video.

mophobia. Unlike the propaganda of other human rights movements, which is more purely political, gay propaganda is a fascinatingly impure genre, juxtaposing news about the latest anti-discrimination bill next to repetitions of key concepts about the goodness of being gay and the necessity of loving yourself. The gay propagandist is not only expected to be a shrewd tactician who strategizes about the next protest rally, but a comforter, a provider of solace, a "gay people-helper"[40] whose work serves as "a kind and comforting guidepost," making homosexuals "feel better about themselves."[41]

If the House Committee on Un-American Activities helped produce the Good Gay, a ventriloquist's dummy who mouthed the patriotic pieties of the right wing, so pop psychology helped produce the Happy Gay, a character that radiates inner contentment, beaming a type of exuberant good cheer that is ultimately as unconvincing as bright yellow smiley face buttons. Emphatic assertions of homosexuals' psychological health became a highly unconventional form of propaganda very early on in the gay rights movement, which sought to repudiate commonly held opinions that gay people were always unhappy and maladjusted, lonely old queens slumped over the bar sobbing into Daiquiris or plunging off cliffs. One of the earliest examples of happiness propaganda was published in a 1955 issue of *One*, a short story appropriately entitled "Smiley," an unapologetically didactic piece premised on the then original notion that homosexuals can and do live normal, productive, and satisfying lives. Appearing immediately after an article that states that "homosexuals are not necessarily neurotic" and that gay activists must "produce a healthy new homosexual literature,"[42] this narrative demonstration of the pleasures of being gay opens with the bungled suicide attempt of a gay man named Bert who, convinced he will never find happiness, leaps off a bridge only to be fished out of the murky, frigid waters by a lovable blue-collar worker named Smiley.

---

[40]*Living Gay*, p. 98.
[41]*On Being Gay*, jacket copy and p. ix.
[42]David I. Freeman, "Literature and Homosexuality," *One*, Jan. 1955, p. 14.

Speaking in an illiterate, pseudo-proletarian dialect ("Im [sic] a regular guy. Or anyway I try ta be"), Smiley explains that before he
plucked Bert out of the river he was "sad," he drank, he engaged
in fist-fights and felt so lonely and incomplete that he "just got ta
be a mope." By story's end, however, he and Bert have moved in
together and are living happily ever after in a fairy-tale romance
that concludes with Smiley's moral of the story: "Bert and me,
we're . . . happy. We're not lonely, neither of us—we're not unhappy now. We couldn't be. . . . Now it makes sense when they call
me Smiley."[43]

The conditions under which homosexuals have been oppressed are
so unusual that something as subjective and intimate as our peace of
mind can actually be appropriated as a form of propaganda, a way
of bestowing on the homosexual a clean bill of psychological health.
Spontaneous effusions of joyfulness attesting to how good our sexual
orientation makes us feel inside form a mainstay of gay propaganda
which assigns political meanings to things as elusive as emotions,
transforming the state of contentment into an unlikely expression of
rebellion and defiance. Gay propaganda often makes political points
through a form of emotional exhibitionism, through ritualistic demonstrations of euphoria. This approach has produced an entire genre
of testimonial literature in which gay people, like born-again Christians vouching for the healing power of the holy scriptures, speak in
distinctly rapturous terms about the delights of being gay. Bert Herrman's *Being, Being Happy, Being Gay: Pathways to a Rewarding Life
for Lesbians and Gay Men* (1990) functions as propaganda simply by
presenting without commentary a series of snapshot portraits of successful, well-adjusted homosexuals, whom he proudly holds up for
view like a communist apparatchik showing the incredulous West
photographs of happy, well-fed factory workers in Russia. He even
offers as an appendix to the book a "happiness test" for homosexuals,
a multiple-choice quiz that quantifies readers' well-being according
to questions that run from their sex lives to their salaries. (Serious
grade inflation seems to have skewed the results in the direction of

---

[43]James Whitman, "Smiley," *One*, Jan. 1955, p. 17.

the deliriously ecstatic, however, since it is possible to have "unusually high well-being" with a score of only 82 percent.)[44]

While obviously well intentioned, the work of the "gay people-helpers" has often had a trivializing impact on the gay rights movement in that it has led some activists to forsake their duties as lobbyists for their work as therapists and comforters. By focusing on the psychological dimension of gay liberation and neglecting the political dimension, the propagandists most influenced by the human potential movement misrepresent the entire process of social change. They often characterize reform as a simple matter of making internal adjustments in the homosexual's self-esteem, as if gay people could create a utopian society of brotherly love and tolerance through acts of introspection alone, through self-acceptance and the power of positive thinking. Many gay activists now spend more time urging their fellow homosexuals to feel good about themselves than they do grappling with issues like fag bashing or derailing antigay ordinances. For the ever-growing number of gay people-helpers, liberation has taken such a dramatic turn inward and become so apolitical that they no longer fight the homophobic enemy directly through the swift mobilization of high-powered lawyers and crafty legislators but mentally through mind games, through silent visualizations, which serve as a technique for neutralizing anger against bigots, a process described in *Being, Being Happy, Being Gay*:

> I will imagine myself in a cloud of white light. I imagine each part of my body full of love and light. When I'm totally full of love, I try to think of the people towards whom I hold negative feelings. . . . Then I imagine that person smiling and happy. Then I do the same with anyone else I think of in that vein. When I'm done with them, I do the same thing with the people I like best and to whom I wish good things. I finish by saying to myself, "And we are all one." . . . One discovers that when you wish people love, especially on a regular basis, that it's hard to keep hating them. This is an effective visualization for forgiveness.[45]

---

[44]Herrman, *Being, Being Happy* (Alamo Square Press, 1990), p. 120.
[45]*Being, Being Happy*, p. 102.

For Herrman, liberation involves, not a legal battle or a picket line or a boycott or even a mass mailing, but a "path to self-discovery," a willingness to be true to yourself, killing your enemies with kindness, annihilating them with joy, smothering them with toxic clouds of forbearance and magnanimity. His unconventionally subjective approach to clamping down on bigots through the telepathic projection of punitive benevolence is echoed in the disproportionate amount of attention that he and many other writers devote to the issue of coming out. Human potentialists place this decisive moment in every homosexual's life at the very center of their psychopolitical agenda, which is frozen on reenactments of a single, emotionally purifying declaration. The vast literature on how to do it and whom to tell often implies that all that is necessary for effecting reform in society is this exhilarating confession which has become the philosopher's stone of gay rights, its open sesame, the universal remedy for oppression that wipes out homophobia through the repetition of the magic words, "I'm gay." Only a culture saturated in therapy could believe that political revolution lies, not in changing minds and drafting legislation, but in unburdening oneself, in making a clean breast of it through a therapeutic disclosure, through the utterance of a forbidden secret. All too often in the propaganda of the gay people-helpers, personal empowerment becomes a substitute for social empowerment, self-acceptance for social acceptance, coming out for fighting back.

The conspicuous consumption of literary propaganda has dominated the intellectual life of homosexuals perhaps even more than it has the intellectual life of other minorities. A thorough course of reading on such subjects as the genetic and environmental origins of homosexuality or the sociological reasons for intolerance is not only crucial to the entire process of coming out but provides us with a way of joining a metaphorical community of readers even before we have mustered the courage to join the real community of flesh-and-blood gay people. As one writer put it in 1965,

It can with safety be claimed that books are even more important to the homophile than to the general class of readers. Why? Because so many homophiles are finding themselves and searching out their way of life alone.
Scattered far and wide, on the farms, smothering in small towns, lost in the
anonymity of great cities, they can turn to books to share vicariously the experience of others while avoiding the dangers. . . . They can . . . take part silently in the debate about their condition, all the while without exposing
themselves to public view.[46]

As we have seen, from the beginning of the gay rights movement, the homosexual transcended his regional and emotional isolation by reading propaganda smuggled through the U.S. mail or obtained through other more surreptitious channels, thus circumventing many of the challenges and pitfalls of a more direct involvement with gay life. This loosely knit fellowship, this book club without walls, was based on an extremely figurative type of socializing, of collective solitude, a community of minds not bodies that enabled us to remain anonymous, alone, and yet connected, in the company of other homosexuals and yet shielded from the liabilities of actually being in their physical presence. Much as people now surf the Internet in the privacy of their homes, communicating with multitudes of other information junkies on the World Wide Web, so reading the same books and magazines provided a sort of early, low-tech Internet, the medium of contact through which homosexuals created intellectual solidarity with other lonely gay people living in rural areas or barricaded in their closets. As we have seen in other chapters, many important aspects of gay culture have provided pretexts for the establishment of an ethnic identity. Their real function was to instill esprit de corps and offer safe and sheltered opportunities for social interaction, as in the case of the Hollywood star who enabled her gay admirers to find unity in fandom or in the case of the motorcycle club which constituted one of the first openly gay social institutions apart from bars. Just as there is no actress behind the diva and no

---

[46]*One*, Nov. 1965, p. 6.

fetish behind leather, so all too often there is no book between the covers. Like the diva and the leather jacket, the book has traditionally functioned less as a vehicle for self-enlightenment than as an instrument for mobilizing an implicit community of readers.

While the use of books as a galvanizing social force may have turned many homosexuals into avid readers, it has ultimately had an ambiguous impact on their intellectual life. Because books often do not serve a rational, intellectual function in gay culture but a symbolic and extraliterary one, the act of reading is for large numbers of homosexuals a basically contentless experience, an academic exercise in group identification in which an author's arguments are all but irrelevant, platitudes preached to the converted. When we read propaganda, many of us suspend both aesthetic and intellectual judgment in order to savor the pleasures of being part of an obedient quorum of party liners who, marching together in lockstep, uncritically concur with ideas that, rather than stimulating thought, merely strengthen social bonds. The historic role that books have played in gay culture has produced a vast audience of readers whose relation to "positive" gay literature is characterized by a mindless spirit of gloating unanimity, as well as by an intolerance of dissent. Both factors have contributed to the intellectual paralysis of the subculture, which year after year—indeed, decade after decade—continues to applaud with wild fervor various permutations of the theme "gay is good."

The gay readership, with its seemingly infinite capacity for repetition, has also provided an economic bonanza for book publishers, who, because they are not held responsible by an alert audience with exacting standards, are able to take the path of least resistance and fill the shelves with the same tautological material with which they have been flooding the market for the last 30 years. Even before Stonewall, gay reviewers expressed dismay about the never-ending hemorrhage of books refuting arguments against homosexuality ("here we go again" and is there "a necessity . . . that the same things be said over and over again in varying tones?"[47]). Long after the 1969 riots, however, this sense of incredulity has not yet succeeded

---

[47]W. Dorr Legg, review of *In Defense of Homosexuality*, *One*, Nov. 1965, p. 11.

in stemming the tide of treatises that reinvent the wheel of gay rights and rehash the same positions in our favor. Nearly 70 years after the appearance of André Gide's *Corydon* (1924), which defended homosexuality with the full panoply of ethical and biological arguments, conservative author Bruce Bawer restated many of them virtually verbatim in his *A Place at the Table* (1993), a book that seems almost breathtakingly redundant given that its primary audience is other gay men. Publishers have been complicit in the stagnation of gay culture in that even in the 1960s they recognized the economic expedience of the yawning, bottomless maw of the gay readership whose interest in books had little to do with their actual contents. The immense social needs of this ideal consumer niche, coupled with its extraordinary indifference to literary quality, could be satisfied by writers who simply dredged up and repeated the fundamental premises of gay liberation which were greeted with the amens and hallelujahs of an enraptured congregation. Once again, as in the case of writers like Clark, who justify the need for their work by holding on to a lingering sense of persecution and by exaggerating the threat of the homophobic enemy, the economics of propaganda has made it intellectually inert and conservative. The very people who should be advancing social change in gay culture, our writers, are in fact obstructing it, accustomed as they are to addressing both indiscriminate readers addicted to the comforting banalities of propaganda and publishers eager to exploit the irresistible opportunities created by our tolerance of mediocrity.

Gay propaganda often takes extremely anomalous forms, and one of the least conventional is that of self-help manuals. Lifestyle guides for homosexuals are not typical how-to books, but a type of literature that has actually been written in code by accomplished illusionists who mask glad-to-be-gay propaganda in an elaborate disguise. The gay audience is so attractive to publishers because we are the ideal self-help audience. As an insecure and apprehensive readership, we eagerly consult books for the answers to such pressing questions as the protocol involved in seating gay newlyweds at a dinner party, as in Daniel Curzon's *The Joyful Blue Book of Gracious Gay Etiquette*; the intricate rituals of snagging hunky numbers in bars, as in Lenny Giteck's *Cruising to Win*; or the most auspicious time, astrologically speaking, for the randy Gemini or Aquarian to find the ideal mate, as in John Savage's *The Gay Astrologer*. Self-help literature in general presumes the self-helplessness of an infantilized readership bereft of common sense, an audience so ignorant of the most elementary techniques of survival that it must be told how to do everything, from purchasing a car and defrosting a refrigerator to sewing on a button and tying a shoe. Homosexuals constitute the ideal self-help audience because many of us are indeed ignorant and helpless, assailed by doubts and consumed by feelings of guilt, infe-riority, and ineffectiveness, especially those of us who are still in the closet facing the ordeal of coming out or, even worse, confronting something altogether more frightening, the prospect of an imminent death from AIDS. While American culture in general is saturated with self-help literature, the fear and insecurity of the gay commu-nity makes it particularly vulnerable to publishers who would re-duce us to befuddled imbeciles unable to make our own decisions, forced to pore over books before we risk the fatal step of venturing out-of-doors. We cling for dear life to the sapient admonitions of gurus and oracles who, as they indoctrinate us with positive propa-ganda about the privileges of being homosexuals, explain to us how to come out, stay alive, fall in love, plan a funeral, and enjoy satis-fying sex.

Mary Borhek's *Coming Out to Parents* is a typical example of a gay self-help manual that patronizes its readers as its author helps them through this potentially stormy announcement, playing the role of an anxious mother hen who lends her audience a comfortingly ma-ternal shoulder to cry on. This modern-day Polonius offers advice about such matters as scheduling the Big Decision, explaining to impetuous spoilsports that "the day after Christmas is better than the day before" and that if they decide to come out in the presence of a counselor they must be sure not to choose one "who wears an earring." She assumes her readers know nothing, that they are grop-ing about in the dark, pondering such thorny questions as what to call ourselves when the time finally arrives, ultimately concluding—no doubt rightly—that "if you are a woman, you want to tell [your parents] you are a lesbian; if you are a man, you want to tell them you are gay."[48]

The self-help literature targeted at homosexuals may appear to offer an encyclopedia of beneficial recommendations about surviving the perilous social and psychological hardships that beset us in everything from dating to dying, from shaking out a rug to rolling on a rubber, but in fact these books belong to a genre in disguise. They are not intended to inform but to flatter. The gay reader enjoys them not because he really needs to be told to wait until after Christmas to make his announcement or to choose a therapist without an earring but because he *enjoys* being told how to perform such self-evident tasks. An act of "pretend" is involved when he reads self-help literature: he makes-believe he is consulting these books to learn how to tie that shoe and defrost that refrigerator (or, mutatis mutandis, how to come out) but in fact what he is really seeking is the assurances their authors provide about how good and normal and healthy it is to tie shoes and defrost refrigerators and how personally empowering he will find it to join together in solidarity with other proud shoe tiers and refrigerator defrosters. He reads these books, in short, not as instructional manuals, but as propaganda that affirms the goodness of being gay and mesmerizes him with a constant flicker of subliminal messages attesting to the normality of gay life. Only secondarily do these guides give him sound, practical advice about where to buy macramé potholders and Rubbermate bath decals for his new apartment or how to tell his boyfriend that, while he loves his eggs Benedict, he abhors his microwaved lasagna.

One of the clearest examples of the way propagandists pose as the authors of self-help books can be found in the recent avalanche of primers on how to have healthier, happier gay relationships. Books and videos like *The Male Couple*, *The Male Couple's Guide to Living Together*, or *Finding True Love in a Man-Eat-Man World* offer such indispensable tips as how to distinguish undying true love for "The One" from a puppy-love crush on some flirtatious swain playing hard to get; or how to avoid annoying one's live-in boyfriend by consci-

[48]Borhek, *Coming Out*, pp. 39, 40, 3.

entiously refraining from squeezing the toothpaste tube in the middle rather than rolling it up "from the bottom like a grownup."[49] Relationship books are the most make-believe of the entire gay self-help genre. While they profess to give the reader pointers about such things as ferreting out a trick's waist size in order to buy him stylish lingerie for midnight drama or dimming the lights with rheostat fixtures in order to establish a suitably romantic ambience for intimate tête-à-têtes, these books are in fact a duplicitous and distinctly sermonizing type of literature that carries on an imaginary dialogue with an absent reader, the heterosexual. Manuals about achieving greater intimacy or having more meaningful sex are intended to refute the notion that gay men are too flighty and fickle to have long-term relationships, that they are incorrigibly sluttish and emotionally immature, and that they are therefore doomed to lead lonely, desperate lives as aged spinsters who drown their sorrows in cocktails while watching reruns of Joan Crawford movies. In her essay "Achieving Success as a Gay Couple," Betty Berzon argues that, because popular culture is saturated with images of the conjugal bliss of heterosexuals, we must counteract this surfeit of oppressive representations by disseminating positive images of unflaggingly devoted homosexuals who will teach us "to believe in the rightness of gay love relationships."[50] Throughout the 1980s, as the AIDS epidemic took its toll and gay men ducked for cover in monogamous relationships that they policed like blood pacts for survival, gay propagandists manufactured and distributed a third major mythical figure next to the Good Gay and the Happy Gay: the Uxorious Gay. This propagandistic device was designed, not only to provide role models for gay men and to curb our suicidal promiscuity, but to negate straight stereotypes of homosexuals as emotionally unstable loners, incapable of making commitments, ordained by fate to an endless succession of romantically bankrupt, slam-bam-thank-you-mam one-night stands.

The propaganda of the Uxorious Gay reaches its most extreme

---

[49]*The Male Couple Video*, A Humanus Home Video Production, 1985.
[50]Berzon and Leighton, *Positively Gay*, p. 31.

expression in *Straight from the Heart: A Love Story*, a first-person narrative in which Bob and Rod Jackson-Paris describe their courtship, betrothal, and ultimate marriage in a Unitarian Church, where they celebrated their nuptials with all of the trappings, from tastefully engraved invitations to tuxedos and cummerbunds. Almost from page 1, the reader encounters the bodice-ripping rhetoric of starry-eyed reminiscences, such as Rod's and Bob's electrifying first glance ("a truly cosmic moment, absolutely magical"[51]) that made Rod's stomach do "little butterflies" and his knees go "woo-ooh."[52] "Woo-ooh" is an understatement for what the reader feels as we relive the distinctly seasick first moments of "this primal, millions-of-years, soulmate type of thing"[53] in which we lurch back and forth on the unsteady deck of their ever-shifting emotions. Their hearts a-pitter-patter, they blow now hot, now cold, as when Rod, pedaling frantically on a stationary bicycle, plucks the petals of an imaginary daisy as he repeats to himself "oh my God, he's interested in me, oh, he's not interested in me. Oh, my God, he's interested in me, oh, he's not interested in me."[54] Within a remarkably short period of time, however, poems are being written and cried over ("Come and take me/Take me to your heart of gold"[55]), joint bank accounts are being opened, and dreams are being dreamt in which Rod imagines himself a dashing Indian brave and Bob a nubile squaw who hurl themselves into a gorge when their tribe refuses to acknowledge their strange and beautiful love. Hearts are drawn on steamy windows with big toes during three-hour phone conversations, new poems get written ("If I could promise you/The moon and stars, in all their azure blue"), more tears are shed (Bob's poem "was beautiful . . . it was brilliant,"[56] Rod sobbed), and jealous spats are staged, such as when Rod is forced to turn down *Playgirl*'s Man of the Year award because

---

[51]Rod and Bob Jackson-Paris, *Straight from the Heart: A Love Story* (Warner Books, 1994), p. 4.
[52]*Straight*, p. 5.
[53]*Straight*, p. 6.
[54]*Straight*, p. 13.
[55]*Straight*, p. 20.
[56]*Straight*, p. 20.

Bob doesn't "want anyone seeing [Rod's] penis." "I'm the only one who should see it,"[57] he insists like any male chauvinist, thus stifling his wife's independence and ruining the first big break in her career.

Oddly enough, on their first date, it is the squaw who actually pops the question, not the Indian brave. After Bob served Rod a romantic candlelit dinner (which neither could eat, since both were on starvation diets to preserve their hourglass figures), they managed to get all the way to first base when Bob suddenly leapt to his feet, snatched up the photograph of his mother and father, and turned it toward Rod, solemnly proclaiming, "I want my family to witness this."[58] With the Paris forebears looming sternly over his shoulder, lending their moral authority to this momentous occasion, he then sank down on one knee and, seizing Rod's hand in his, asked, "will you marry me?" One can only imagine the thoughts that raced through Rod's head as he told Bob "he was crazy, that this was ridiculous, that this was just . . . too soon."[59] "We didn't have sex that night," Rod explained after he agreed to become Bob's fiancé, for although "we wanted each other badly . . . it went unspoken that we would"—one utters a silent prayer for the values of Western civilization—"wait a while."[60]

The propagandistic fictions surrounding the Uxorious Gay operate by reenacting the rituals of heterosexual courtship and by deliberately de-exoticizing gay relationships, turning homosexual lovers into glamorless hausfraus who wash socks, entertain in-laws, pick up laundry from the dry cleaners, and agonize over their dishpan hands. Relationship books rarely make gay love seem very appealing but in fact go out of their way to trivialize it, to describe it as a perfectly vapid and matter-of-fact arrangement between two men who weather the ups and downs, the feasts and the famines, of sexual affairs as pedestrian and unthreatening as those of their heterosexual counterparts. Manuals about homosexual relationships underscore

---

[57]*Straight*, p. 157.
[58]*Straight*, p. 30.
[59]*Straight*, p. 30.
[60]*Straight*, p. 30.

the similarities of gay romance with traditional straight love affairs, dwelling on the things they have in common, on the universal stresses and strains of cohabitation, from the tantrums we throw in the produce aisles of grocery stores to our constant haggling over how to split the chores, from the insomnia we experience at night listening to the stertorous snoring of our asthmatic partners to our quarrels over the pee stains of our pets. The propagandistic aim of relationship self-help books is to relocate the ideological center of gay romance from the bedroom to the kitchen, a far less problematic stage setting, where self-help writers can underplay the importance of steamy sex acts and emphasize instead the mundane domestic realities of living together. What is so troubling about these political manifestos posing as Harlequin romances is that, far from representing a triumphant assertion of the value of gay love, relationship books revolve around disfiguring acts of impersonation in which gay men perform travesties of the sort of reactionary behavior that many heterosexuals have rejected. In remaking ourselves in the marzipan images of the bride and groom on a wedding cake, we are performing the gay equivalent of ethnic hara-kiri and submitting to a vicious process of self-cancellation. Once again, as in the case of the Good Gay, the propaganda of the Uxorious Gay has had a negative impact on the homosexual sensibility itself, which must be suppressed and camouflaged in order for us to achieve complete social acceptance.

While books about coming out or having successful relationships profess to instill us with confidence, they in fact fill us with doubt and insecurity, with a constant demeaning sense of our inadequacy in dealing with the most elementary problems of our lives. The self-help industry is an immense comfort machine, a dispenser of pats on the back, of maternal hugs and sloppy wet kisses, of the bland pap of enthusiastic affirmations whose monotonous taste we have come to crave. It is in the financial interests of both publishers and propagandists to keep us in this childlike state of dependence and to reduce the debate over important social issues to the crudest form of sloganeering, never letting it get beyond the truisms that are the bread and butter of self-help authors. Writers like Borhek and McNaught are our own worst enemies, exerting as negative an impact on the emotional life of gay people as the shrillest of bigoted Bible thumpers. They claim to be telling us how to cope, but in fact they make us feel incompetent, in dire need of the moral support that turns us into a timid group of self-help addicts forced to make a mad dash for the bookshelf every time we are faced with the horrible necessity of defrosting our refrigerators or tying our own shoes. One of the great ironies of glad-to-be-gay propaganda is that, in the final analysis, it does precisely the opposite of what it is ostensibly intended to do: rather than making us feel bolder, more courageous, and more "empowered," it makes us feel more insecure and powerless, devoid of common sense, reliant upon the self-evident advice of writers who profit from our emotional confusion and keep us from growing up, from getting on with our lives, from advancing to a higher state of intellectual awareness about the psychological and political issues surrounding homosexuality. A subculture addicted to propaganda is not a liberated subculture but a fettered one, enslaved to a class of mercenary homilists paid to cheer homosexuals up with platitudes.

The commercialization of gay men has had a profoundly detrimental impact on our images of our bodies, which have been complicated by the intimidating techniques used in the sale of both cosmetics and pornography, products that draw the consumer's attention by implicitly denigrating him and instilling him with fear. But a far more disturbing consequence of commercialization is the intellectual paralysis of the subculture, whose uncritical acceptance of gay positive propaganda has allowed the book trade to publish with impunity second-rate purveyors of moral support who, rather than expanding our horizons or enriching our understanding of our homosexuality, produce a consistently mediocre type of feel-good literature. Just as the gay man is now suspended in a state of agonizing doubt about the appearance of his body, which he constantly judges according to the inflated aesthetic standards he acquires from porn films, so he is now kept in an infantilized state of dependence on uplifting bromides by an industry so eager to profit from our literary vulnerability that it feels no obligation whatsoever to seek out new

authors with new ideas to challenge our assumptions. In every regard, the commercialization of gay culture has had a trivializing
effect on our lives, producing unhappiness and dissatisfaction while
reinforcing our intellectual inertia.

It is not just economic forces that are to blame for the decline of
the subculture but gay liberationists themselves, who are in some
sense at war with the gay sensibility, anxious to tone down or eliminate altogether our idiosyncrasies as a minority, which some activists
treat as the necessary casualty of progress, the price we must pay for
social acceptance. In the three chief fabrications of gay propaganda—
the Good Gay, the Happy Gay, and the Uxorious Gay—we have
seen that the obliteration of the gay sensibility, of our effeminacy,
campiness, promiscuity, and aestheticism, is actually built into the
program of the gay movement, which, far from being an ally of
traditional gay culture, is its worst enemy, a savior that will ultimately strip us of our distinctive ethnic features. The gay movement
is bent on disseminating images of happy, healthy homosexuals who
have abandoned their compulsive cruising and their bitchy, self-
loathing sarcasm and become instead unthreatening replicas of mild-
mannered heterosexuals who, like Rod and Bob Jackson-Paris, go to
church, play sports, get married, adopt children, and take turns doing
the dishes and taking out the garbage. Gay liberation has thus in
many ways been as corrosive of the subculture's identity as our exploitation by large corporations.

In the sentimentalization of our minority status after Stonewall,
we see how the subculture's romantic vision of the glamor of ethnicity comes at the tail end of the gay sensibility, in its extreme
decadence, at the very moment when our identity as a distinct group
has begun to lose its definition and our differences from mainstream
society are no longer the source of the same discomfort they once
caused. The gay man's cult of his outsider status can arise only when
the psychological anguish triggered by his alienation has significantly
diminished. Before gay liberation, it was impossible for those who
experienced nothing but shame about their proclivities to romanticize
them as something they should be proud of, as if they could console
themselves, while being hounded out of jobs and carted away from

bars in paddy wagons, with the belief that their misery was one of the privileges of belonging to a colorful if oppressed minority. Only when we have achieved a considerable degree of acceptance and social mobility as open homosexuals does our former ostracism begin to exert a certain fascination for many of us. It has become the source of the subversive ethnic identity lauded by multiculturalists, the marginality that is now the plaything of a minority no longer on the run from the law, forced to exercise the utmost stealth to escape humiliation and even ruin. Nostalgia is the death knell of the subculture, a sure sign that it has entered its final stages of decay. The social conditions that shaped the gay sensibility have changed so irrevocably that we use this uncanny embodiment of grief and surreptitiousness as a way of cultivating an exotic persona, of acquiring the much coveted cachet of illicitness and nonconformity, the stigma that once brought with it so many hardships but has now become glamorous and even fashionable.

The end of oppression necessitates the end of the gay sensibility. When gay men no longer feel degraded and insecure and therefore driven to prove their worth to the heterosexual mainstream, they will cease using culture as a means of achieving social prestige and, as a consequence, will stop flocking to art schools, the stage, the concert hall, or the opera house, becoming much more conventional in their aspirations and gravitating to less creative jobs in the business sector. To the immense impoverishment of fields like painting, poetry, and choreography, gay culture will gradually be eliminated as one of the essential ingredients of artistic culture in general, which was fueled by the reservoir of persecution and inferiority that first motivated homosexuals to pursue careers in the arts. Moreover, once it becomes possible to communicate openly with other gay men without the protective screen of innuendo that formerly ensured we could at once identify ourselves to others of our persuasion and avoid the humiliation of being exposed to potentially hostile outsiders, our national treasure, camp, will become obsolete, a charming anachronism in an age that has witnessed the proliferation of gay Witches Support Groups, Stitch & Bitch Sewing Circles, Gay Esperanto Language Clubs, and Digital Queer chat rooms on the Internet.

Is the demise of gay culture such a great tragedy after all? Certainly, it is an inevitable tragedy, and only a nostalgic fool would want to prevent it from happening in light of the fact that the flourishing of gay culture depends on the persistence of the oppression we have struggled so hard to eliminate. And yet the fact remains that we feel sentimental about things like camp, drag, and aestheticism now that they are disappearing into the oblivion of a world dominated by Coke commercials and sitcoms. The process of assimilation itself is unpleasant, and we recoil from the sight of the extreme homogenization of American culture, of a monolithically uniform melting pot gobbling up its minorities, wiping them out through television and mass marketing. It is this complex and ambivalent attitude toward assimilation, toward both its necessity and its ultimate ruinous impact on us as a minority, that marks the pages of this book.

Index